# Long-Term Care

## Management, Scope
## and Practical Issues

Edited by

John A. Toner, EdD
Lynn M. Tepper, EdD
Beverly Greenfield

The Charles Press, Publishers
Philadelphia

Dedicated to the memory of Catherine T. Fisher,
mentor, friend and an Auntie Mame to all who knew her.

Copyright © 1993 by The Charles Press, Publishers, Inc.

The Charles Press, Publishers
Post Office Box 15715
Philadelphia, PA 19103

The Charles Press acknowledges the American Institute of Life-Threatening Illness and Loss, a division of the Foundation of Thanatology, and the Daughters of Israel Geriatric Center.

**Library of Congress Cataloging-in-Publication Data**

Long-term care: management, scope, and practical issues / edited by
  John A. Toner, Lynn M. Tepper, Beverly Greenfield.
      p.    cm.
  Includes bibliographical references.
  ISBN 0-914783-66-1
  1. Aged—Long-term care—United States. I. Toner, John A.
II. Tepper, Lynn M. III. Greenfield, Beverly. IV. Title: Long-term care
  [DNLM: 1. Health Services for the Aged—organization & administration.
  2. Long-Term Care—in old age. 3. Long-Term Care—organization & administration. WT 30 L8485]
  RA564.8.L655    1993
  362.1'6'0973—dc20
  DNLM/DLC
  for Library of Congress                                    92-49112
                                                                 CIP

ISBN 0-914783-66-1

Printed in the United States of America

# Editors

**John A. Toner, EdD**
Senior Research Scientist and Assistant Professor
Center for Geriatrics and Gerontology
Columbia University
New York State Office of Mental Health
New York, New York

**Lynn M. Tepper, EdD**
Director, Institute of Gerontology
Mercy College, Dobbs Ferry, New York
Associate Clinical Professor
Columbia University School of Public Health
New York, New York

**Beverly Greenfield**
Program Assistant
Center for Geriatrics and Gerontology
Columbia University
New York, New York

# Contributors

**Tobi A. Abramson, PhD**
Private Consultant in Geriatrics
New York, New York

**Virginia W. Barrett, DrPH, RN**
Senior Research Scientist
Hebrew Home for the Aged, Riverdale, New York
Associate Research Scientist
Columbia University Center for Geriatrics
and Gerontology
New York, New York

**D. Peter Birkett, MD**
Medical Director, Riverside Nursing Home
Haverstraw, New York

**Lauren Birns, CMT**
Co-owner, At Ease, Inc.
Westfield, New Jersey

**Marcie Cooper, MSW, RMT**
Special Events Coordinator
Daughters of Israel Geriatric Center
West Orange, New Jersey

**Peter S. Cross, MPhil**
Geriatrics Research Scientist
New York State Psychiatric Institute
New York, New York

**Sharon Gallo, CMT**
Co-owner, At Ease, Inc.
Westfield, New Jersey

**Lawrence Gelfand**
Executive Vice President
Daughters of Israel Geriatric Center
West Orange, New Jersey

**Lois Grau, PhD, RN**
Associate Professor of Clinical, Environmental
and Community Medicine
University of Medicine and Dentistry of New Jersey
Robert Wood Johnson Medical School
New Brunswick, New Jersey

**Seymour Herschberg, MD, FACP**
Medical Director, Medigroup Health Centers
Trenton, New Jersey

**Fay Hortz, MTRS**
Formerly, Director of Public Relations
Daughters of Israel Geriatric Center
West Orange, New Jersey

**Terry Kinzel, MD, FACP**
Associate Professor, Department of Medicine
Michigan State University, East Lansing, Michigan
Chief of Geriatrics and Gerontology
Veterans Affairs Medical Center, Iron Mountain, Michigan
Medical Director, Copper County Mental Health Services
Houghton, Michigan

**Austin H. Kutscher, DDS**
President
American Institute of Life-Threatening Illness and Loss
Department of Psychiatry
College of Physicians and Surgeons
Columbia University
New York, New York

**Theresa Martico-Greenfield, MPH**
Assistant Administrator
The Jewish Home and Hospital for the Aged
New York, New York

**Patricia A. Miller, MEd, OTR**
Assistant Professor in Clinical Occupational Therapy
and Clinical Public Health
Division of Geriatrics and Gerontology
Columbia University, New York

**Susan Sataloff, BS**
Recreation Therapist
Daughters of Israel Geriatric Center
West Orange, New Jersey

**Shura Saul, EdD, BCD, CSW**
Educational Consultant, Kingsbridge Heights Nursing Facility
Adjunct Professor
Columbia University School of Public Health
New York, New York

**Sidney R. Saul, EdD, BCD, CSW**
Mental Health Consultant
Kingsbridge Heights Nursing Facility
New York, New York
Adjunct Professor, Mercy College
Dobbs Ferry, New York

**George Serban, MD**
Senior Clinical Research Psychiatrist
Department of Psychiatry
New York University/Bellevue Medical Center
Clinical Associate Professor of Psychiatry
New York University Medical School
New York, New York

**Margaret M. Shannon, MS, RN**
Assistant Director, Clinical Review Department
Calvary Hospital
Bronx, New York

**Roger H. Sherman, PhD**
Assistant Professor, Department of Public Administration
Director, University Center on Aging
Long Island  University
Bronxville, New York

**Roberta K. Sutler, MSW**
Edison Estates
Edison, New Jersey

**Sister Robert Clare Swarts, MA, LNHA, RN**
Assistant Administrator
St. Vincent's Nursing Home of St. Joseph's
Hospital and Medical Center
Program Director
St. Vincent's Medical Day Care Program
Paterson, New Jersey

**Lynn M. Tepper, EdD**
Director, Institute of Gerontology
Mercy College, Dobbs Ferry, New York
Associate Clinical Professor
Columbia University School of Public Health
New York, New York

**Terry Tirrito, MSW, DSW, CSW**
Assistant Professor, College of Social Work
University of South Carolina
Columbia, South Carolina

**John A. Toner, EdD**
Senior Research Scientist and Assistant Professor
Center for Geriatrics and Gerontology
Columbia University
New York State Office of Mental Health
New York, New York

**Stanley F. Wainapel, MD, MPH**
Associate Professor of Clinical Rehabilitation Medicine
College of Physicians and Surgeons
Columbia University
New York, New York

# Contents

# 1

# The Evolving Continuum of Long-Term Care

*John A. Toner, EdD and Austin H. Kutscher, DDS*

## INTRODUCTION

Long-term care refers to a range of health and supportive services for individuals who have lost some capacity for self-care due to a chronic illness or condition and who are expected to need care for an extended period of time (Brickner et al. 1987). Long-term care services can be provided either formally—by individuals or agencies who are paid for their services—or informally—by relatives or others who provide the services without compensation. The theoretical framework for the development of formal and primary group services to the elderly will make up part of the introduction to this chapter.

This introduction addresses a number of issues pertaining to community and institutional services available to elderly individuals, such as health, housing and social services. Long-term care services are defined here as services whose purpose is to provide prevention, therapy, rehabilitation, support and maintenance to persons over age 65 who have chronic physical or mental impairments* (Health Care Financing Admin-

---

*Sections I and II discuss the rationale for long-term care services, including family versus public involvement. Section II defines long-term care, introduces the concept of "functional disability" as it relates to the need for long-term care, and describes the characteristics of the elderly who are most in need of long-term care services.

istration 1981). Although the emphasis is on the elderly, much of the discussion here is relevant also to others receiving long-term care services.

The continuum of services is identified here by setting and an array of services from least restrictive to most restrictive (Brody and Maschiocchi 1981). Long-term care constitutes a wide variety of services offered in diverse settings to individuals with differing needs and preferences. The continuum stretches from total institutional care in hospitals to a variety of social services to patients in their own homes, with a large number of services in between. Ideally, they begin with an effort to prevent deterioration or dependency and end only after death and suffering have been made as bearable as possible.

The need for long-term care can be confused with the need for formal services, which in reality is determined by the absence of informal support and the presence of a disabling condition. Despite its importance to an increasing number of people, long-term care remains misunderstood. The evolving concept of the continuum considers long-term care needs as varied and changing, and not limited to patients who receive services in such formal settings as nursing homes, hospital outpatient departments and physicians' offices.

The concept of a continuum of long-term care services evolves from policy; policy is the implementation of legislation, such as the Older Americans Act or the various Social Security Act amendments, and derives from the government's responsibility to carry out the law. The fact remains, however, that in reality a continuum of coordinated services for the elderly does not exist in U.S. legislation or policy and probably cannot be achieved without Congressional action.

The long-term care population has two segments: the impaired or chronically ill who need assistance in activities of daily living, and the residents in long-term care institutions, including large numbers of younger, mentally retarded patients, as well as the aged.

Although long-term care ranges along a continuum of required services, public programs disproportionately support institutional care, notably nursing home care. The U.S. Health Care Financing Administration (1981) reports that less than 10 percent of public funds are devoted to home-delivered services. And, while many disabled persons receive no long-term care, there is evidence that 20 to 40 percent of those in nursing homes could be cared for at less intensive levels if adequate community services were available. (Studies of the institutionalized elderly report large percentages of unmarried or childless residents without sufficient community supports.)

Current long-term care services have three main characteristics:

- They are dominated by the Medicaid program, which stresses medical and institutional rather than community social and support services for people with chronic impairments.
- They result from fragmented federal programs, which inadequately assess the needs of persons requiring long-term care. Each program deals only with an isolated aspect of an individual's need. For example, the Supplemental Security Income (SSI) program raises income above the poverty level, but neglects to address the issue of quality of life.
- Title III of the Older Americans Act and Title XX of the Social Security Act have provided opportunities for developing community services, but neither has achieved the volume of services or the specific focus on long-term care that might make such services a major element in the delivery of long-term care.

Koch (1989), Armour, Estes and Noble (1981) and Ruchlin and Levey (1976) provide a review of long-term care financing. Current federal programs finance a variety of long-term care services at the local level, primarily under Titles XVIII, XIX and XX of the Social Security Act (Medicare, Medicaid and Social Services) and Title III of the Older Americans Act (Social and Nutrition Services and Senior Centers). Of these, Medicaid, Title XX and Title III are administered by states, while Medicare is federally administered. Income maintenance is provided mainly through Social Security—Old Age, Survivors and Disability Insurance and the Supplemental Security Income Program—and is federally administered. Housing programs are financed by the U.S. Department of Housing and Urban Development, but are often under state and local administration. Although these programs contribute to meeting long-term care needs, the system emphasizes health services because that is where federal financial support is concentrated.

While current programs are neither comprehensive nor uniform across the states, all states cover some range of services critically important to the health and continued independence of many chronically impaired persons. Because each state has some discretion in setting Medicaid eligibility standards, the resulting variation contributes to the inequities of the system. Medicaid coverage, for example, does not extend to every elderly person in need of these services.

## Impairment, Disability and Handicap

Cole (1979) focuses on the concepts of disability and rehabilitation and their implications for elderly populations. Disability is an instrumental factor in determining whether a person seeks long-term care.

It is important to make a distinction among the concepts of impairment, disability and handicap. Impairment is an abnormal physiological or mental process that occurs in an individual. Disability is the physical manifestation of such abnormality. Handicaps are the effects these manifestations have on the individual, and particularly whether they limit the person in a function deemed crucial to independent living. According to some definitions, disability and subsequent handicap imply chronic conditions (those that last longer than 3 months) rather than acute conditions (Cole 1979).

Fifteen percent of the U.S. population is handicapped due to disability, and of this percentage the elderly constitute the greatest proportion. Although age and disability are directly proportional, most aged persons do not become handicapped until they reach the "frail elderly" age, which begins at 85 years. U.S. Bureau of the Census data (1986) indicate that more than 34 percent of those over the age of 85 require assistance in performing at least one activity of daily living (ADL), such as dressing or bathing, and 39 percent of this age group require assistance in performing at least one instrumental activity of daily living (IADL), such as shopping. This is a substantial increase from the population between the ages of 75 and 84 years, in which only about 11 percent and 14 percent, respectively, require assistance in ADLs and IADLs. Therefore, the older one gets, the greater the chances that one will spend the rest of one's life unable to perform ADLs or IADLs. It is when the individual becomes completely dependent on others for these activities that long-term care is initiated.

In most cases rehabilitation is the final phase of the medical care continuum, after prevention and acute care. It has as a primary goal the improvement of the quality of a patient's life by optimizing abilities. In a sense, rehabilitation is prevention because it can restore an individual's capacity to perform all types of activities of daily living, which can, in turn, prevent the individual from seeking institutional long-term care. Thus, rehabilitation will allow some individuals to remain in the community and function independently. Considering the costs of long-term institutionalization and home care services, rehabilitating services could become an instrumental facet of long-term care policy in the future.

In addition to its potential monetary benefits, rehabilitation is beneficial by definition. As human beings and living organisms, we all strive to maintain our optimal state of existence; rehabilitation can mean the difference between independence and institutionalization.

Finally, by way of introduction to the long-term care continuum, it is important to consider the prevalence and significance of disability as it relates to the community and to homebound, hospitalized and nursing home elderly, as well as the estimates of prevalence and their significance in the development of services in the long-term care continuum.[*]

## THE EVOLUTION OF LONG-TERM CARE SERVICES

This section introduces the history of long-term care in the United States. Moroney and Kurtz (1976) describe the growth and development—and attempt to predict the future—of American programs of long-term care. They employ a systems-analysis approach in their examination, which is based on four assumptions: that the total system has a goal that is common to its subsystems; that the subsystems are interdependent; that functions develop within the system in response to the needs of the system; and that no single part or subsystem completely controls the whole system. The authors contend such an analysis of long-term care identifies the strengths and weaknesses of linkages between subsystems.

Because a systems analysis requires a clear statement of goals, four goals are suggested for the U.S. health care system: prevention of disease, treatment of disease, rehabilitation of patients, and maintenance of health. Long-term care has a primary goal of maintenance, although each of the other three goals may impinge on long-term care at various times.

### Early History

Moroney and Kurtz (1976) undertake a historical analysis of care of the aged in the Western world and point out that in Greek and Roman times

---

[*]The HCFA report (981; pp. 3-16) provides a discussion of the issue of prevalence and significance of disability. Also to be noted is the definition and measurement of "functional disability"; see HCFA Tables II-1 and II-2. Saxon and Etten (1987), which is concisely written for those without a background in science, and Pizer (1985), which emphasizes the diseases commonly associated with older age (and other health-related topics) provide a review of the normal physical and biological changes associated with aging, age-related changes in the major organ systems, and diseases commonly associated with aging.

the disabled and the elderly were considered a drain on society, and abandonment was almost a social norm. With the advent of Christianity, tending the sick became an exercise of charity that earned spiritual rewards for the caretakers. This type of church-sponsored care reached its peak in the Middle Ages.

Under a system of Poor Laws enacted in 17th-century England, parishes put able-bodied paupers to work and provided places of habitation for the needy and elderly who were unable to work. It was a system that lasted well into the 19th century. If the needy or elderly had relatives who could provide support, they could not enter the system. If they were without family, they entered the system and usually ended up in human warehouses called "almshouses"—along with the insane, the feeble-minded, the blind and the chronically diseased, as well as criminals, prostitutes, epileptics, mothers of illegitimate children, orphans and deserted children. In colonial America care of the elderly followed the English mode.

## Modern History

The modern period, which begins roughly with the dawn of the present century, includes four subperiods.

### 1900 to 1935

The 20th century inherited a troublesome legacy of mistreatment and neglect of the elderly. In the previous century, the Charitable Organization Society moved to get the aged out of public almshouses and to eliminate the need for public administration of relief. Efforts were made to develop a system of privately financed boarding homes (Miles 1949).

In 1910, the Flexner[*] reports resulted in a marked improvement in physician training and in better standards of medical care. These efforts at improvement, however, were directed toward acute care in hospitals

---

[*]Abraham Flexner, concerned with the disparity between American and European standards of medical practice, documented the need to establish controls in medical education and was instrumental in the closing of many marginal medical schools. Over the next 40 years, through the American Medical Association, he initiated changes in both medical education and in hospital practice (Moroney and Kurtz, 1976; p. 89).

rather than long-term care; the boarding homes that had been established for the elderly in this era were outside of the medical system.

The Great Depression created severe financial difficulty for hospitals. Health insurance designed to help with high medical costs began to
appear and was looked at with much interest by the financially strapped
hospitals. During this period the primary source of health care was the
physicians who determined the place and course of treatment for elderly
patients.

### 1935 to 1949

Two important changes affecting the future linkages among the health
care subsystems occurred during this 15-year period; they were the expansion of voluntary health insurance and passage in 1935 of the Social
Security Act. The health subsystems linkages during the period, however,
remained much the same as in the earlier years of the century. The trends
in health care continued to center on hospital-based medical services.
Boarding homes and convalescent homes became more popular as modes
of care for the elderly. Some of the homes began to provide nursing
services for their sick residents and thus evolved into nursing homes.
These nursing homes, however, were not integrated into the medical care
system.

### 1950 to 1964

During this period there was a marked increase in the number of elderly
persons requiring health care. Chronically ill, elderly patients were filling
acute-care beds in hospitals, so much so that the hospitals themselves
began to look for means to ease the overcrowding.

Health insurance continued to expand—both in numbers of persons and benefits covered—until, by 1960, 87 percent of the total population had some form of hospital coverage. In the high-risk group over
age 65, however, only about 47 percent were covered. Government intervention appeared to be necessary.

A most dramatic economic change for the elderly had occurred with
the passage of the Social Security Act of 1935. Included in the Act were
Old Age Survivors' Insurance (OASI) and Old Age Assistance (OAA). The
latter program was administered by the federal government and state
welfare departments. These programs gave the elderly the choice of
remaining in their own homes or going to boarding and convalescent

homes. The federal grants were not available, however, to persons in "such public institutions as almshouses or county farms." The elderly, therefore, had little incentive to go to public institutions.

Experience also indicated that cash OASI and OAA payments did not satisfactorily cover the medical expenses of the elderly. States, if they wished, could pay for additional medical services for the aged, but such additional payments were not contributed to by the federal government. In 1960, however, federal matching funds became available to states which provided medical assistance to the elderly when Congress passed the Medical Assistance for the Aged (MAA) legislation, also known as the Kerr-Mills Bill. Kerr-Mills substantially increased federal funds for states to make medical-services vendor payments; in return, states were expected to expand their medical care programs for the aged. Nevertheless, few states were willing to allocate additional funds for such care programs, even with matching federal monies—thus a relatively small number of states used the bulk of MAA funds. Also during this period, hospitals discovered they needed nursing homes, and slowly their reluctance to establish relationships with them waned and linkages between hospitals and nursing homes improved.

*1965 to 1972*

In this period efforts were made to bring the nursing home industry into the mainstream of the health care system. The most significant legislation passed was the Social Security Amendments (PL 89-97) that initiated the Medicare and Medicaid programs; the programs were designed to aid medically high-risk groups, notably the aged and the poor. The legislation made two major assumptions:

- The insurance program, Medicare, would meet the needs of the aged. The welfare component, Medicaid, was a secondary program to meet the needs of a few individuals. (This assumption proved to be erroneous.)
- Given financial incentives, the nursing home industry would respond by developing additional resources (it did to some degree) and comply with federal certification standards for participation (it did not).

By July 1969 the number of fully certified homes—now called skilled nursing facilities, or SNFs—had almost doubled and a demand for nursing home care for the elderly had been created. Politically and socially, the government found itself with only one option: to certify nursing homes that failed to meet the nursing-home standards as extended care facilities, or ECFs. Costs spiraled.

Medicaid faced similar problems. Under Title XIX the federal government agreed to match state payments for care of patients at the level of skilled nursing homes. If the patient was classified as needing a lower level of institutional care, the state was reimbursed at the former OAA rate. With this kind of financial incentive, some states reclassified lower-level facilities to SNFs and patients as in need of skilled nursing care. There was no incentive to lower costs.

In 1967 Congress enacted PL 90-248, which authorized federal matching funds for a lower level of care in the ICFs, with the understanding that as many as 50 percent of the SNF patients could have their needs met in lower-cost ICFs. In general, however, states have made no substantial effort to classify ICFs. Rather than improve care and reduce costs, many states have simply licensed those nursing homes that fail to qualify as skilled facilities as ICFs with decreased levels of services. Thus, up to 1972, the federal government assumed a central role in financing medical care but adhered to the principle of noninterference (Moroney and Kurtz 1976). Legislative programs likewise have been disappointing, and despite increased funding, nursing homes did not notably respond to opportunities to upgrade services and standards or to extend care.

Vogel and Palmer (1985) focus on the question of alternatives, primarily on costs, cost-effectiveness and cost-efficiency. These issues are extremely controversial. It is important to analyze costs relative to the quality of care provided. Indeed, for Pollak (cited in Vogel and Palmer), the cost of long-term care is a function of care at a given level of quality for a given level of impairment; the trick is to define and measure quality. In fact, families and patients do not agree with most professionals and see less need for services than do professionals (Coe and Kahana 1976).

During this period a number of research efforts were begun to evaluate the costs of community services as an alternative to institutional care. The Channeling Initiative was a multi-state research project that was designed primarily to determine—once and for all—if community care was a cost-efficient alternative to nursing home care. Three articles—Carcagno and Kemper (1988); Weissert (1988); and Kemper (1988)—provide the core of information on the channeling demonstration program.

The concept of channeling, particularly the role of basic case management in channeling, and the financial control model described by Carcagno and Kemper are critical. It is also important to consider the intended effects of the demonstration program, including the increased use of community services, reduced use of nursing homes and hospitals, and reduced cost of long-term care. A review of the information learned from the demonstration and the current focus of research efforts in this area is important.

*1973 to 1985*

During this period, two major legislative initiatives relating to long-term care focused attention on the pressing need to cut costs in health care. These initiatives were the Tax Equity and Fiscal Responsibility Act of 1982 and the Social Security Amendments and introduction of the DRG (diagnosis-related group) system in 1983. The impact of the trends in public health care financing during this period yields one continuing theme: the evolution of a competitive health care system and the recognition of accountability on the part of the health care providers. There have been major provisions, revisions and budget cuts that have resulted in a Medicare system far different from that brought into effect by the enactment of Medicare in 1965. Estes (1982) proposes three general factors that shaped the development of health care policy during the period and made it possible for the Reagan and Bush administrations to control federal expenditures in regard to health care from 1980 to the present. These factors follow:

1.  There was a political declaration of fiscal crisis at the federal level that generated a climate of intense psychological uncertainty and vulnerability in the American public to proposals to dismantle major social programs.
2.  There was a growing perception that the problems of the elderly and other disadvantaged groups could not be solved by instituting national policies and programs; rather, the solutions had to come from the efforts of state and local government, or from private sector or individual initiatives.
3.  There was a popular perception in the United States that old age was a problem resulting largely from the biological and physiological decline of the aging individual; it was further believed that the dependency of the elderly was a consequence of individual default.

The passage of the Tax Equity and Fiscal Responsibility Act (TEFRA) of 1982 was fueled by many of the perceptions described above and dramatically limited public expenditures for health care of the elderly. For the first time since the "Great Society" programs of the 1960s, the political legitimacy and utility of the elderly came into question. Collins (1982) indicates that the Tax Equity and Fiscal Responsibility Act of 1982 had sweeping, negative effects on long-term health care for the elderly. Those effects had a direct impact on (1) Medicare Part A, by increasing patient deductibles and co-insurance; (2) Medicare Part B, by increasing the annual deductible for physicians' services; (3) limiting the enrollment period for Medicare Part B coverage and restricting coverage to the first 3 months of the year, as opposed to the open-ended enrollment that was previously allowed; (4) limiting outpatient services; and (5) reducing reimbursement to hospitals and home health agencies.

Hospital reimbursement under the TEFRA legislation outlined a plan that placed a ceiling on growth for charges to patients given health care covered by Medicare. The basis for the legislation was the adoption of the plan to reimburse hospitals according to the established cost per case. Thus, beginning October 1, 1982, no hospital could exceed 120 percent of the established mean cost per case for all hospitals of similar types. This ceiling was then lowered to 115 percent in 1983 and 110 percent in 1984 (Verville 1982). On March 24, 1983, Congress approved a Medicare prospective pricing plan for most inpatient services as part of the Social Security Amendments of 1983. Thus, Medicare payment for inpatient services on the basis of prospective prices replaced the cost-per-case limits imposed by TEFRA. This new legislation applied to all hospitals except children's, psychiatric, rehabilitation and long-term hospitals. The basic features of the Medicare prospective payment system were the following: (1) all patients were classified into one of 468 diagnosis-related groups (DRGs); (2) with the exception of a limited number of "outlier" patients, the hospital would receive a fixed payment per DRG to cover operating costs; (3) the payment per DRG received by a hospital would be a function of area wages, whether it was in a rural or urban area, and the number of full-time interns and residents on staff; and (4) capital costs and direct education were to be passed through, but the secretary was to report to Congress on methods of including these costs in the prospective rates (Lave 1984).

The legislative initiatives described above had the effect of revolutionizing the long-term health care delivery system. Home health agencies became the prime benefactors in this system as fierce competition arose between the emerging health care corporations. Likewise, the nursing home industry experienced a shift in its market and in its position in the health care field.

*1986 to Present*

This period has been characterized by further cost-containment measures but also by an attempt on the part of the federal government to develop a mechanism of long-term health care insurance, which would at the very least prevent catastrophic financial losses on the part of older people and their families. To this end, the Medicare Catastrophic Coverage Act was passed in 1988. The act was designed to put cost ceilings on out-of-pocket expenses related to health care for catastrophic illness. Although the Catastrophic Coverage Act was repealed one year after being passed, many of its provisions have been restored.

Current initiatives in long-term care focus primarily on developing a system for federal coverage of nursing home care. However, at a time of immense fiscal constraints, most initiatives for the development of long-term care health insurance programs have not been successful.

## EVOLVING THEMES IN LONG-TERM CARE

### Family, Formal, and Informal Support

The increased concern regarding the role of the family in caring for the chronically ill elderly led to the early studies of family caregiving characteristics (Shanas 1979). This led to the early studies of caregiver burden (Lebowitz 1978) and work on old age and family functioning (Fengler and Goodrich 1979) and ultimately to studies of how formal services might reduce caregiver stress by providing relief from caregiving responsibilities (Rathbone-McCuan 1976; Horowitz 1978). The acknowledgment of the critical role that families play in the care of their older family members and the need that family members have for formal services to supplement the care they deliver eventually led to the development and expansion of formal support services for the elderly and their families.

Providing the elderly with long-term care services presents complex and multidimensional problems—problems of financial, physical and emotional dependence-independence for both the elderly person and the caregiver. There are no facile answers; the solutions are often imperfect and frequently as complicated as the problems themselves.

The issue of funding for long-term care has become more and more pronounced as health care costs continue to spiral. A Congressional Budget Office (CBO) study provides startling statistics about providing home health care benefits (CBO 1988; "Administration cuts spending" 1988). The CBO examined Reagan administration Medicare cuts and found $2.4 billion less was spent on home health and nursing home benefits since 1984 than the amount Congress had estimated was needed. In the same period, studies have shown a doubling of demand for some home health services. The growth rate of home health care coverage plummeted from 20 percent in 1984 and 16.7 percent in 1985 to 4.3 percent in 1986 and 6.4 in 1987. The emphasis on cost containment and reduction in services can be found in the CBO's view of the reason for the drop in services—"coverage restrictions imposed by the Health Care Financing Administration."

Another important issue related to the utilization of services, but independent from the issues of cost containment and reduction in services has to do with the distinctions made between formal services and informal support. In this regard, it is important to note the distinctions identified by Litwak (1985) regarding formal institutions and primary group structures and apply his model of formal organizations and primary group structures. In the model, Litwak compares and contrasts formal organizations and primary group structures in terms of recruitment, commitment and tasks.

Comparison of Formal and Informal Group Structures

|  | *Formal* | *Informal* |
| --- | --- | --- |
| *Recruitment* | Technical knowledge | Birth/marriage/ friendship |
| *Commitment* | Limited; based most often on fee for service | Long-term; life based on internalized level of commitment, duty and love |
| *Tasks* | Technical skills | Skills developed through socialization, companionship, assistance with basic and instrumental activities |

It is clear that informal networks, particularly primary groups, provide the majority of long-term care services for the chronically ill elderly and their caregivers (Stone 1987). It is also clear that this limits the demand for formal, community-based, long-term care programs. The primary group or informal network accomplishes this by:

· Diffusing the primary caregiver's stress, which in turn enables the primary caregiver to continue caregiving until another crisis arises.
· Providing emotional support and supplementary assistance with

basic and instrumental ADL, which reduces the need for formal respite services.
- Serving as the primary caregiver's only referral source to the outside world.

Treas (1977) and Shanas (1979) contributed most to the study of long-term family caregiving. The following summary of their work highlights the major issues—past and present—in formal and informal support services for the elderly and may also serve as a means of organizing future efforts in regard to these types of services.

- The long-term demographic trends of mortality and fertility have had startling consequences for the kin network.
- The aged's share of the population has grown relative to younger age groups.
- The older population has experienced not only growth, but also changes in composition.
- If family support systems are now taxed by the high ratio of aged to younger family members, the future promises little relief.
- Children routinely provide aging parents with services, companionship, financial aid, gifts, advice and counsel. These family exchanges often reveal a gender-biased division of labor.
- To a greater extent than their predecessors, the cohort of women aged 41 to 55 have husbands and children whose interests must be balanced against those of aging kin.
- The role of filial piety in caregiving is significant.
- Historical changes in the economic organization of society have operated to reduce the economic clout that aged parents can exercise over grown children.
- By the time parents reach old age, children have established careers and independent lives and hence are in a position to resist whatever economic threats or inducements parents might muster. Rather than being motivated by economic coercion, assistance to kin rests on delicate sentiments such as affection, gratitude, guilt, or a desire for parental approval.
- Public opinion will be increasingly disposed in favor of the nevitable growth of governmental and private intervention in the care of the aged.
- Individual and informal assistance to elderly relatives and assistance based on intimacy may avoid the unpleasant consequences often associated with caregiver stress.
- There are significantly more unmarried and never-married elderly

in institutions for the sick and frail compared to elderly living at home.
· Persons without close family are more likely to be institutionalized when they are ill. This includes the very old, who are largely widowed women, as well as the never-married.
· About one of every four persons who report spending one or more days in bed because of sickness also report having no help at all.
· The elderly have regular and frequent contact with their children.
· The presence of immediate relatives makes it possible for bedfast persons to live outside institutions.
· It is not necessary for older people to have many visitors. It *is* important that they have regular and concerned visitors.
· Old people turn first to their families for help, then to neighbors, and finally to the bureaucratic replacements for families—social workers, ministers, community agencies and others—because they expect families to help in case of need.

### The Continuum of Long-Term Care Services

The continuum of long-term care services can be defined by the identification of an elderly population to be served, the types of services available and the purpose of the services. The target populations include well elderly, temporarily ill elderly, frail elderly residing in the community and frail elderly residing in institutions. The types of services available include nutrition; health and medical; home support; recreational, educational, social and cultural; mental health; housing; transportation; legal; life management and financial assistance. The purposes of the services, singly or in combination, can include prevention, therapy, rehabilitation, support and maintenance.

At this point, the issues pertaining to community services available to elderly individuals, including health, housing and social services, must be addressed. According to the definition cited by Monk (1985), social services are "a flexibly organized system of activities and institutions to help attain satisfying standards of life and health while helping people develop their full capacities in personal and social relationships." Clearly, this asserts the value of social service providers in assisting the chronically or functionally disabled elderly to maintain independence. Therefore, social service providers must shift from focusing on symptom-oriented treatment to focusing on disease-prevention and health-promotion strategies. This shift is imperative to encourage the elderly to enhance their health status and develop self-reliance.

Now that the Tax Equity and Fiscal Responsibility Act (TEFRA) is more than ten years old, problems inherent in the legislation have been identified and corrected. The TEFRA-mandated patient classification system based on diagnostically related groups (DRGs), in particular, appears to adversely affect health services and treatment received by the elderly under Medicare and the elderly and others under Medicaid. Designed to pay hospitals standard rates based on a combination of diagnosis and length of stay, DRGs also prompt hospitals to save money by beating the game—that is, by discharging patients "quicker and sicker." As a result of the early discharges, elderly patients have developed higher-than-before utilization rates of SNF services and rehospitalizations (U.S. GAO 1985; Monk and Stuen 1988). Clearly, the system must be reevaluated to guarantee that the elderly are provided with quality health care in both hospital and community settings.

In regard to community care, particularly home care, there are few educational or training requirements for those who provide most of the care for home-bound elderly. Home care services reimbursable under Medicare and Medicaid are, for the most part, provided by caregivers who are not subject to educational or licensure requirements. The Home and Community Based Services for the Elderly Act of 1985 (S 1181) calls for training of home care personnel providing medical services to the elderly, which may be seen as a possible solution to home care abuses.

## Model Long-Term Care Service Systems

A coordinated system and continuum of care for the elderly does not yet exist in the United States, yet the creation of such a system should be a main objective of the organization of services. Achieving this objective will require defining the components of a good system of care, reviewing examples of successful systems, and identifying means of improving, expanding and generalizing these efforts. In this direction an International Invitational Consensus Conference on Long-Term Care was sponsored by Columbia University's Center for Geriatrics and Gerontology in October 1986. The conference stimulated multidisciplinary group discussions on the desirability, feasibility, progress and achievements in building a complete system of health care for the elderly. A major focus of these discussions was cross-national comparisons of systems of health care for the elderly and resulted in a monograph that represented the recommendations of the international experts regarding long-term care and cross-national comparisons of systems of care (Gurland et al. 1988).

A review of model long-term care programs in the United Kingdom and Canada is provided by concentrating on three areas of long-term care services—physical, social and mental health. In addition, it is helpful to review the impact of various state long-term care assessment and service initiatives, including those of Connecticut, Florida, Massachusetts, Minnesota, New York, Oregon and Wisconsin (Benjamin 1985). Among the state projects are demonstration and pilot projects, multiple funding streams, Medicaid waiver opportunities, established statewide agency networks, strategies for the elderly to get access to services before becoming poor and slotted to institutional care, breakdown of boundaries between acute and long-term care through informed discharge planning and prescreening of potential nursing home clients, and the role of hospital planners and client management staff in community care networks.

Different countries have addressed long-term care in ways influenced by cultural tradition and social policy. It is useful to look at these long-term care systems with an eye to their appropriateness to establishing a system of care for the elderly in the United States.

The spectrum of care in the United States presently includes acute care, community services, day care and respite care. Within this spectrum, individuals get a mixture of benefits and services that depends on their economic status, the economic status and generosity of the particular state, and the ability of their case manager to assign or broker these services. Model programs, mostly concerned with issues of service delivery, are underway, but rarely are these connected with other programs. In addition, most long-term care strategies fail to consider clients as members of family units. New approaches, including the Lombardi program in New York State, multifunctional hospitals (nursing homes) and social HMOs, are also being implemented in an effort to serve long-term care needs. But overall in the United States, the system is a non-system; it is fragmented, duplicative, and often inaccessible.

*National Health Service*

With the development after World War II of the National Health Service, Great Britain established a range of programs and retirement benefits for their elderly through national budget appropriations. In contrast to the situation in the United States, Great Britain placed a high priority on health and social services at the national level and set forth a national plan for such services. Property taxes fund these programs, which are then administered through local geographic authorities. A general practitioner (GP) acts as gatekeeper to community services and as a member of a community health care team.

Community health care teams also include social workers, district health nurses, geriatric workers, community psychiatric nurses, the MESS squad (household cleanup crews dispatched by the public health department) and home-chore helpers. Other community services—such as day care and meal programs—are available; specialized geriatric hospitals, which are reserved for acute cases, and geriatric consultants are also available by referral from a GP.

Local authority homes, developed from retirement homes, are administered under the auspices of Social Services and have social workers as matrons. They do not have a medical director or institutional atmosphere; they utilize the services of a community GP and health care team in the same manner as these services are used in the community. As the numbers of frail elderly increase, however, there are signs that local authority homes may need to provide more medical services.

The major differences and similarities between London and New York elderly can be seen in the treatment of dementia. Prevalence of the disease is about 40 percent in both cities. Sixty-seven percent of the care given to dementia patients in New York, however, is given in nursing institutions, while 64 percent of the care provided in London is given in residential settings. Moreover, a higher percentage of patients in New York are likely to be in skilled nursing beds. In New York, 90 percent of the demented are institutionalized; in London only 50 percent reside in local authority homes.

Compared with London facilities for long-term care, New York facilities are more medically oriented, have more staff and larger physical plants. In New York dementia patients are often separated or segregated from others, while in London there are small, residential facilities with little segregation of patients and a more heterogeneous mix (due largely to the size of the facility). Thus, New York appears to devote much more of its long-term care resources to institutional care: larger, more sophisticated, more technological and more expensive facilities with little to suggest that care or the quality of life for the demented elderly is any better than it would be in less expensive community settings.

*Canadian System*

As long-term care benefits have been introduced over the past decade in various Canadian provinces, that country's rate of health care spending—

expressed as a proportion of the Canadian gross national product—has remained consistently below that of the United States.

Kane and Kane (1985a, 1985b) have studied the Canadian long-term care system. It is an extension of Canada's national health insurance program, which has been in effect for many years. Certain aspects of Canada's economic system and sociocultural ethos likely impact the national long-term care program. The parliamentary system, for example, has fostered widespread public acceptance of a large government role. So too has the density of Canada's population; Canada is slightly larger than the U.S., but with only one-tenth the number of people. Canada's federal system is also smaller, with only 10 provinces and two territories—all of which may make health financing and planning somewhat less complex. And fewer hospitals, medical schools and government agencies make coordination of services less cumbersome.

The long-term care system in Canada consists of a mix of for-profit and nonprofit agencies and institutions. Although a person's income is considered, every older person is assured nursing home care without a means test. The level of functional impairment is the basis for eligibility. Institutionalized persons pay room charges designed to leave even those who depend solely on government pensions with some discretionary income. Typically, for-profit facilities are paid a per diem rate, which is negotiated annually by province. Nonprofit facilities, on the other hand, receive payments based on prospectively negotiated global budgets.

In 1982, Canadian public expenditures per nursing home bed averaged $9600 (U.S. currency equivalent), compared with combined state and federal expenditures of approximately $10,000 in the United States. In Canada, remaining costs are paid directly by the consumer; each province establishes a maximum daily ward rate, which is keyed to the minimum pension. Additional charges for private rooms and specified amenities are permitted but strictly controlled. The highest annual per-bed rate (Manitoba Province) is $15,400—compared with the U.S. average of $18,200.

The long-term care provisions of three Canadian provinces—British Columbia, Manitoba and Ontario—provide the central theme of Kane and Kane (1985a), who describe the salient features of the system in each province. They note that in Ontario there is a fixed daily amount for skilled nursing care that clients have to pay ($15.68), leaving them with approximately $96 of their monthly pension for discretionary personal expenses.

Homes for the Aged were started before the provincial long-term care program in Ontario, and were established by municipalities and nonprofit organizations to provide residential care to senior citizens who could not, or preferred not to, live in the community. Residents pay according to means; deficits the homes incur are met by the sponsoring organization or municipality and the province. There are now 13,000 persons in extended care beds in Homes for the Aged. Ontario also has chronic care hospitals that provide long-term care, some in free-standing settings but most in sections of general hospitals. These beds are paid for as part of the hospitals' global budget from the province and are free to patients. (After the 60th day, however, patients in such beds—as well as all patients in acute care awaiting a lower care level of bed—are charged the $15.68 per day fee.)

Since 1968, Ontario has had an acute home care program as part of its insurance benefit. The benefit is free; it was introduced in 1975 as a pilot program, but as of 1984 covered all 38 health districts. It covers nursing and therapeutic services, but it also provides homemaking services—80 hours in the first month and 40 hours in each subsequent month per admission, assuming that at least three medical visits per month are required for professional care.

The amount of homemaker care provided to each client is determined by home-care case managers in each health district. The Ministry of Health purchases nursing services from voluntary agencies at rates negotiated at a provincial level; homemaking devices are purchased from nonprofit and proprietary agencies. Although home-care case managers have a limited role, they represent an important resource for rationalizing home-based services. Some health districts in Ontario also have placement coordinators who complete assessments of all extended care applicants in their assigned districts and manage a centralized waiting list of these patients.

Manitoba has four levels of nursing home care, ranging from level one for those patients who require no more than 30 minutes of nursing care per day, to level four, which is analogous to Ontario's chronic care hospitals and is also offered in extended care units of general hospitals.

Since 1975, community care and case-management services in Manitoba have been provided by continuing care programs in each local health and social services department. Nurse-social worker teams serve as continuing care coordinators who assess eligibility for all long-term care services, including skilled nursing facility, home and day care. Homemaking is provided directly by public employees up to a maximum number of hours authorized by the coordinators. Nursing and therapies are also provided directly, but may be purchased from nonprofit agencies as well.

Applicants may not enter a skilled nursing facility without their cases being reviewed by an interdisciplinary panel. Home-care coordinators are responsible for assessing the applicants, organizing the information for the panel hearing, and managing the waiting list of persons who have been granted facility placement. The panel reviews medical information (provided by the applicant's physician), as well as social information, which helps to decide the appropriate plan for the individual patient. Home-care per-client expenditures are capped at the nursing home patient level, with exceptions possible for short-term terminal care if a skilled nursing bed is not available. Applicants are encouraged to make their own first and second choices of facilities. If forced to enter a different facility to free a hospital bed, they are put on the waiting list for the facility of their choice.

In British Columbia there are five levels of nursing home care—personal care, three intermediary levels, and extended care for persons unable to get out of bed independently. The province is divided into districts, which administer long-term care benefits. In each district, managers assess the functional status of applicants and determine their level of care. The managers may authorize homemaker services up to maximum limits set for each level of care; they may also authorize day care.

Homemaker services are purchased from nonprofit and for-profit agencies. Home nursing visits are provided by health department nurses. Case managers review each case every six months, after every intervening hospitalization, or as requested by the client or care provider. Case managers follow up their assessments of the client's needs no matter what level of long-term care the client is receiving.

## CONCLUSIONS: TOWARD A COORDINATED U.S. SYSTEM OF LONG-TERM CARE

Examining Canada's nationalized system of long-term care leads to a consideration of the lessons to be learned from it. These lessons can be used in the development of a national system of long-term care in the United States. In considering ways by which the U.S. system could be improved, it must be stipulated that proposed solutions address issues of service comprehensiveness, coordination and financing as part of the overall program. The following examples are supplied as a possible approach to improving the U.S. system and are not meant to be definitive or exhaustive.

A national system, jointly financed by the federal and state governments, might provide a productive solution to the current dilemma in long-term care in the United States. In addition to joint federal and state funding, a certain portion of the elderly's monthly pension should be withheld for use by the government in the continued financing of long-term care.

States would be compelled to implement the long-term care program developed at the national level. Each state government would administer its own program. Programs would be organized into geographical units or districts, each with a public health department to determine the medical and social needs of each candidate for long-term care. Case managers would be responsible for monitoring the progress and ongoing needs of each patient and adjusting the care plans for the patient accordingly. There should be no means testing for the elderly to gain access to the system; all should be eligible for long-term care services.

For more and more health care consumers and providers, a national system of long-term care in the United States is an idea whose time has come. However, it can only become a reality if citizens and legislators alike are willing to declare that good health care is a right, not a privilege.

## REFERENCES

Administration cuts spending. *The New York Times*, February 7, 1988.

Armour, P., C. Estes and M. Noble. Implementing the Older Americans Act. In R. Hudson, ed., *The Aging in Politics: Policy and Process*. Springfield, IL: Charles C Thomas, 1981.

Benjamin, A.E., Jr. Community-Based Long-Term Care. In C. Harrington et al., eds., *Long-Term Care of the Elderly*. Beverly Hills: Sage, 1985.

Brody, S.J. and C. Maschiocchi. Data for long-term care planning by health system agencies. *Am. J. Public Health* 70(11):1194-1198, 1980.

Brickner, P., A. Lechich, R. Lipsman and L. Scharer. *Long-Term Health Care*. New York: Basic Books, 1987.

Carcagno, G. and P. Kemper. The evaluation of the national long-term care demonstration: an overview of the channeling demonstration and its evaluation. *Health Services Res.* 23(1):1-23, 1988.

Coe, R. and E. Kahana. Alternatives in Long-Term Care. In S. Sherwood, ed., *Long-Term Care: A Handbook for Researchers, Planners and Providers*. New York: Spectrum Publications, 1976.

Cole, P. Morbidity in the United States. In E. Jaco, ed., *Patients, Physicians and Illness*. New York: Free Press, 1979.

Collins, J. Medicare and Medicaid: cuts and concerns. *Geriatrics* 37:33-39, 1982.

Congressional Budget Office. Memorandum to Kathy Gardner, Subcommittee on Health and Long-Term Care, House Committee on Aging: Preliminary Estimates of Medicare SNF and Home Health Outlays. Washington, DC: Congressional Budget Office, February 5, 1988.

Estes, C. Austerity and aging in the United States: 1980 and beyond. *Int. J. Health Services* 12:573-584, 1982.

Fengler, A. and N. Goodrich. Wives of elderly disabled men: the hidden patients. *The Gerontologist* 19:175-183, 1979.

Gurland, B., et al. The Organization of Mental Health Services for the Elderly. In L. Lazarus, ed., *Essentials of Geriatric Psychiatry.* New York: Springer, 1988.

Health Care Financing Administration. *Long-Term Care: Background and Future Directions.* Washington, DC: Health Care Financing Administration, January, 1981.

Horowitz, A. Families who care: A study of natural support systems of the elderly. Paper presented at the Annual Scientific Meeting of the Gerontological Society, November, 1978.

Kane, R.A. and R.L. Kane. *A Will and a Way: What the United States Can Learn from Canada about Caring for the Elderly.* New York: Columbia University Press, 1985a.

Kane, R.A. and R.L. Kane. The feasibility of universal long-term benefits: ideas from Canada. *N. Engl. J. Med.* 312(21):1357-1364, 1985b.

Kemper, P. The evaluation of the national long-term care demonstration: overview of the findings. *Health Services Res.* 23(1):161-174, 1988.

Koch, A. Finance and Reimbursement in Long-Term Care: Paying the Price. In *AUPHA Modules for Management Education.* Arlington, VA: Association of University Programs in Health Administration, 1989.

Lave, J. Hospital reimbursement under Medicare. *Health Care Financing Management* 35:62-74, 1984.

Lebowitz, B. Old age and family functioning. *J. Gerontol. Social Work,* Winter, 1978, pp. 111-118.

Litwak, E. *Helping the Elderly: The Complementary Roles of Informal Networks and Formal Systems.* New York: Guilford Press, 1985.

Miles, A. *Public Welfare.* Boston: D.C. Heath, 1949.

Monk, A., ed. *Handbook of Gerontological Services.* New York: Van Nostrand Reinhold, 1985.

Monk, A. and C. Stuen. *The Impact of Medicare and Prospective Payment System on the Elderly Patient: Study of Three New York City Hospitals.* New York: Columbia University, Brookdale Institute on Aging, October, 1988. .

Moroney, R. and N. Kurtz. The Evolution of Long-Term Care Institutions. In S. Sherwood, ed., *Long-Term Care: A Handbook for Researchers, Planners and Providers.* New York: Spectrum Publications, 1976.

Pizer, H., ed., *Over 55, Healthy and Alive.* New York: Van Nostrand Reinhold, 1985.

Rathbone-McCuan, E. Geriatric day care: a family perspective. *The Gerontologist* 16:517-521, 1976.

Ruchlin, H. and S. Levey. An Economic Perspective of Long-Term Care. In S. Sherwood, ed., *Long-Term Care: A Handbook for Researchers, Planners and Providers.* New York: Spectrum Publications, 1976.

Saxon, S.V. and M.J. Etten. *Physical Change and Aging: A Guide for the Helping Professions, 2nd Ed.* New York: Tiresias Press, 1987.

Shanas, E. The family as a social support system in old age. *The Gerontologist* 19(2):169-174, 1979.

Stone, R. National profile of caregivers. *The Gerontologist* 27:616-631, 1987.

Treas, J. Family support systems for the aged: some social and demographic considerations. *The Gerontologist* 17(6):486-491, 1977.

U.S. Bureau of the Census. *Statistical Abstract 1986. U.S. Census of the Population 1980.* Washington, DC: U.S. Government Printing Office, 1986.

U.S. General Accounting Office. *Information Required for Evaluating the Impact of Medical Prospective Payments of Post-Hospital Long-Term Care Services: Preliminary Report.* GAO/PEMD 85(8):1-90, February 21, 1985.

Verville, R. A look at the new Medicare-Medicaid provisions. *AANA J.* 51:505-508, 1982.

Vogel, R.J. and H.C. Palmer, eds. *Long-Term Care Perspectives from Research and Demonstration.* Rockville, MD: Aspen Systems Corporation, 1985.

Weissert, W. The national channeling demonstration: what we knew, know now, and still need to know. *Health Services Res.* 23(1):175-187, 1988.

# 2

# The Process of
# Long-Term Care

*Shura Saul, EdD, BCD, CSW and
Sidney R. Saul, EdD, BCD, CSW*

We have long ceased to regard "old age" as a fixed point on the life cycle, but rather we have come to recognize that senescence (the process of aging) is a developmental stage of life that may span as many as 20, 30 or even 40 years of an individual's lifetime. While the aging process is a phase of the life-cycle continuum, it also comprises several specific phases of its own. Therefore, senescence must be viewed also as its own continuum of conditions, circumstances and complexities.

If we are to comprehend the process, it becomes important to recognize, identify and understand the changes and differences that develop for and within an individual between the early and late stages of this lengthy time span. Mental health is an integral dimension of a person's total health, involving physical, emotional, psychosocial and intellectual components. It is also a vital dimension of human survival. Practically speaking, it is the ability of a person to cope in individually unique and self-constructive ways with the ups and downs of life; to adapt to what cannot be controlled; to control what is reasonable and possible.

Every person develops a range of strategies and coping mechanisms to maintain survival and to protect it when it seems to be threatened. Individual behaviors will differ. The common denominators, however, are that the mentally healthy person strives to live constructively, finds ways to adapt to the challenges of the immediate situation, and learns to accept realistic limitations and to deal with disappointments. The goal is to sustain the positive and negative stresses of life, to behave in both a socially and individually appropriate manner, and to seek and develop a socially and individually suitable style of enjoying life.

The aging process, replete with its diversity of changes, presents every individual with situations that call upon all earlier coping capacities, especially the skills of adaptation and flexibility. The elderly must determine which of their earlier responses to life have been constructive and useful, in what ways they require adaptations, and what new responses are needed to meet the challenges of situations previously not experienced.

Change itself, whether positive or negative, constitutes a stress upon the personality. The quality of loss inherent in many changes during aging, coupled with societal and individual unpreparedness for the entire process of aging, may exert a negative impact upon the emotional, psychosocial and mental strength of the person, and therefore affect his health. The entire concept of care to be offered throughout this lengthy time span (i.e., long-term care) must relate to the needs generated by these phenomenal changes and to the environment, both social and individual, of the person who requires it.

> The modern aging person performs his/her developmental tasks with consideration for the range of changes, discontinuities, unpreparedness and crises of his/her own life....The very content of the changes in senescence offers unique, qualitative differences from the earlier stages....For the aged person these discontinuities may be experienced one at a time, or in combination. They may occur suddenly and traumatically, or in slow progressions. How they occur is also important (Saul 1983, pp. 44-45).

Some of the discontinuities that strain the older person's capacity to function in keeping with lifelong patterns of control include physical and biological changes, economic and social discontinuities, crises, trauma and death.

## RETIREMENT AND ITS ACCOMPANIMENTS

A prevailing circumstance of sharp discontinuity, which generally occurs early in senescence, is retirement and the entire constellation of events that accompanies it. Even though it is an accepted reality of aging in modern society, retirement is a point of discontinuity. Individual expectations of this change vary from a very positive outlook ("Now I can do everything I couldn't do while I was working") to a totally negative one ("When I stopped working, I died"). These are actual statements by alert, high-functioning, skilled members of the work world, anticipating or coping with separation from the work role. These comments describe the parameters of thoughts and feelings about the changes in the organization of their lives and the consequent impact upon some important relationships and meaningful activities.

In retirement, the inner and outer person must deal with an identity crisis to answer the questions, "Who am I?" and "What am I now?" The struggle to answer these questions, and answering them to one's own satisfaction, is an ego activity that continues throughout life. Especially reminiscent of adolescence it becomes very pressing at the point of retirement when one's identification with the work role is altered or lost. A worker from any walk of life (business, professional or blue-collar) has generally identified, even if only in part, with some aspect of the work role. Work for some is a source of status and accomplishment and expresses the meaning of life. For others it may have represented solely a source of income. But even to those with the least meaningful jobs, the work role has organized life routines, provided structure and a set of relationships and challenges that have been met over a long period of time. Even for these people, who are eager to be rid of the burdens of their jobs, the changes wrought by their retirement call for major adaptations.

Those who have identified more deeply with the work role may experience real confusion when they retire.

"How do I introduce myself?" asked a former director of a department of a major urban hospital. "I used to be the Director of Housekeeping. Now what am I?"

A social psychologist once commented, "The saddest remark I ever heard was I used to be a doctor.'"

These are commentaries on the significance of work role to the person's identity and self-esteem. For some men the loss may be very threatening and even devastating, especially for those whose work has been all-enveloping and who have relegated other life activities to lesser status. This may be just as true for many women in the work world.

The aging homemaker and housewife also experiences role losses. In fact, this may even occur at two different points in her life. The first of these may have occurred earlier than her spouse's (or her own) retirement. The syndrome of the "empty nest" may present a serious, even traumatic, circumstance of discontinuity as the woman's nurturing role is drastically altered. Some women may turn to the work world at this point, and then at retirement they must again cope with separation from the new identity that they developed.

The homemaker who does not enter the work world has also found new ways to organize her life during the empty nest period while her husband is still at work. She too faces change and must make alterations when he retires. ("I married him for better or for worse, but not for three meals a day!") Both husband and wife must find ways to renew their marriage contract, to reassess their relationship and to establish a new homeostasis in the organization of their lives.

All retired people—married or single, rich or poor—must revise daily schedules, alter the balance of their activities, cope with new or renewed relationships and set new expectations. All this work must be performed within the context of other changes, such as economic, health and energy differences, to name an obvious but significant few.

These are stressful demands. Although not necessarily negative ones, they do require a rallying of one's healthiest and most powerful emotional, mental and psychological capacities. They affect people in all walks of life. However, individuals with better access to and control of the necessities of life (e.g., finances, housing, daily living arrangements and physical health) may be more free to cope with psychological concerns.

It is at this point on the continuum of the aging process that intervention can begin to be helpful. There can be some preparation for anticipating, through planning and forethought, some of the major changes imposed by retirement. Pre-retirement counseling should include concrete information and offer appropriate assistance in planning. Such counseling should also help the pre-retiree to develop some awareness and anticipation of the psychosocial aspects and forthcoming pressures on the inner self. At this point in time, the meaning of life to the individual becomes a paramount issue.

## HEALTH AND MENTAL HEALTH

Another important prevailing circumstance is the cluster of physiological and biological changes that accompany the aging process and require awareness and adaptation for healthy functioning. These include sensory losses (waning of vision or hearing), a slowing down of certain physiological processes, and possibly some diminished energies and endurance. These are, of course, individually unique circumstances that develop at different points in time for different people. The manner in which an individual responds to these changes is related to and has an effect upon that person's mental health. Those who have integrated the stereotype of aging as a period of inevitable breakdown and regard these changes as threats to their survival may well develop such emotional responses as anger, depression, anxiety, self-deprecation or a negative self-image. Some people practice the mechanism of denial, sometimes with positive affect ("Never mind, I'm going to function anyway as well as I can!"). Others, however, may utilize denial to such an extreme point as to negate important reality factors with extremely negative consequences.

The syndrome of "This isn't happening to me—I can keep going just as I always did" may well result in an inability to recognize one's growing dependency needs in given areas and a refusal to accept help. Under these conditions, unattended physical problems will undoubtedly escalate, and the individual's ability to function in a normally healthy manner may become severely impaired. One's very survival may be threatened. The quality of the person's life becomes poorer and the problems that proliferate usually wreak great hardships upon family, friends and neighbors. To put it mildly, this individual's judgment may be described as "impaired" and their mental health is not good.

Another type of discontinuity is experienced by the person who suffers a traumatic illness such as stroke, heart attack, or other sudden catastrophic condition. This, of course, may happen to anyone at any age and have a deleterious effect upon mental as well as physical health. Some older people experiencing a life-threatening illness may feel less capable of surviving it. They may become despondent and even uncooperative in treatment. Some of these physical conditions are known to cause brain damage (e.g., stroke); others directly affect mood (e.g., diabetes is closely connected with depression).

Another dimension of the physical condition and its treatment is the use of medications and their effect upon mood, cognitive abilities and libido. In the U.S., it well known that a leading cause of confusion and disorientation in people over 65 is the misuse of drugs and their interactions. The aging body metabolizes medications much more slowly and the tendency for the older person to become overmedicated is not adequately appreciated.

The interrelationship of physical and mental health is very clear in the diagnoses of a number of physical conditions. Equally important, however, is the relationship between diminution of capacity, energy and sensory acuity and the development of altered mood and diminished enjoyment of life. In many cases, catastrophic illness may short-circuit the normally expected continuum of aging. Such an event may force elderly persons to enter a long-term care facility where their life follows a very different route from what may have been anticipated. This may occur under circumstances of severe chronic illness as well. Even when the person remains at home, but chronically ill and home-bound, life is inexorably altered.

## FINANCES

Older Americans are financially better off today than they were 50 years ago, mostly due to Social Security income and improved retirement plans. Yet the economic situation for most retirees is far from glowing. The "rich old geezers" are few—most American seniors may be old and getting older, but they are not very rich (ABC News: "Growing Old in America" 1989). Most blue-collar workers who retired ten years ago on what had seemed to be an adequate income (Social Security plus a pension) may now find themselves unable to meet mortgage payments and medical costs. People in these circumstances are often forced to sell their retirement dream house and many have returned to jobs requiring a lower level of skill and at significantly lower pay. "I never worked so hard in all my life," said one such retired skilled machinist who, at age 70, could only get a job moving refuse in a factory (ABC News: "Growing Old in America" 1989).

Because of increased taxes, inflation and rising medical costs, the average worker today may still retire into poverty. Poverty spawns medical neglect and illness. The health and mental health of elderly people can be significantly affected by their economic circumstance. The 1990 Census reports that "People with incomes under $10,000 a year spent an average of 26 days with an illness or disability, while those with incomes over $35,000 spent less than ten" (Bureau of the Census, 1990).

Rising medical costs and inadequate health insurance may also lead to the neglect of health problems. These problems, which might be amenable to treatment or cure in the early stages, may well become major or chronic health problems leading to the need for long-term care at an earlier age than necessary. Again, this circumstance short-circuits the "normal flow of life."

## SOCIETAL AND FAMILY CHANGES

Societal changes and their impact upon the families of elders must also be considered. The anticipated progression of events in the aging process offers an expectation of grandparenthood and relationships with adult children. Today's world, with its stresses upon families (children as well as adults) such as the high incidence of divorce, unemployment, homelessness, substance abuse and AIDS, has affected the lives of many seniors as well. In many families, grandparenthood has brought a renewed demand for parenting—this time, of grandchildren. This may occur because of a variety of family situations, such as single-parent households, families requiring two earners to make ends meet or parental incapacity. Grandparents have entered these situations to assist with their own limited funds and waning energies. As in the Great Depression of the 1930s, some young families now have moved in with the older folks.

Family circumstances may affect even the middle-class elderly. Geographical separation occurs when younger families move far away to improve employment or living opportunities. Or, the older folks may have moved away for personal or economic reasons, especially after retirement. Problems develop when either the elders or the younger people develop new needs because of health, unemployment or other crisis situations. It is well known that the "sandwich generation" is deeply affected. Also affected are the elders who face either their own increased dependency needs or, sometimes, those of their "children." Again, the planned flow of life is interrupted by trauma.

## DEATH OF OTHERS

A most significant point of discontinuity in the lives of elderly people is the increasing experience of losses through death. Lives are changed and expectations altered when siblings, relatives or close friends of long standing become ill or die suddenly. The older person's social world diminishes. Opportunities for new relationships also dwindle. "It's not easy to make new friends," observed a charming, sparkling older woman who moved to a housing development for retirees. "Anyway," she added, "I don't want to get too friendly with anyone. Too many people are dying around here."

The death of a spouse is a most significant loss and probably causes the greatest pain for most older people, leaving a person feeling alone, abandoned and lonely. Most often an elderly couple will have spent from 40 to 70 years together. Such marriages are more than a "coupling," they are significant lifetime relationships. A person who is in their seventies, eighties or nineties who becomes widowed may lose not only a mate, but a very close friend as well. One octogenerian said tearfully, "I've lost the last person who knew me when I was young."

Reactions to such loss can vary greatly. The grieving process may last a long time. Denial, or lack of acceptance of the reality of the loss, may be very strong. One 94-year-old woman awakened every night for two years to prowl around the house, asking "Where is my husband?" She had denied his death completely. Similarly, another 75-year-old man spent hours looking down the street for his wife of 50 years, who had died suddenly in the hallway of their home. Some people eventually overcome their sorrow and grief and go on with their lives. Many others do not achieve such resolution. Sidney Saul (1968) found that the primary significant factor triggering a request for placement in a home for the aged was the loss of a caring person, most often the spouse. Lives are significantly altered by this type of loss.

## INSTITUTIONALIZATION

Placement in a residential care facility is another threatening disruption. The personal losses inherent in this move are enormous. The prevailing concept about placement in a long-term care facility is that it is the "last stop" and the person has come there to die. This in itself sets the stage for hopelessness, a first step toward depression and intensified mental illness. It is safe to say that almost every new resident comes into a nursing care facility with some level of depression from mild to severe. Depression stands out as the most prevalent condition prior to the suicide attempt. According to the World Health Organization, two types of losses are cited as major motivations for suicide: loss of health and loss of a loved one (Weiss 1968). While "waiting to die," the elderly nursing home resident must learn to live in this setting. This involves a singularly difficult set of tasks as the person must cope with a range of losses and changes—over and above those suffered by most older people who live at home.

In addition to conditions of physical (and often emotional as well as mental) illness, there are the limitations of the institution's rules and routines, which restrict personal freedom and opportunity to control one's life (Saul and Saul 1974). For some, suicide presents itself as a viable option, just as it does for other people who face seemingly insurmountable problems of living. The dependencies of illness are exponentially exacerbated by the emotional impact of separation from one's own home, familiar surroundings and people; of coping with alien life styles; of being cared for by strangers and of living and dying among them.

Loss of one's sense of identity (as established for decades prior to placement) and loss of self-esteem accompany and emphasize other changes and losses. Sadness, depression and frustration are common denominators of the elderly resident's existence (Gossett 1966). These dimensions of life in the institution are qualitative exacerbations of the life circumstances of some elderly people residing in the community— circumstances that may account, at least in part, for the high rate of suicide among old people (Choron 1972). The nursing home resident becomes a prime candidate for suicide as, for this person, almost all the apparent "requisites" prevail, including physical illness, widowhood, depression and hopelessness (Saul and Saul 1988-89).

The remarkable point to note is that so many elders adapt to institutional life and even find ways to appreciate some of its little-known positives (e.g., the security of food, clothing, shelter and needed care). This suggests a clue for improving institutional care. Effort must be directed toward improving the quality of institutional living so that the other common human needs described by Maslow may also be met. Indeed, the challenge to institutions is to find ways of helping a resident achieve some measure of self-actualization in spite of the obvious deterrents in this communal living arrangement. Studies of the various models of a therapeutic community, especially the model implemented by Maxwell Jones at Dingleton Hospital in Scotland, provide a fruitful and useful framework for improving residential health care facilities along these lines (Jones 1976). Also, the increasing numbers of Alzheimer's patients suggest the need for developing special programs within these facilities.

## SUICIDE AND FACING ONE'S OWN DEATH

The highest rate of suicide in the U.S. occurs among people aged 75 and older (Choron 1972). In 1974, elderly American males and females committed suicide three to four times more often than did younger persons of the same sex.

> The elderly account for a dispropotionately higher number of suicides. While many more young persons attempt suicide than commit suicide, the number of older people attempting suicide is roughly the same as the number actually committing suicide. These data indicate that suicide remains a serious problem among the elderly (Busse and Blazer 1980).

Weiss found the major factor in the high suicide rates among older people to be "isolation along with deprecating sociocultural attitudes, low socioeconomic status with loss of psychologically and socially rewarding occupation, biological decline and clinically recognized psychiatric disorders" (Weiss 1968). Concerns about one's own death are also to be noted. Fear of dying, related to the fear of the unknown, may be a constant concern for those elderly people who have not come to terms with their own mortality. This fear may be exacerbated by those who work with the elderly. The lecturers at a recent Elder Hostel program were instructed by the administration of the local university not to mention or introduce the subject of death. This was said despite the fact that the presentation was about the life cycle. (Interestingly enough, the subject was brought up by the elders themselves in the ensuing discussion.)

In the nursing home, where death is a daily occurrence, when given the opportunity residents are quite free to talk about and face the fact of death as a normal consequence of life. They are willing to talk freely and without fear of the death of a fellow resident. They often say that they do not fear their own death, only the pain and distress that may precede it. One resident said clearly, "If I could be sure to fall asleep and not wake up, and not feel any pain, I'd be willing to die tonight." This comment is typical of many elders, whether at home or in a nursing home.

## OMNICONVERGENCE

Any of these discontinuities, traumas and crises may and do occur in the lives of younger people as well as their elders. An important complicating factor for elderly persons, however, is the fact that several of these may, and usually do, occur simultaneously or consecutively within a very concentrated time period. This convergence of several disruptive situations, a seriously complicating feature of the aging process, has been described by Stanley Cath as "omniconvergence":

> For ease of communication and conceptualization, a new topographical and dynamic psychological construct is useful—omniconvergence ("omnicon"). This term includes not only phenomena in the personality structure (ego, superego and id) but also in the physical structure of the organism (the body and the body ego) and the socioeconomic ethical and purposeful environment. Omnicon thus signifies that the total human being and his personal cosmos are involved in the various epigenetic phases of loss of self and others....The ego's attempts at restorative processes will best be understood when seen in this total perspective of multiple converging epigenetic variables, and we are thus spared from taking sides in what appears to be a re-creation of the conflict between theories on the significant external and internal factors (Cath 1965).

This conceptualization suggests that the whole is greater than the sum of its parts. That is, the need to cope with several crises and changes converging within a relatively short period of time imposes an enormous stress upon an individual and affects all aspects of that person's life.

> This concept of omniconvergence suggests that when an older person requires help, the situation may call for several helping agents to merge their expertise for individual assistance within a unique situation. Such a merging is the interdisciplinary approach to service (Saul 1983).

## TOWARD A CONTINUUM OF SERVICE

This view of aging as a continuum within a developmental phase of life requires a parallel view of services on a continuum related to the developing needs of elderly persons. If the Maslowian idea of self-actualization is to be applied to the area of aging, efforts must be directed to support a person's healthy growth and development, to find the strengths and accentuate the positives. This approach, of course, suggests a simultaneous process of identifying all possible dependency needs that may develop (psychosocial, physical, mental and emotional), meeting and treating them to prevent deterioration, anticipating further needs and providing opportunities for their prevention and treatment.

Older persons, like any others, are helped best when they are perceived as individuals with a life style and integrity of their own. Help is given and received best when it is offered in harmony with the personality of the individual, family or group of people to be helped. In the aging process, just as in any other stage of life, there are normal dependency needs to be met. Usually, these needs are met through the organization of an individual's ongoing life style. However, as these needs may increase in number or intensity, the individual (as well as the other involved parties) may require supports or interventions. It is at this point that the continuum of long-term care should begin for the elderly, not as a system of intensifying dependency, but one that helps to meet their needs, thus freeing them to conduct life at the highest possible individual capacity for independent functioning. This, indeed, should be the goal of any caring system from cradle to grave: the freeing of individual strengths through the meeting of individual needs.

This approach calls for a very high level of individualization, support, interventions and caring modalities. This point of view is not very popular because of the myth that it is too costly for implementation through social policy. However, as any caregiver knows, individualization is the only way a person can be helped with dignity and humanity. The notion that this is too costly may be open to question on two counts. The first, a philosophic query, asks what is the "cost base"? That is, if we measure in terms of human cost, this is not a very expensive approach. In fact, it is humanly economical. If we measure within a financial frame of reference, it may or may not be expensive, depending on how the system is conceived, organized and administered.

> We asked the nurses in a very successful rehabilitation center in Scotland, "How do you organize the tasks of daily living? Does everyone get up at a certain time, bathe on a certain day, etc?" The nurse responded, "We used to do that, of course. That's how we were taught at school. But we found it took too much time and energy to coax the patients...and the cost in staff-patient relationships was too high. Now we work with the patients...those who want to rise early, do. Others want to breakfast in their dressing gowns, they do. We find that the unit is straightened up at the same time as ever, but with much less stress on the staff or the patients (Saul and Saul 1975).

This account contradicts the tenets of our current continuing categories of service "slots" with an emphasis on financial rather than human cost. This view even suggests that individualization of care costs less in terms of human stress and probably not more in dollar terms. However, to achieve this balance requires a sophisticated look at needs and how they may be met creatively, with imagination and insight, new methods of administration and task organization.

In the United State we have developed a range of need-meeting service models, many of which are very innovative, creative, imaginative and sound. It is not that we do not know what to do; it is that we have not implemented what we know. Demonstration projects and programs have been developed, conducted and concluded. Reports have been written and conferences held. More often than not, these are followed by little or no continuity; no implementation is instituted and no use is made of findings and recommendations. This wasteful practice must be ended. The findings and creativity of such caring programs must be implemented beyond the "demonstration project." This country's multicultural, multi-ethnic social network requires a wide diversity of need-meeting models and methodologies. There are many ways to serve, support and help people. Intergenerational, interdenominational, interethnic, interagency and interdisciplinary approaches should all be utilized appropriately.

## THE CONTINUUM OF NEED

The ongoing set of needs presented by older persons may vary at different points and with different individuals, depending on circumstances. Ideally, these needs should be met through a flexible system of services that can be described in general as follows:

1. For the person living at home: The range of supports begins with family, friends and neighbors. Preventive services may be offered through senior centers and other agencies: nutrition programs, social supports, group services, recreational and cultural activities, counseling and problem-solving, preventive health care (e.g., exercise programs, screening for physical health care needs, mental health services, information and referral). This suggests a major revision of the current concept of senior centers. Centers must extend their foci beyond the recreational, social, cultural and nutrition programs toward developing multipurpose, multi-generational and multiservice offerings, thus becoming true community centers. Center members themselves should be involved in planning and implementing such changes.

2. Should the elderly person living at home become less independent and develop new needs, services should be available such as:
   a. Family assistance programs: Where there is a family willing and able to meet the older person's needs, family members may be helped through any of a variety of plans. Some of these are: a range of respite programs, meals-on-wheels, tax exemptions for elder care, and support services for multiproblem families.
   b. Programs to support quality of life for home-bound elderly: health access programs, developed throughout the nation, which offer library and museum services; beauticians and barbers; telephone reassurance and telephone emergency assistance; friendly visiting; and special services for the visually handicapped and hard-of-hearing as well as other disabled persons. Many of these, currently in place, need to be extended with greater imagination and individual appropriateness.
   c. Housekeeping and home care services: These can and must be individually tailored to meet needs. For example, some people may need only morning or afternoon assistance; others only weekend or weekday care. Flexible programs such as these would enable the family and elderly person to maintain some

homeostasis and independence. Coordination of such home care services is important.

d. Transportation and home visiting services from health care workers.

e. Mental health professionals should make home visits and maintain an ongoing mental health care program. Referral in and out of mental hospitals should be possible, with follow-up after discharge. Community programs for outpatients should be in place.

f. Day care programs for physically dependent elderly people living at home.

g. Day care programs for mentally ill elderly people living at home (e.g., Alzheimer's patients and depressed elderly). A special note about care for Alzheimer's patients is in order here. There is no treatment for Alzheimer's disease, no "magic bullet," no cure. At this point in time we do not even know the cause. However, we can treat the accompanying psychiatric conditions that almost every Alzheimer's patient experiences: depression, anxiety and the loss of impulse behavior controls. Group and individual programs, which focus on alleviating these conditions, can and do help the Alzheimer's patient to be somewhat more comfortable during the course of the illness. They also help families and caregivers.

3. For the older person who may elect to live in a retirement home: A range of support services in retirement communities and facilities would offer needed preventive measures. Too often retirement communities overlook the needs and ignore the possibilities for such prevention. Support groups, counseling and problem-solving, assistance with family concerns, physical and mental health programs, and information and referral are some of the important services that would be useful in retirement communities.

4. When catastrophic illness strikes, hospital care is usually most appropriate. But hospital programs for elderly persons must be revised toward an improved understanding of the physical needs of the older patients as well as their psychosocial and emotional concerns when hospitalized. It is especially important to know and understand the total person; important information may not be included in the presenting diagnosis of the acute condition. Specially organized and specially staffed geriatric units are needed for certain elderly patients, although many may be treated in multigenerational units. The criteria for placement in a geriatric unit

would be highly individualized, depending on both physical and psychological condition and needs of the patient.

5. Discharge planning must be related to the individual circumstances of the patient, rather than to some general directives about "the elderly." There should be options beyond the "either-or" of nursing home placement or return to home. These should be discussed with the older person (when possible) and the family or other caring persons. Discharge to a rehabilitation center, to a coordinated home care program or a "nursing home without walls" should be considered. Such discharge planning is almost impossible in the current climate of pressure to discharge within a stipulated period that is determined by diagnosis and regulations. Elderly people generally require a longer recovery time from a catastrophic illness. The hospital discharge system must realize that a person's life and the quality of that life are being determined for a long time to come.

6. Nursing home placement: This is often used as an expedient, rather than because it is the best possible decision. When discharged from the hospital, elderly patients are often routinely sent to nursing homes without much exploration of alternatives or future planning. When an elderly person is living at home, families often feel pressured to place him because there has been little or no counseling, and there are few, if any options. Nursing home placement must also be viewed as part of a total treatment plan rather than an end in itself. Too often, it is seen as the "last stop"; the person is placed and all bridges burned (e.g., the home or apartment is given up). Yet it does happen that with nursing home care and treatment a person may achieve a better level of functioning and may even be able to eventually return home. There are enough such instances to warrant more attention to this possibility.

7. Hospice: Finally, there is a real need for developing a range of hospice care services for elderly people. The idea of helping a person to die with dignity has finally penetrated our health care system, but there are very few programs to implement it. The notion of hospice, so beautifully and humanely developed for certain categories of patients, must be extended to help elderly patients who may not fit these categories. The elderly are the group most aware of the fact of death. The hospice concept, as conceived and developed by Cecily Saunders, can be adapted to serve terminally ill older people and to enable them to die with dignity and without suffering, whether at home, in the hospital or in a long-term care facility.

## CONTINUITY IN THE CONTINUUM

In general, a more humane philosophy of elder care is required. A flexible philosophy rooted in a caring and need-meeting matrix must be adopted. The continuum of service should be seen as a chain of helping hands, ready to buoy the individual (and the family) when the aging process and its accompaniments suggest the need for this.

Services should reach out to seniors. Information, support and caring should be evident, so that the needy are encouraged and not intimidated when they seek help. The continuum requires a two-way flow and should not be viewed as a continual "downward spiral." People can and do return to improved and healthier levels of functioning when care and treatment are available. They should be enabled to assume increased independence with appropriate supports.

Coordination of efforts and follow-through between and among helping agents is a requirement. Too often a person is offered assistance with no reference to another context. This makes for duplication of effort, which is wasteful, and it also can result in inappropriate effort, which is unacceptable.

Social policy should make available enough options and services within these options to allow for individualization and appropriateness of services. Contrary to current thinking, this would not necessarily result in greater dollar cost, and would definitely enhance the quality of life for all generations.

Finally, training for all health care professionals and workers must be revised to flow with these perspectives. Persistent myths and stereotypes of aging must be consistently eradicated. Each new generation of students must learn about the aging process as a developmental phase of life not to be feared, but to be lived with creativity and hope.

## REFERENCES

ABC News. "Growing Old in America." Video documentary narrated by Hugh Downs, 1989.

Busse, E. and T. Blazer. *Handbook of Geriatric Psychiatry*. New York: Van Nostrand Reinhold, 1980.

Cath, S.H. Some Dynamics of the Middle and Later Years. In Howard J. Parad, ed., *Crisis Intervention: Selected Readings*. New York: Family Service Association of America, 1965.

Choron, J. *Suicide: Incidence of Suicide by Age.* New York: Scribners, 1972.

Gossett, H. *Restoring Identity to Depersonalized Residents in a Nursing Home.* New York: United Hospital Fund, 1966.

Saul, S. *Aging: An Album of People Growing Old,* 2nd Ed. New York: John Wiley & Sons, 1983.

Saul, S.R. *Family Factors Precipitating Request for Institutional Care.* Unpublished doctoral dissertation, Teacher's College, Columbia University, 1965.

Saul, S. and S.R. Saul. *Notes of Discussions with Scottish Nurses in Scotland.* Edinburgh: Borders Health Board, 1975.

Saul, S. and S.R. Saul. Old people talk about suicide. *Omega* 19(3):237-250, 1988-9.

Saul, S. and S.R. Saul. Group psychotherapy in a nursing home. *Gerontologist* 14(5):446-450, 1974.

U.S. Bureau of the Census. *Statistical Abstract of the United States, 1990.* Washington, DC: U.S. Government Printing Office, 1991.

Weiss, J.A. Suicide. In H.L.P. Reznick, ed., *Suicide in the Aged.* Boston: Little, Brown, 1968.

# 3

# Reimbursement Mechanisms and Their Impact Upon Nursing Home Patients

*Terry Tirrito, MSW, CSW, DSW*

The federal and state financing mechanisms that are used to reimburse nursing homes for the care they provide to patients has developed into a system that is often detrimental to older people. Both the federal and state governments have created systems that were intended to improve the quality of care for patients, increase access to care for the elderly, and reduce the costs of nursing home care to the taxpayer. Have these systems met their intended goals? It is my contention that they have not and that they have created adverse situations for the elderly. Quality and access have not improved and cost reductions to the taxpayer have not been realized.

## GROWTH IN THE AGING POPULATION

As is well known the population in America is aging and the numbers of elderly people are growing dramatically. Ken Dychwald tells us about the coming of an "Age Wave" (Dychwald 1989). In 1990 the population of those over 65 years was reported to be over 31 million (U.S. Census Bureau 1991). It is projected to be over 39 million by the year 2010. Added life expectancy in the over 80 age group will add to the population most at risk. Currently there are 61,000 people over 100 years old, 229,000 between 95 and 99 years and 790,000 between 90 and 94 years of age (U.S. Census Bureau 1991). These numbers are increasing at unexpected rates. It is projected that the over 80 group will grow from 3 million in 1990 to 8 million in 2010. These changes have great significance for nursing home care.

The elderly who are 80 years and older have used the largest proportion of health care services and nursing home care. The typical nursing home patient is 82 years old, female and needs assistance in at least five activities of daily living (ADLs). In 1990 there were over 27,000 nursing homes in the United States and over 1.4 million nursing home patients. Nationally, the need for nursing home beds and the growth in the population needing these beds have not kept pace with one another. The nursing home population is expected to double from 1.4 million to 2.8 million by 2010 and to double again in 2020 to 5.4 million (National Center for Health Statistics 1984).

## GROWTH OF NURSING HOMES

As previously stated there are over 25,000 nursing homes in the United States compared to 11,000 in 1960 (National Center for Health Statistics 1984). While the number of nursing homes has increased, the number of hospitals has declined from over 7000 in 1970 to fewer than 6000 in 1990 (U.S. Census Bureau). The nursing home industry grew dramatically with the use of public funds for reimbursement through the Medicare and Medicaid systems (1965). The use of public funds has contributed to the increased use of these facilities as well as a system of regulation linked to reimbursements. With regard to ownership of nursing homes in the United States, 75 percent are privately owned, for-profit facilities, 5 percent are owned by churches, 5 percent are owned by government and about 15 percent are owned by secular not-for-profit corporations.

For-profit homes dominate the industry. The largest chains (those owned by corporations) have 22.4 percent of the nation's licensed beds. Nursing homes usually have 92 percent of their beds filled. The South and the Midwest typically have more nursing homes than the Northeast and the West (National Center for Health Statistics 1984).

## GROWTH IN HEALTH CARE COSTS

The costs of health care have grown rapidly since 1965. The problem is such that controlling these costs has become a national priority. The rise in health care costs has affected state governments throughout the country. The Medicaid program is an increasing burden and is creating havoc on state budgets. The cost of health care in the United States is the highest of any industrialized country and is 11.6 percent of the Gross Domestic Product. At the lower end of the spectrum, the United Kingdom and Japan were spending 6.2 and 6.7 percent, respectively, of their Gross Domestic Product on health care in 1989. In terms of general public expenditures, the health care industry ranks third after national defense and education (National Center for Health Statistics 1984).

In 1970 Americans spent 74 billion dollars on health care. In 1990 Americans spent $604 billion on health care, $232 billion for acute care, $47 billion for nursing home care and the remainder for physicians' services. Sweden and France came closest to the United States in spending for health care. Health care costs rose steadily after 1965 when Medicare and Medicaid were implemented.

As health care costs rose, financing mechanisms were developed to control costs.

## THE MEDICARE PROGRAM

On July 30, 1965, President Johnson signed the Medicare bill into law as Public Law 89-97. The passage of the Medicare bill provided millions of people over age 65 with hospital insurance and, later, with physician insurance. The rise in costs in health care following Medicare's passage has been dramatic. In 1989, the elderly, numbering over 31 million, and others who are disabled are insured by Medicare at a cost of $98,305,000 annually (U.S. Census Bureau). In 1985 the federal government, through the Medicare program, expended only $600,000 on nursing home care in contrast to $48.5 billion and $17.1 billion on hospital and physician services respectively (Kane and Kane 1989). Medicare has developed into one of the federal government's most costly domestic programs. Medicare has been primarily responsible for coverage of acute care services. Part A is hospital insurance and Part B covers physician services, diagnostic tests, medical devices, outpatient hospital services and laboratory services. Part B is paid for by the recipient. Medicare reimbursement for nursing home care is limited. Coverage is provided for what is called "skilled nursing services" only. Medicare does not provide payment for custodial care which is generally classified as nursing home care. Medicare provides payments to nursing homes if patients are determined to meet the specific criteria for "skilled nursing services." Patients and families often have difficulty deciphering these classifications for coverage. In 1989 the Medicare Catastrophic Act attempted to increase the criteria for "skilled nursing services" and offer more Medicare coverage. However since it was rescinded, the prior status of coverage remains minimal. Therefore, payment for nursing home services are severely limited. When a patient's treatment needs are determined to require "skilled nursing services," payment by Medicare to the nursing home is restricted to 80 percent of charges for 20 days and 20 percent of charges for 80 days for a total of 100 days. This Medicare reimbursement system has adversely affected nursing home patients who rely on Medicare coverage as a source of payment for nursing home care. Access for Medicare patients to nursing homes is limited unless they met reimbursement criteria.

## THE MEDICAID PROGRAM

The Medicaid program (Title XIX of the Social Security Act) was enacted in 1965 to provide medical insurance for the needy. Those who qualify are provided with coverage for inpatient hospital care, outpatient care, nursing home care, limited home health care, laboratory tests and optional health care services as determined by the state such as dental care, drugs, eyeglasses, homemaking services and other community services. The cost for state Medicaid programs has escalated tremendously and state governments are struggling to finance these increases. The majority of nursing home patients (56 percent) are Medicaid recipients. Medicaid has become the nursing home industry's primary revenue source. The Medicaid program spent $14.7 billion on nursing home care in 1985 (Kane and Kane 1989). The program is administered by the states, with matching funds from 50 to 78 percent provided by the federal government. Although all participating states must offer certain mandatory services, there is some flexibility in determining eligibility, choosing optional services, and establishing limits on the amount, duration and scope of services.

In an effort to control Medicaid's escalating costs, states have utilized various controls. Some states control costs by limiting the number of Medicaid beds certified in nursing homes. In 1986 New York state developed a reimbursement system that was to control the rising nursing home costs called RUGs (Resource Utilization Groups). Prior to this system, payment to nursing homes for patient care was based on a retrospective system not a prospective system as had been the DRG system. In the retrospective system costs were payed to nursing home operators as they occurred. With the prospective system costs of the nursing home operator were determined by a formula anticipating future expenses. The RUG system will be discussed in more detail later in this chapter.

Eighty-five percent of the long-term care provided to New York's 100,000 nursing home residents in 1986 was paid by Medicaid at a cost of $2.5 billion annually (New York Medicaid 1991). The reimbursement system was crippling the state's budget and the growth in the numbers who would need this care was alarming.

## DIAGNOSTIC RELATED GROUPS (DRGs)

On October 1, 1983, the implementation of the DRG system for the financing of acute care in hospitals was a major impetus for change in the treatment of hospital patients. DRGs (diagnostic related groups) are a classification system whereby the diagnosis of a patient is allotted a set monetary value. It is a method of payment to hospitals for patient care based upon the diagnosis of the patient selected from 467 diagnostic related groups. The system was developed by a federal agency, the Health Care Financing Administration (HFCA), as a prospective payment system for acute care hospitals in the United States. Its primary purpose was to curb the rising costs of health care. It was initiated in 1983. Using this method in New Jersey resulted in lower hospital costs per capita for the state (Harrison 1985). The major shift had been in reimbursement to the hospital for a diagnosis rather than for costs incurred per patient. Under the DRG system the hospital is paid a set fee for the diagnosis with a set time for treatment of the patient with that diagnosis. If the hospital's costs are above the fee, the hospital absorbs the loss. If the period of treatment is less than stated, the fee remains the same and the hospital profits.

The DRG system changed the emphasis in acute care treatment. Discharge planning became the focus for hospitals. Patients were to be treated and discharged from the acute care setting as quickly as possible. The fewer inpatient treatment days, the better the reimbursement for hospitals. With this new focus, new systems developed such as ambulatory care centers, home health care agencies, day treatment centers and short-term rehabilitation centers. Hospital costs seem to have decreased for acute care inpatient days. However, new costs developed in the health care system.

## RESOURCE UTILIZATION GROUPS (RUGs)

The RUGs system, a Medicaid reimbursement classification system for reimbursement in New York, was initiated in 1986 to reimburse nursing home operators for the costs incurred for a patient's care as determined by a classification system of the physical treatment needs of each patient. This classification system uses nursing staff to analyze the patient's treatment needs. For example, the activities of daily living, the diagnoses, the treatments given, the potential for independence, behavioral indicators or psychiatric symptomatology, medications given, rehabilitation services and physician visits are tallied into a classification system for each patient called their RUG score. The sixteen classifications are:

1. Heavy Rehabilitation A
2. Heavy Rehabilitation B
3. Special Care A
4. Special Care B
5. Clinically Complex A
6. Clinically Complex B
7. Clinically Complex C
8. Clinically Complex D
9. Severe Behavioral A
10. Severe Behavioral B
11. Severe Behavioral C
12. Reduced Physical Functioning E
13. Reduced Physical Functioning D
14. Reduced Physical Functioning C
15. Reduced Physical Functioning B
16. Reduced Physical Functioning A

Each of these classifications has specific criteria that can include diagnosis as well as treatments. The highest score for reimbursement is allotted to number one (Heavy Rehabilitation A) and the lowest reimbursement value is number 16 (Reduced Physical Functioning A). All patients in the facility are assessed at six-month intervals and assigned a RUG score. Scores are totaled and an average score is determined, called a CMI (case mix index). The CMI is linked to a dollar value per patient per day of care. For example, heavy rehab patients may be assigned the value of $120 per day, while reduced physical functioning patients are valued at $30 a day. The calculations are complex and different for each facility according to a preset Medicaid daily rate. Medicaid and Medicare rates for days of care differ for each facility in each state as well as from state to state.

## Problems with Access to Care

In 1986 the implementation of the RUGs system brought changes in access to nursing home care. Admissions of patients were now determined by their RUG score. How much care the patient needs and whether these needs can be met without increases in cost of supplies, staffing, medications treatments and training became the priority. Prior to 1986, the patient requiring the least time for care was the patient of choice because reimbursement was the same for all patients. Why should a facility admit a patient with many special needs and higher costs when all patients were reimbursed at the same daily rate?

After 1986 the scenario changed. The RUG score of the patient determined reimbursement and so the patient game began. What type of patient brings the highest reimbursement to the nursing home? What type of patient requires the least increase in costs or has the longest return on the investment? The balance of patients with the correct RUGs scores for a high case mix index was paramount in admitting patients to nursing homes. Problems of access for the elderly patient who was now being quickly discharged from the acute care hospital due to DRGs increased dramatically.

Nursing homes were interested in admitting the more highly classified patients and barriers developed for the admission of those patients at the lower end of the classification scale. Nursing homes specialized and some became rehabilitation centers. Patients scored as "Heavy Rehabilitation A" were most sought after since they had the highest numerical score for reimbursement purposes. Patients classified "Reduced Physical Functioning A" were no longer desirable patients for admission to nursing homes.

*Case Examples*

Heavy Rehabilitation A: Mr. Jones

Mr. Jones, age 75 years, had fallen and fractured his hip. He was currently receiving physical therapy and was responding well. His family and his wife were pleased with his progress and hoped he would return home as soon as possible. However he needed two people to assist him to meals, toilet, and to bed. He had been hospitalized for over two months and was to be released. His wife could not manage his care at home since she was frail and had a serious heart condition and arthritis herself. He was not financially eligible for home care services. He has Medicare coverage and some private funds to pay for his nursing home care. He is able to manage some of his care needs such as eating. He cannot bathe himself or dress himself and he cannot transfer to his bed or toilet unassisted. Nursing home care is recommended until his rehabilitation is complete.

This patient is a good candidate for nursing home reimbursement. His classification is very high. Medicare will cover some portion of his nursing home stay with his private funds supplementing the costs of nursing home care. In addition his "high RUG score" will increase the facility's case mix index and raise the reimbursement schedule. However, this patient with some changes in his social situation, would not be a desirable long-term candidate for nursing home reimbursement. For example, if the patient did not have a family or home to which he could return, and he progressed in his treatment to be somewhat independent but continued needing some assistance in activities of daily living such as bathing or toileting, his RUG score would decrease to Reduced Physical Functioning C, a very low reimbursement rate, and he would be a liability to the reimbursement schedule of the nursing home.

What about patients with Alzheimer's disease? Where do they fit in the reimbursement schedule? Why is it so difficult for these patients to gain access to nursing homes? Is it management of behaviors or is it reimbursement? What are their reimbursement capabilities? The Alzheimer's patient in the early stages of the disease will score at the least treatment care level such as Physical A, B or C. Actual assistance with activities of daily living by nursing staff are scored with the RUGs classification such as assistance with eating, assistance with walking, or assistance with bathing, dressing and toileting. The Alzheimer's patient may need supervision of these tasks and personal assistance. Supervision of these tasks is not calculated in this system. Physical treatments are reimbursable items, but psychological and social treatments are not measured in this system. The Alzheimer's patient is therefore not a "good reimbursable patient."

## Mrs. Temple, Age 74 Years

Mrs. Temple is a widow. She lives with her daughter in a suburban area of a large city. Mrs. Temple's daughter is 50 years old and her husband is 57 years old. Both are employed full-time in the city. They have three children attending college, ages 19, 21 and 24 years. Mrs. Temple has been diagnosed as having Alzheimer's disease, early stage. She is confused, anxious, wanders out of the house, does not remember to eat, cannot bathe herself and often forgets to use the toilet. Her family is distressed and unable to manage her care at home. She is not eligible for a personal care aide through the Medicaid or Medicare long-term home health programs. She does not qualify for Medicaid since she has assets of $40,000. She does not meet the criteria of skilled nursing services for the Medicare program. Private paid help will deplete her savings in a short period, which the family recognizes they may need in the later stages of her disease. Mrs. Temple's RUG score is Reduced Physical Functioning A since she requires no physical treatment services. Thus, she is not a desirable nursing home candidate.

### Problems with Quality of Care

Quality of care diminishes under these reimbursement systems because all services are not measurable for reimbursement. Patients who are to receive costly treatments or high-priced medications are not desirable patients. For example, patients who need dialysis treatments are not cost-effective; patients who need chemotherapy are not cost effective; and patients who need frequent blood monitoring drugs are not cost effective. Patients who need suctioning and daily oxygen require costly nursing services. Many of these patients are not admitted to facilities that want to keep costs low and reimbursements high. For example, there is the clinically complex patient (high reimbursement score). This type of patient may have many treatment needs such as tube feedings, dressings to be changed, suctioning, oxygen, transfusions or chemotherapy. These treatments need to be managed by skilled, well-trained professionals, and do require expensive equipment, sometimes high-tech beds or other high-tech equipment. Usually this type of patient will have a diagnosis that will impede improvement in their condition. Are these patients "good reimbursable patients"? It depends on whether or not the costs will exceed the reimbursement for the patient. Some questions are: Will this patient require expensive equipment? Will the staff need additional training? Psychiatric treatment is not reimbursable and has not been considered a priority for patients. However, OBRA 91, the Omnibus Budget Reconciliation Act of 1991, has required an assessment of psychotropic medications and restraints for patients that will necessitate the involvement of psychiatric services. Mental health treatments have not been measurable and reimbursable items and the facilities that provided them had done so to improve the quality of care for patients.

## Problems with Cost Reductions

There is great concern nationally regarding the continuing rise in health care costs and especially long-term care costs. In New York evidence has not been found that costs are declining under the RUGs, system and rising Medicaid costs continue to be a state priority. New York State's projection for fiscal year 1991 indicates that Medicaid costs were soaring and care for the poor was lagging behind. New York's Medicaid costs were $12.2 billion annually, $5.15 billion for long-term care in nursing homes and home care (42 percent of the budget) and $4.08 billion for inpatient hospital care (33 percent of the budget). Outpatient care at clinics and hospitals cost $1.33 billion and ambulatory care at doctors' offices cost $1.67 billion (New York Medicaid 1991). Most other states are struggling with their Medicaid budgets and are looking for solutions to the long term care problem. Many states are reporting difficulties in meeting federal mandates to provide services while the federal government is not willing to assist in sharing more of the costs. Obviously Medicare costs and Medicaid costs have not been reduced and continue to spiral upwards uncontrollably.

## CURRENT TRENDS

In 1990 a new assessment tool was developed in New York called the Minimum Data Set, or the MDS. It began as an 80-page assessment form and has been streamlined to a 35-page form. Data is collected from multidisciplinary staff members and statistically analyzed by state examiners. Costs of care for each patient are determined and a reimbursement schedule developed. The potential for linking patient care to reimbursement has become more sophisticated with this evaluation. Linking treatments more closely to reimbursements seems to be the goal of this new technique.

Some studies have been undertaken to assess different reimbursement incentives. One such study (Thorburn and Meiners 1986) was conducted as a demonstration project in San Diego, California. Thirty-six proprietary skilled nursing homes were studied for two years. Eighteen of the facilities operated under what is described as an incentive reimbursement system. A total of 823 patients were in the experimental system and 872 patients in the control system. From this experiment there was no evidence that goal-related reimbursement incentives improved patient outcomes. Goals for patients were developed but were not effective. The goal achievement rates were low. Facilities that did not receive any reimbursement other than the standard Medicaid rate did not achieve patient goals.

## CONCLUSION

Reimbursement mechanisms such as RUGs and MDS, which attempt to link treatments to a dollar figure, have not improved access and quality in nursing homes, nor have they reduced the costs of health care to the public. The classifications of Heavy Rehabilitation A or Reduced Physical Functioning A did not offer assistance to Mary Jones, who is 82 years old and had a stroke. She needs physical therapy and psychiatric services for her depression, which is related to her illness and fear of the future. Her family is devastated by the changes she is experiencing and needs social services to help them. She needs assistance with the toilet, bathing, dressing and eating. She cannot be managed at home without someone in the home 24 hours a day. To restore her to some level of independence would require therapists on a daily basis. The treatment and care of Mary Jones now depends upon her classification, her RUG score and how she fits into the classification scheme of the nursing homes in her area and not on her health care needs.

The questions to ask now are not only Who will pay? but How much is the patient worth? Undoubtedly this was not the intention for reimbursement mechanisms in the long-term care continuum. What is evolving is a health care system that is obsessed by measurement of treatments and costs. Although attention must be paid to the spiraling costs of high-tech equipment, excessive services and unnecessary treatments, the health care dilemma cannot be solved by the development of increasingly sophisticated measurement tools. "Long-term care comes down to people caring for people" (Kane and Kane 1989). Caring and helping is what the future should hold for the patients of today and the patients of the future.

# REFERENCES

Dychtwald, K. *Age Wave.* New York: St. Martins's Press, 1989.

Feather, J. *Resource Utilization Groups: An Introduction for Health Care Professionals.* State University of New York Press, 1986.

Harrison, D. Cost containment in medicine: why cardiology? *Am. J. Cardiol.* 56(5):10c-15c, 1985.

Hing, E. Use of Nursing Homes by the Elderly (From the 1985 National Nursing Home Survey). *Advance Data from Vital and Health Statistics* 135 (DHHS Publication No. PHS 87-1250). Washington, DC: National Center for Health Statistics, 1987.

Kane, R. and R. Kane. *Long-Term Care: Principles, Programs and Policies.* New York: Springer Publishing, 1989.

New York Medicaid: Costs surge, but care for poor still lags behind. *New York Times,* April 12, 1991.

Thorburn, P. and M. Meiners. Nursing Home Patient Outcomes: The Results of an Incentive Reimbursement Experiment. Long-Term Care Studies Program Research Report (DHSS Publication No. PHS 86-3400). Washington, DC: U.S. Department of Health and Human Services, National Center for Health Services and Research and Health Care Technology Assessment, 1986.

# 4

# Frustrations of a Nursing Home Administrator in the 1990s

*Lawrence Gelfand*

The long-term care industry has grown by leaps and bounds over the last three decades mainly because of the increasing number of elderly people, particularly those who are over the age of 85. Now that there are so many elderly people, a key issue seems to be how much money the American people are willing to spend to give them a reasonable quality of life. Even those who have gained significant wealth often do not value spending it on health care, and while nobody wants to pay higher taxes, there is an unspoken belief held by a growing number of citizens that health care is a right that every elder person deserves, not a benefit only for those who have insurance or money. Medicare pays almost nothing for long-term care, and Medicaid requires indigence for an applicant to become "eligible" for basic services. While no one has the solution to this major crisis, everyone knows clearly who the "bad guy" is in this drama. It is always the nursing home industry.

Nursing homes are one of the most regulated, underpaid, poorly regarded and least understood industries in the United States. The public has been led to believe that nursing homes are in business to provide mediocre care in the worst possible conditions and to overcharge for these services. Our own facilities are inspected, re-inspected, criticized and put on display constantly. The federal government, the state government and local health officials are all around us, as are the families, board members (in the case of non-profits) and, in some cases, Ombudsmen to handle special complaints. This, of course, doesn't include the need to respond to the Occupational Safety and Health Administration (OSHA), a trade union, or the fire department. Everybody is launching an investigation, they are all ready to sue, and nobody wants to pay the bill. A recent magazine article called nursing homes the new target for litigation.

Is it any wonder that long-term care administrators are "stressed out?" A recent poll taken by *McKnight's Long-Term Care News* rated the level of stress among nursing home administrators across the country on a scale from 1 to 5, with 5 being the highest level of stress. The results showed 82 percent rated their stress level at 4 or 5, 18 percent rated their stress level at 3, and nobody rated their stress level at either a 1 or a 2. And while the McKnight's article goes on to indicate that stress is universal in today's workplace, it is certainly more exaggerated in the health care industry. Why is the stress level higher now than, say, ten years ago? Probably because the problems of today's nursing home administration are more complex and the stakes are higher. Take, for example, the problem of caring for AIDS patients. It is not so much the issue of providing care that complicates matters, but the education of staff and families who are panic-stricken by the mere mention of the word.

Administrators must worry about the potential loss of income if families refuse to use the nursing home facilities that serve AIDS patients because it will reduce the census numbers as well as income. Cost is another factor, and while the government doesn't recognize the "by-prod-uct" or "fall-out" cost of managing AIDS patients, facilities have had to pay premium rates for their staff who work with AIDS patients, and even keep empty "buffer" rooms between AIDS patients to prevent other families from removing their relatives from the facility. Yet nursing homes cannot discriminate against caring for AIDS patients.

New OBRA requirements attempt to give residents more individual rights and protect their decision making. However, if someone has a communicable disease, you must find him a private room, rights or no rights. This usually means bumping someone else out of a private room. Of course, the family members of the residents being bumped are far from delighted with this change and they will call the State Ombudsman charging that the facility has moved their relative because he or she is a Medicaid recipient, and claim that this would never happen to a paying resident.

The modern nursing home administrator wears many hats. During any given day, he may get involved in a legal, medical, social, funding, fund-raising, budget, maintenance, supervision, political or counseling, crisis, or just another normal complaint about last night's dinner or a missing pair of dentures.

Nursing home residents of the '90s are no longer subject to the use of restraints, and while many administrators support this change, it will certainly cause a few ulcers until the industry learns to cope with it. Surely there will be more falls; in fact, one ought to suspect that something is amiss if too few people seem to be falling. Anti-wandering systems of all varieties will become the theme, and no one is really quite clear on how much liability attaches to the home and the administrator when a resident "escapes" and is severely injured or even killed.

The functional competency level of residents is a growing issue and an aspect of the decision-making rights of individuals. Very few elderly residents have legal guardians, while many are somewhat competent, at least part of the time. Family members often disagree with treatment alternatives, and while recent legislation such as the new New Jersey Advanced Directives may be of some help, it will not clear up such questions as hospitalization for those who, in the opinion of the treating doctor, can benefit from hospital care, while the family with no guardianship refuses to allow their relatives to be hospitalized.

High on every administrator's list of frustrations is Medicaid reimbursement. The name of the game for most nursing home administrators is private pay. This enables most facilities to maintain a reasonable bottom line. Of course, most families believe that nursing homes overcharge residents, but the fact remains that nursing home care is far less expensive than hospital or home care. The private pay rate for nursing homes ranges from approximately $100 to $250 per day. If one compares this to the cost of a good hotel or for a 24-hour-a-day babysitter at $5 an hour, it is easy to see that nursing home costs are not inordinately expensive, especially considering that the home supplies food, nursing care, recreation, social activities, housekeeping, laundry services, and often medications.

The fact that many families do not wish to deplete their parents' estates does not alter the fact that nursing homes, in general, give a good value for cost. And while institutional care has many shortcomings, it still is the least expensive method of providing the full range of services needed, with the possible exception of at-home care by a relative, but even then, the adequacy of care may be questionable. Medicaid is the single largest payer for long-term care. They do their best to pay less and demand more. Many states have either settled or are in the process of being sued by the nursing home industry for underpayment in reimbursement in their Medicaid rates. New Jersey nursing homes claim that over 80 percent of the homes throughout the state do not even get back from Medicaid the amount they spend on nursing services to their residents. For-profit facilities claim that they cannot exist on a census of less than 40 to 50 percent private pay and that they must charge higher rates for private pay to help offset the shortfall they receive from the Medicaid program. Some facilities have decided against taking any Medicaid patients at all.

Families, on the other hand, are working diligently on shifting assets so that their parents can become eligible for Medicaid. Lawyers have set up special counseling for people to help them legally shelter their assets. They say it is just like getting good tax advice. Nobody seems to remember the true spirit of the Medicaid legislation or that it was set up for the financially indigent, not for the rich to figure out ways to legally beat the system.

Notwithstanding the host of problems that have beset nursing homes in the past, they now must face the enforcement policies of OBRA. Noncompliance provisions stipulate only "A" level deficiencies for which a variety of so-called remedies can be imposed. These include a freeze on admissions, fines of up to $10,000 per day, and the replacement of the administrator with full authority to act on behalf of the facility by the government. The judgment of the surveyor is supreme, and if an administrator admits guilt with respect to a deficiency, his remedy may be reduced. Under the circumstances, it is a wonder that anyone still wants to own or operate a nursing home in the 1990s.

It is clear that government is a force to be reckoned with in the running of a nursing home, but it is only one of many factors that can add to an administrator's plight. The residents can be demanding, but more often than not, it is the residents' family that creates the greatest turmoil. Many families cannot distinguish between a nursing home and a hospital, and their expectations of the services of the home are often quite unrealistic.

One of the most common examples is the family that says, "My mother hasn't seen a doctor today." They do not realize that daily visits by a physician are neither required nor necessary in a nursing home, unless there is an acute episode. At our facility we give all the families of new admissions *The Nursing Home Handbook* by Jo Horne. It is one of the most accurate books ever written about what families can reasonably expect from a nursing home. Almost everything related to care in the nursing home is dealt with, from selecting a facility and moving in, to how to handle a relative's complaints. The author suggests that the family can best assess the nursing home's performance by comparing the experience of the first few weeks with the terms of the admissions contract. Nine basic questions should be asked. They are:

1. Did the home staff make a care plan for your relative?
2. Was your relative a party to the formation of that plan and were you?

3. Does the home make provision for regular meetings with the family members to go over the resident's progress and their care plans and to make any adjustments and hear any concerns?
4. Does the staff encourage your involvement with the care of your relative?
5. Does the staff listen when you ask questions and receive your concerns as genuine rather than as nuisances?
6. Does the home staff seem to work hard to foster independence on whatever level is possible or do you see signs that they are really "too helpful" to residents?
7. Does the staff infantilize residents with pet names and lack of such basic respect as knocking before entering the residents' rooms?
8. Do you see teaching going on with the staff?
9. Are there signs that this home seeks innovative ways of making life better for all residents through the use of novel and creative programming?

If we assume that the administrator can satisfy the federal government, the state government, the local government, the residents and the families, he can then focus his attention on satisfying the board of directors, if the home is a not-for-profit facility. This can be far more difficult than it sounds. Volumes of material have been written about how to work with boards of trustees, and about some of the nightmares that have become a reality for administrators all over the country. The most basic reason for the failure of administrators to function effectively with their boards is the lack of distinction and understanding of the roles of each. Problems arise when an administrator has a board that is not sufficiently involved with the home. On the other hand, many problems arise from boards that are overly involved in day-to-day operations. Ordinarily, the board's function is to set policy and to raise funds. Administration is supposed to carry out these policies and run the operation. This may sound simple, but board-administration relationships are very high on the list of administrators' frustrations.

Boards are more sophisticated today than ever before. The expectation for the administrators is high. The understanding of board politics and the managing of board members' ego needs would require a full seminar in itself. Suffice it to say that the administrator continually walks a fine line between being in charge of running his facility and helping his board members stay motivated and appropriately active without obstructing the facility's operations.

Some nonprofit nursing homes have the added concern of having to answer to a funding source in addition to their own board, such as the

United Way, Catholic Charities or the Jewish Community Federation. Here again one must be ever ready to demonstrate how donated money is being spent and be able to graphically dramatize the agency's needs in order to secure their piece of the money pie.

A relatively new frustration of administrators is the need to compete for residents, particularly those in the private-pay category. The need for advertising and marketing strategies is a fairly recent one for nursing homes. As a result of an aging population with greater affluence and many more alternatives to the institutional setting, such as day care, home health care and residential health care, many nursing home facilities are experiencing vacant beds. Vacant beds are a serious problem for profit as well as nonprofit facilities for they represent lost income with no counterbalance of lower expenses, resulting in a negative bottom line.

Competition for staff, particularly nursing personnel, is yet another frustration for the administrator of a nursing home in the '90s. For the most part, nursing homes cannot compete with hospitals in meeting nurses' salary expectations. And while working with the elderly is exciting for some people, many still consider it to be a dead-end occupation with little job satisfaction. To further complicate matters, in calculating nursing home rates, some states do not recognize agency nurses in the reimbursement calculations. Thus another "Catch 22" exists—nursing homes can't find nursing staff and are therefore forced into using nursing agency pool nurses, and they can't get paid for this even though it costs them more.

One final source of frustration for administrators is labor unions. A significant portion of the nursing home industry in the Northeast is unionized. Labor contracts not only raise the cost of care, but often make deploying the workforce difficult by bargaining for extra benifits and holidays, such as every-other-weekend-off schedules for employees. Significant time, effort and money are spent on negotiating labor contracts and on labor issues that arise form time to time, not to mention the need to prepare for a potential strike every time the contract expires.

So, you may ask, why would anybody want to be a nursing home administrator, especially now? It might seem as though one would have to be either a masochist or totally insane, or perhaps the prospect of high pay is a factor. I personally don't believe it's any of these things. I think it is the combination of a challenge coupled with the firm and sincere belief that older people are worth something, and that every day in the life of an older person that is enriched in some way by our facilities is as important a reward as anyone can hope for. And underneath it all, we know that someday we, too, may need care and kindness in our old age.

# 5

# Special Care Units in
# Nursing Homes

*Virginia W. Barrett, DrPH, RN*

## THE SPECIAL CARE UNIT

Among the greatest challenges in long-term care is how to provide for people with Alzheimer's disease and related disorders. One response has been the development of special care units, or SCUs. SCUs are segregated living areas, located within nursing homes, designed for residents with Alzheimer's disease and related disorders. Although there is great diversity in types of SCUs, most provide special training for staff members who are assigned to these units, maintain staff support groups, have family support groups and have structured the environment in ways to decrease the risk of patient accidents. Typically, SCUs are committed to provide services that will decrease negative aspects of the disease, increase independence where possible and maintain optimum quality of life for their residents.

According to the results of a survey of 42 facilities with SCUs conducted by the Hebrew Home for the Aged at Riverdale, New York (Weiner and Reingold 1989), the program objectives most frequently reported included: (1) provision of a safe, secure and supportive environment; (2) improvement of the environment and community of the mentally intact; (3) reduction of feelings of anxiety and confusion through environmental and communication support; (4) help in reaching or maintaining optimal levels of physical and cognitive functioning; (5) holistic patient care; (6) offering care providers understanding, training, education and freedom from excessive stress; (7) recognition that dementia patients are entitled to experiences and activities that will enhance the quality of their lives; (8) recognition that patients are autonomous and that they can expect that their needs and their family's needs will be met with sensitivity and appropriateness; and (9) provision of opportunities to succeed that build on a sense of self-esteem, dignity and hope.

SCUs are a care modality that is growing rapidly throughout the United States, but not without some controversy. Those opposed to the proliferation of SCUs state that they have been allowed to grow without the proper controlled studies to demonstrate whether they improve quality of care and quality of life or are detrimental to these desired outcomes. The literature abounds with reactions to the existence of SCUs and suggestions for improvement, and there is an obvious lack of clarity surrounding what constitutes the best environment in which to provide care to elderly patients with dementia.

Those critical of SCUs focus on the segregated design, which does not allow Alzheimer's patients to be exposed to the social interactions and activities of the other residents (Lawton 1981); the lack of fairness to those residents who would also benefit from many of the environmental changes that help people with dementia (Office of Technology Assessment [OTA] 1987); the dangers of staff burnout associated with working continually with severely impaired people whose disease follows a pattern of progressive decline (Pynoos and Stacey 1986; Wilson and Patterson 1988); the higher cost involved in operating a specialized unit; the difficulty of hiring and keeping staff, creating a virtual ghetto in which no one is able to report abuses or be a legally capable witness; and the potential for SCUs to develop the kind of reputation that is often the subject of negative press that can make families reluctant to enroll their elders. The factors presented as beneficial aspects of SCUs are discussed later in this chapter.

## THE NEED FOR SCUs

Because the American population is aging and the number of persons over the age of 80 is steadily increasing, there are ever more cases of Alzheimer's disease. It is estimated that 1.5 million persons in this country have chronic and severe dementia, a number that will increase by more than half in the next 10 years (OTA 1987). In fact, over 20 percent of the population over 80 years of age is estimated to have Alzheimer's disease, and it has been estimated that as many as 75 percent of residents in skilled nursing home units have cognitive impairment.

Because people with Alzheimer's disease and related dementias often present management problems to staff and have needs and capacities that are different from other patients, there has been a tendency for nursing home staff to view them as disruptive and burdensome. It has been suggested that many nursing homes have been reluctant to admit Alzheimer's patients because of the intensity of care they require. By segregating them from residents who are cognitively intact, and by providing separate activities and services, it is believed that the quality of their life and care is maximized. Added to this is the fact that with more women in the work force, there is less availability of care provision to the frail elderly in the home and more dependence on nursing homes to provide care.

## THE SCU RESIDENT

Among clinicians and researchers on SCUs, there is general agreement that SCU residents are usually less alert than other nursing home residents and display more behaviors that result in care management difficulties and the need for special care planning. Although there is diversity in performance abilities, SCU residents in general are also more dependent in personal care activities such as eating and grooming, owing to their cognitive impairment.

Among the special programs reviewed by OTA, the type of client was described fairly consistently as ambulatory, occasionally incontinent, exhibiting problem behaviors, in a middle stage of dementia, and able to participate in activities and assist in self care (OTA 1987).

The benefits that SCUs can provide residents are numerous and generally focus on safe environments and activities that are specially planned for the cognitively impaired. Safety is an important factor, since cognitively impaired persons are unable to perceive the potential risks involved in operating mechanical devices, using a stove, an iron, hot water, knifes or other sharp objects, and are often unable to find their way around their environment.

The environment of the SCU is usually specifically designed for the cognitively impaired, minimizing distracting and confusing stimuli. This environmental consciousness is part of the "milieu therapy" concept described by Dr. Dorothy Coons, director of the Alzheimer's Disease Projects, which includes physical designs impacting on the physical, psychological, social and cultural aspects of life for persons with dementia. In 1989, the American Association of Homes for the Aging (AAHA) issued guidelines for special care programs stating that characteristics of a good physical design include a space of a unit or program area that "must be a safe, prosthetic, and enriching environment that accommodates the changing needs of the resident and that can be modified to meet a changing population" (AAHA 1989, p. 13).

Often architects who specialize in creating these environments are hired to plan walking areas for people who wander, as well as unobstructed views of activity areas such as the dining room, activities room and nurses station. Other design features of SCUs that are beneficial to the patients include the carefully planned use of color and lighting to serve as sensory stimulants and orienting clues to the resident, and extensive use of signs and strong visual contrast between walls, floors and ceilings. Careful attention is also paid to eliminate environmental stress that may be aggravated by drafts, elevated doorway thresholds that can cause tripping, irritating noises, and shiny surfaces that might reflect images that could be perceived as unfamiliar and frightening (Riley 1988).

The desired outcomes of creating physical designs specific to the needs and capacities of demented residents, as stated by the AAHA, include: (1) minimizing the use of physical and chemical restraints; (2) reduction of disruptive behavior; (3) positive emotional quality on the unit; (4) comfort for the residents, a sense of belonging and a homelike feeling; (5) less disorientation, the ability to distinguish sites and travel unaccompanied to their rooms, the bathroom and dining room; and (6) increased ability of more physically active residents to exercise and walk safely in personal and public areas (AAHA 1989, p. 14).

The professional staff on SCUs are generally recruited and trained specifically to care for cognitively impaired residents, thus enhancing the quality of care provided. Because problem behaviors often typify the residents on SCUs, much attention is paid to developing appropriate and effective interventions that, in a specialized setting, can become part of policy.

According to the OTA's 1987 report on SCUs and the concept of special care, a few programs claim that residents showed changes as a result of special care and others reported an initial improvement followed by gradual, but less precipitous decline. Changes reported included less resident wandering, agitation, screaming, depression, incontinence, hallucinations, and other problem or socially inappropriate behaviors. There was also a decline in the need to use chemical and physical restraints on patients. Other favorable outcomes included weight gain or improved eating; better sleeping habits; improved sense of humor; better socialization and formation of friendships; the initiation of interpersonal exchanges; happy, relaxed appearance; and improved orientation. Some clinicians also reported that people with dementia can improve in behavior, social function and life satisfaction (OTA 1987).

The concentration of resources on these units allows for more individualized activities that are tailored to the short attention span, poor concentration abilities, forgetfulness and disorientation frequently seen to varying degrees in the cognitively impaired. The therapeutic structure reduces the pressure on residents to participate beyond their ability, and adjusts to the changes that result from the inevitable decline in function.

Special decorations, games and activities are often incorporated to encourage the patient's recognition of time and place. Activities that focus on reminiscence help in stimulating interest and provide continuity with the past. A more subtle benefit of SCU care to elderly dementia patients is the attention that it brings to the rights of this group, thereby reducing the risk that they will be poorly served (OTA 1987).

## THE NURSING HOME AND SCU STAFF

Nursing homes that establish SCUs sometimes have the opportunity to receive special funding with which to design and support dementia-centered environments, activities, care plans, staff training and support programs. The specially designed environment decreases the possibility of patient accidents and diminishes the need for staff supervision. It also allows for activities that can be more individually planned.

The staff-resident ratio on SCUs is often much better than that of many nursing homes and the staff is usually recruited because they have expressed an interest or demonstrated special skills in caring for the cognitively impaired older person. Special training helps to provide them with the knowledge and sensitivity needed to ensure quality care and at the same time avoid burnout. An all-dementia unit allows staff to gain expertise in caring for such residents, which benefits patients and is rewarding to staff members (OTA 1987). In addition, staff support groups provide the opportunity to express feelings, share concerns and receive support and problem-solving suggestions from coworkers.

On a well-developed SCU, the staff consists of an interdisciplinary team that is constantly interacting. Depending on the availability of specialties at the facility, the SCU nursing and support staff may interact with physicians; activities or recreational therapists; music or dance therapists; rehabilitation, occupation, speech and physical therapists; volunteers; family members and councils; pastoral counselors and social service workers.

When an SCU has positive relationships with family members of its residents in which families are actively involved as caregiving partners, staff members can feel relieved of some of the stress involved in care. Positive relationships with families, and their incorporation into care planning, require that the staff be carefully trained to interpret this involvement as beneficial.

Innovations in caregiving such as the formation of family/staff care partnerships involve change, and change can be seen as threatening, especially if it is interpreted as a negative criticism of the care provided by either source in the past. However, with a well-thought-out training curriculum, changes can be introduced in ways that are sensitive to the feelings of staff and family members, enhance their job satisfaction and improve their sense of self-worth, while ultimately benefiting the residents as well.

## THE FAMILIES OF SCU RESIDENTS

The families of people with Alzheimer's disease or a related dementing disorder are affected by its impact, as demonstrated by the great attention paid to family caregiver stress in the literature. Caregiver stress is associated with the patient's need for around-the-clock care and supervision in activities of daily living, including bathing, toileting, dressing and feeding, ambulation, transportation to appointments and financial management, to name just a few. Families generally do not shun this responsibility and provide the majority of care required, sometimes at great cost to their own health, to relationships with spouses and other family members, friends and social life, to pursuit of their career or education, and to their pocketbooks.

There inevitably comes a time, however, when the family requires assistance from outside services such as adult day care, home care and respite care. If supplemental care is not sufficient to help them maintain the older person in the home, they turn to nursing home care, especially in the advanced stages of the disease. With fewer available family caregivers in the home, nursing home care has become the focus for care of the cognitively impaired elderly who require continual supervision and management.

Placing the impaired family member in a facility can be traumatic for family members who do so as a last resort and with many conflicting feelings about the decision. Being able to place the impaired older person on a unit specifically designed to meet their needs and in the care of specially trained staff can lessen anxiety about the placement. Of course, this transition to specialized care requires that the facility present a careful and positive orientation to residents and their families.

Many families, although unable to maintain impaired elders in their homes, want to remain actively involved in their care. Families can be a resource to SCU staff if their interest in caregiving is encouraged and their participation is made a part of the care plan. In this way families become caregiving partners with the staff, rather than feeling alienated from their elders and the environment. One major contribution families can make to care planning and the staff's understanding of the resident is made possible by their unique knowledge of the older person prior to the onset of the dementing illness. Families can provide important insights to the staff by sharing information about the resident's prior occupation, social life, hobbies, interests, skills and idiosyncrasies.

Similar to the growth of family caregiver support groups in day care settings is that of support groups for families of persons in nursing homes, who require special care because of their dementing illness. These support groups assist families in two important ways. First, they provide opportunity for expression of feelings about their relationship with their relative and how it has been affected by the dementing illness, and second, they allow families to become involved in the activities on the unit. In some situations, SCU family groups have become active in promoting educational programs and volunteer recruitment and in developing positive and constructive ways to communicate with staff members through the formation of family councils.

## REFERENCES

American Association of Homes for the Aging. Best Practices Guidelines for Special Care Programs. Presented by the AAHA's 1987-88 Task Force on Alzheimer's Disease at the 28th Annual Meeting and Exposition, Baltimore, November 6-9, 1989.

Coons, D.H., ed. *Specialized Dementia Care Units.* Baltimore: Johns Hopkins University Press, 1991.

Cluff, P.J. Alzheimer's disease and the institution: issues in environmental design. *Am. J. Alzheimer's Care Related Disorders Res.* May/June 1990, pp. 23-32.

Getzlaf, S.B. Segregation of the mentally impaired elderly: debunking the myths. *J. Long-Term Care Admin.* Winter 1987, pp. 11-14.

Gold, D.T., et al. Special care units: a typology of care settings for memory-impaired older adults. *The Gerontologist* 31(4):467-475, 1991.

Holmes, D., et al. Impacts associated with special care units in long-term care facilities. *The Gerontologist* 30(2):178-183, 1990.

Lawton, M.P. Sensory Deprivation and the Effect of the Environment on Management of the Patient with Senile Dementia. In N.E. Miller and J.D. Cohen, eds., *Clinical Aspects of Alzheimer's Disease and Senile Dementia*. New York: Raven Press, 1981.

Office of Technology Assessment. Programs and Services that Specialize in the Care of Persons with Dementia. In *Losing a Million Minds: Confronting the Tragedy of Alzheimer's Disease and Other Dementias*. Publication No. OTA-BA-323. Washington, DC: U.S. Government Printing Office, 1987.

Pynoos, J. and C.A. Stacey. Specialized Facilities for Senile Dementia Patients. In M.L.M. Gilhooly, S.H. Zarit and J.E. Birren, eds., *The Dementias: Policy and Management*. Englewood Cliffs, NJ: Prentice-Hall, 1986.

Rabins, P.V. Establishing Alzheimer's disease units in nursing homes: pros and cons. *Hosp. Community Psychiatry* 37:(2):120-121, February 1986.

Riley, J.F. Nursing homes for Alzheimer's patients require special design. *Consulting/Specifying Engineer,* August 1988.

Schiff, M.R. Designing environments for individuals with Alzheimer's disease: some general principles. *Am. J. Alzheimer's Care Related Disorders Res.* May/June 1990, pp. 4-8.

Weiner, A.S. and J. Reingold. Special care units for dementia: current practice models. *J. Long-Term Care Admin.* Spring 1989, pp. 14-19.

Wilson R.W. and M.A. Patterson. Perceptions of stress among nursing personnel on dementia units. *Am. J. Alzheimer's Care Related Disorders Res.* July/August 1988, pp. 34-39.

# 6

# The Professionalization of Nurse's Aides

*Tobi A. Abramson, PhD*

Between the years 1980 and 2050, the population in the 85 and over age group has been projected to increase in size seven times (U.S. Senate Special Committee on Aging 1985-1986). With increasing age, this group also becomes more vulnerable to and is likely to have a higher incidence of chronic physical and mental disabilities (Abdellah 1981). Consequently, many of these chronically ill elderly will require admission to a long-term care nursing facility at some point in their lives.

As the number of elderly seeking nursing home placement swells, so does the need for more nurse's aides, and the need for a change in the role that these formal caregivers provide. Nurse's aides are typically considered to be nonprofessional staff members in long-term care facilities. The demographic composition of this population, their actual role and work experience in long-term care facilities, and society's and researchers' perceptions of them have all contributed to their unprofessional status. Recent regulatory reforms established by the federal government clearly reflect the evolving role of nurse's aides within this system. It is the onset of these regulations that has initiated the process by which these formal caregivers can begin to be perceived as professionals. These areas structure the following discussion on the changing role and status of nurse's aides in long-term care.

## WHO ARE THE NURSE'S AIDES?

Nurse's aides are a vital component in long-term care facilities. They provide upward of 90 percent of total resident care despite the variety of levels of nursing personnel within these facilities (Cohn et al. 1987). An overall picture of this population reveals a minority group of workers with little formal education and low socioeconomic status. More specifically, the majority (92 to 95 percent) of aides working in long-term care facilities are women (Abramson and Fisher 1989a; Johnson-Pawlson and Goodwin 1986; National Nursing Home Survey 1981; Toner 1980; Waxman, Carner and Berkenstock 1984). According to the National Nursing Home Survey of 1977, 76 percent of nursing home caregivers, including nurse's aides, LPNs and RNs, were white. This, however, differs widely by locale. For instance, the majority of nurse's aides working in New York City facilities are black and foreign-born (Abramson and Fisher 1989a; Toner 1980).

Demographic data reveal the average age of these women to vary slightly between samples. Abramson and Fisher (1989a) and Toner (1980) found the mean age of these workers to be 40.8 years, whereas Waxman and co-workers (1984) reported an average age of 33.8 years. A large portion of these women have completed high school, with an increase from 57 percent in 1980 to 72 percent in 1984 (Toner 1980; Waxman et al. 1984). In Abramson and Fisher's (1989a) sample, 49 percent had completed high school and 26 percent completed half a year to four years of college. This latter finding may be indicative of older workers having had less formal educational opportunities than their younger counterparts.

This population also differs in the length of time they have been employed in their current facilities. Toner (1980) reported that 40 percent of nurse's aides were employed in the nursing home for 6 to 10 years, whereas 38 percent were employed between 1 and 5 years. Conversely, Waxman and co-workers (1984) found 53 percent of their nursing home aide sample to be employed between 1 and 5 years. Participants in Abramson and Fisher's (1989a) study were employed in their current facility for an average of 7.96 years (the range was 1 month to 24 years). The National Nursing Home Survey (1977), composed primarily of nurse's aides, reported that more than half (60 percent) of these caregivers had less than 5 years of nursing home experience and were employed in their current positions for under 2 years. These findings suggest a work force that has a fairly high degree of turnover. Nurse's aides are crucial to the quality and continuity of care that nursing homes provide, and turnover of these important staff members can seriously impact care.

## THE ROLE OF NURSE'S AIDES

By the sheer nature of their responsibilities, the job of nurse's aides is both physically and emotionally demanding. One of their major duties is to meet and satisfy the bodily needs of their residents. This includes fundamental activities of daily living such as dressing, feeding, bathing and management of incontinence. Aides are expected to monitor food and fluid intake, take temperatures, maintain proper body positioning and ambulate residents to whom they are assigned. In doing these tasks, they must also document their observations and report them to the unit charge nurse. Household types of chores (i.e., changing soiled bed linens and bed pans) also comprise some of their duties. The nurse's aides must ensure that residents receive their proper meal trays from the dietary department, resolve any food tray discrepancies that arise, and occasionally obtain or return trays to the kitchen (Brannon and Bodnar 1988).

Providing personal and emotional support, especially with depressed, demented or dying residents (Johnson-Pawlson and Goodwin 1986), is one of their most vital roles as it impacts the residents' quality of life. The nurse's aides become the residents' major link to the social world by encouraging involvement in activities and peer interactions (Brannon and Bodnar 1988). Not only are nurse's aides required to deal with daily resident care, but they will occasionally have to tolerate abuse from residents (Johnson-Pawlson and Goodwin 1986). Often it is the aides who first notice any behavioral changes in residents' functioning (Cohn et al. 1987), such as changes in mood, eating and sleeping habits, verbal exchanges, peer interactions and physical abilities. This knowledge is critical to daily functioning and nursing routines (Waxman et al. 1984). Nurse's aides must also interact with family members, and must be able to provide information about their experiences with each resident. In addition, the aides need to be aware of when to refer the family member to the charge nurse. As one can see, nurse's aides provide a wide variety of caregiving services and functions.

## THE CAREGIVERS' WORK EXPERIENCE

Providing direct care services to the elderly, whether at home or in an institution, can be a very stressful task. Individuals choosing to work in the human service field are plagued by higher levels of stress than their counterparts in other types of service jobs. The responsibilities of nurse's aides are fraught with potential job stressors.

Stressors can result from the physical, psychological and social aspects of the job. In other words, stress can arise from actual patient contact and care, or it may be caused by organizational variables. An aide's job demands are often menial and monotonous with inadequate amounts of time to complete her work. At the same time, she is faced with psychological stressors resulting from continual contact with death, confused or agitated residents, resident dissatisfaction, working with residents from culturally different backgrounds and uncertainties regarding treatment (Smyer 1988; Vesperi 1983). Insufficient supervision and conflict with peers can easily create social stressors for the aides. According to Gray-Toft and Anderson (1981a), nurse's aides and other nursing personnel experience similar types of stress. In measuring stress of nursing personnel, these authors found job stress to stem from the workload, dealing with and caring for dying patients, and feeling inadequately prepared to meet the emotional demands of patients and their families.

To further compound these job stresses, nurse's aides enter a work milieu for which they are relatively unprepared. They tend to lack formal training (including mental health training and practical instruction) prior to their first caregiving position. As a result, they may have difficulty distancing themselves emotionally from resident issues (Brannon and Bodnar, 1988). This coupled with the job's demands and potential physical, psychological and social stresses can lead to an explosive situation for both the caregiver and the resident. Despite their difficult, often stressful jobs, these formal caregivers are looked upon as doing menial, nonprofessional work.

## SOCIETY'S PERCEPTIONS OF NURSE'S AIDES

Despite the central and crucial role of nurse's aides in resident care, they are considered to have low-status jobs. The low status attributed to nurse's aides seems to be a by-product of both society's view of the elderly and the nursing profession's view of aides and the long-term care field. Our society holds a pervasively negative view of the elderly, a finding well documented in the literature (Austin 1985; Butler 1975; Nuessel 1982). Negative views, beliefs or attitudes toward the elderly often manifest themselves in the form of negative stereotypes, prejudices, myths or misconceptions. Negative attitudes toward older people have been so rampant in our society that the language we use to refer to them often reflects this perspective. The elderly are often portrayed in derogatory ways and described as possessing traits that are considered undesirable (e.g., dirty old man, old hag, etc.), with few positive expressions to counterbalance them.

These negative views, myths and stereotypes exist not only for society in general, but have been carried over to the professionals who work in the health fields (Chaisson 1980; Michielutte and Diseker 1985), including personnel in long-term care facilities (Boling 1984). According to Cook and Pieper (1986), society's negative attitudes toward aging often discourage individuals from choosing geriatrics and gerontology as a profession. For many, a job as a nurse's aide in a long-term care setting is an unappealing choice of occupation. The position is viewed as having the lowest status in the nursing field. Caregivers in nursing homes are less respected than their counterparts in the hospital setting (Chaisson 1980).

Families of residents often manifest society's views. This attitude might be observed when family members visit the resident. Some will not acknowledge the nurse's aide's involvement in their relative's care. An example of this is when a family member walks past the aide to ask the charge nurse questions about their relative. The nurse may often have to ask the aide for the information requested by the family member as she has more hands-on knowledge. Families may be more likely to turn to the charge nurse since she is perceived as the cognizant professional.

Within the long-term care environment, nursing home aides have historically been the least educated of those who provide care (Johnson-Pawlson and Goodwin 1986). This too has contributed to their unprofessional status. Traditionally, these workers have received the least amount of training among members of the nursing home staff. Compared to nurses in the same setting, their training has also been less rigorous. Whereas most nurses are now required to receive formal college training and be licensed to ensure a basic level of knowledge, nurse's aides have not followed a similar course. Nevertheless, the aides have played and continue to play a crucial role in actual patient care.

## NURSE'S AIDES AS VIEWED IN THE PROFESSIONAL LITERATURE

The view that nurse's aides have low-status jobs is also reflected by the dearth of professional literature about this population. Compared to nurses, nurse's aides as a group are very understudied. The literature has focused primarily on nurses (Rountree and Deckhard 1986) and nursing students (Cook and Pieper 1986) and has examined variables such as the impact of training, age, education and professional level on the attitudes of nursing personnel and nursing students toward the elderly.

Recently, there has been an increase in studies on nurse's aides in long-term care facilities (i.e., Abramson and Fisher 1989a, 1989b; Toner 1980; Waxman et al. 1984). When nurse's aides have been studied, the variables investigated have included demographics, attitudes, job performance, job turnover, job stress and job satisfaction. The cultural diversity of nurse's aides and residents has been a topic of recent interest (Tellis-Nayak and Tellis-Nayak 1989). This development is indicative of an increased recognition of the value and importance of the role that aides have assumed.

## NURSING HOMES AS CONTRIBUTORS TO THE STATUS OF NURSE'S AIDES

Nursing homes themselves have also perpetuated the low, unprofessional status attributed to nurse's aides. This is clearly evidenced in both their hiring and training procedures. Traditionally, nursing homes were able to hire whomever they determined was appropriate for the position of nurse's aide. In other words, nursing homes used their own discretion in choosing and hiring their staff as there were no guidelines for them to adhere to. Those who are responsible for providing care largely determine the quality of the long-term care setting (Eisenstat and Felner 1983) and this employment pattern meant that resident care would vary between nursing homes depending on the facility's hiring policy, the subjectivity of the hirer, and the amount of scrutiny given to the character and quality of the person hired.

The type of training a newly hired aide received was determined by individual long-term care facilities. Prior to 1989, New York State did not have a certified or state-approved nurse's aide training program. According to a report by the Institute of Medicine (1986), only 17 states had a minimum training requirement for nurse's aides, and preemployment training was only required in two states. In most instances, a person who assumed a position as a nurse's aide was not likely to have any formal training prior to the first job. Taken together, these factors have led to a great inconsistency in the caliber of nurse's aides and the resulting care provided.

Within New York State, the quality and delivery of care to the institutionalized frail elderly is closely monitored by the state's Department of Health. The DOH monitors the treatment of residents and the quality of care provided from a multidisciplinary perspective. However, this agency has had little involvement in improving the consistency, competence or professionalism of the state's nurse's aides.

## IMPROVING THE QUALITY OF NURSING HOME CARE AND PROFESSIONALIZING THE ROLE OF NURSE'S AIDES

In a recent effort to improve the quality of nursing home care, a federal regulatory reform has been implemented. This legislation, known as the Omnibus Budget Reconciliation Act (OBRA), was passed by Congress in 1987, with nursing homes directed to begin compliance as of October 1990. Since each state has different standards for nursing home care, the federal government sought to standardize various aspects of such care.

Two major impetuses led to the enactment of this reform. The first was the growth of the Medicaid program. This funding program incorporates both federal and state monies to pay for medical assistance to needy citizens, and the low-income elderly (Smyer 1989). The second was the deinstitutionalization of psychiatric hospital residents. Many of these residents were inappropriately placed in nursing homes because federal Medicaid funds would pay for a large share of their costs (Cole 1987). Nursing homes have not been able to provide enough day treatment programs or follow-up care for these individuals. As a result, nursing homes were becoming more of a mental health facility than a setting for physical care.

OBRA is a detailed and lengthy reform with almost all areas of nursing home care specified. Its overall focus is on improving the quality of care and quality of life for residents of nursing homes. The training and certification of nurse's aides is a major component of this reform. For the purposes of this chapter, this reform will be discussed only in terms of its relevancy to nurse's aides.

### Qualifications for Nurse's Aides

Under OBRA, the role of nurse's aides and the credentials that they must possess are clearly specified. Nurse's aides are expected to "provide personal resident care and services including, but not limited to, safety, comfort, personal hygiene or resident protection services" (National

Citizens' Coalition for Nursing Home Reform 1990, p. 34). These functions are to be performed under the supervision of a registered or licensed practical nurse. All nurse's aides are now required to be certified and registered in the New York State Residential Health Care Facility (RHCF) Nurse Aide Registry. In order for the nurse's aide to receive certification and be listed in the Registry, the aide must complete a state-approved RHCF nurse aide training program, pass the state-authorized clinical skills competency examination, and pass the written or oral competency examination.

However, persons may be employed as aides if they are waiting to take the next state licensing examination or are waiting for the results of the exam and have graduated from either a state-approved RHCF nurse aide training program or a nursing program approved by the New York State Commissioner of Education. Nurse's aides certified in another state and listed in that state's nursing home nurse aide registry may work as aides if the facility verifies their certification and their listing in a registry, and if the hiree is applying for new certification. Nurse's aide trainees enrolled in an approved training program may work in a nursing home as long as they complete this program within 90 days of being hired. They are allowed to provide direct resident care and services if they have completed at least 16 hours of classroom instruction in several required areas and are supervised directly by a nurse when they work with the residents.

## The Training Program

OBRA specifies that the training program must be supervised and conducted by qualified nursing staff. The aides must receive 100 hours in both classroom and clinical training, with a minimum of 30 supervised hours of clinical training in a nursing home. The training should consist of specific goals, measurable performance criteria relevant to the curriculum content, information on the resident population and the purpose of the facility. As outlined by the National Citizens Coalition for Nursing Home Reform in 1990, the curriculum should include, at a minimum, the following topics: (1) normal aging; (2) psychological needs of the resident; (3) communication in health care facilities; (4) personal care needs; (5) resident unit and equipment; (6) nutritional needs; (7) elimination needs; (8) mobility needs; (9) sleep and rest needs; (10) nursing care programs for the prevention of contractures and decubitus ulcers; (11) observing and reporting signs and symptoms of disability and illness;

(12) infectious control; (13) resident safety; (14) nursing care of residents with special needs due to medical conditions; (15) mental health and social service needs; (16) resident rights and (17) care of the dying resident. Each broad area is subdivided into more detailed specific areas. According to these guidelines, the curriculum is geared to a 4th to 6th grade level of English literacy with provisions made for special populations.

As part of the training program, a performance record is kept of the duties and skills taught in the training. Every performance record includes a measurable criterion for each duty and skill covered in the program, a satisfactory or unsatisfactory performance rating, and the date and name of the training supervisor. Upon satisfactory completion of the performance record, nurse's aides must pass two competency tests—a clinical skills examination (given by a licensed registered nurse) and a written or oral examination. The clinical skills portion must be passed prior to the administration of the written or oral competency examination. Aides have three consecutive opportunities to pass these exams. They must be taken within four months of completing the RHCF training program. Once the last exam has been passed, the nurse's aides receive certification and are listed in the Registry.

**Recertification**

Nurse's aides must be recertified every 2 years. To maintain certification, aides must have worked in an RHCF for compensation over the previous 2 years and participate in 12 hours of mandatory inservice education every 6 months.

**Nurse Aide Registry**

The establishment of the Nurse Aide Registry is one of the most important developments under OBRA. The Registry contains the full name, address, date of birth and Social Security number of the aide; the name and date of the successfully completed state-approved training and competency programs; the certification number and description of the certification process; and the most recent recertification date. One of the main functions of the Registry is that it contains the final findings of instances of resident abuse, mistreatment or neglect with the date of the hearing or finding, and a record and date of criminal conviction for abuse, mistreatment, neglect or misappropriation of resident property. In addition, the Registry contains a written statement by the aide disputing such findings.

Before nurse's aides may be hired, the long-term care facility must check with the New York State RHCF Nurse Aide Registry. The facility may make initial contact by telephone. The Registry then provides verbal verification of certification as well as indicating the findings of any resident abuse, mistreatment or neglect, and any criminal convictions in these areas. Following this the facility may receive further documentation once a written request is submitted.

### Professionalizing Nurse's Aides

The implementation of the OBRA regulations is the first step in helping to improve the status and professionalism of nurse's aides in long-term care facilities. OBRA has established the minimum requirements that every nurse's aide must obtain, making it a more difficult process than in the past. As evidenced in the previous sections, nurse's aides must fulfill much more stringent criteria to be employed in long-term care settings. It is the implementation of an abuse registry, standardized training from state-approved programs and competency examinations that is beginning to move nurse's aides toward an increased level of competence. These requirements also serve to minimize the inconsistency in the hiring policies and training previously employed by facilities.

It is to be hoped that over time nurse's aides will begin to receive recognition for the important job they perform. The OBRA reform is the first step in acknowledging the vital role nurse's aides play in the life of nursing home residents and how pivotal their caregiving role is to the quality of care provided by nursing homes. Nurse's aides have a long way to go before they are truly perceived as part of the professional staff, but these new guidelines will assist them in obtaining the status they deserve.

### REFERENCES

Abdellah, F.G. Nursing care of the aged in the United States of America. *J. Gerontol. Nursing* 7:657-663, 1981.

Abramson, T.A. and C.B. Fisher. Stress in Nursing Home Aides. Unpublished doctoral dissertation, Fordham University, 1989a.

Abramson, T.A. and C.B. Fisher. Correlates of Job Satisfaction in Nursing Home Aides. Paper presented at the 42nd Annual Meeting of the Gerontological Society of America. Minneapolis, November 1989b.

Austin, D.R. Attitudes toward old age: a hierarchical study. *The Gerontologist* 25:431-434, 1985.

Boling, T.E. A new image of long-term care: a challenge to management. *J. Long-Term Care Admin.* 12:15-17, 1984.

Brannon, D. and J. Bodnar. The Primary Caregivers: Aides and LPNs. In M.A. Smyer, M.D. Cohn and D. Brannon, eds, *Mental Health Consultation in Nursing Homes.* New York: New York University Press, 1988.

Butler, R.N. *Why Survive? Being Old in America.* New York: Harper & Row, 1975.

Chaisson, G.M. Life-cycle: a social-simulation game to improve attitudes and responses to the elderly. *J. Gerontol. Nursing* 6:587-659, 1980.

Cohn, M.D., M.A. Smyer, A.J. Garfein, A. Droogas and E.E. Malone Beach. Perceptions of mental health training in nursing homes: congruence among administrators and nurse's aides. *J. Long-Term Care Admin.* 15:20-25, 1987.

Cole, T.R. Class, culture, and coercion: a historical look at long-term care. *Geriatrics* 11(4):9-15, 1987.

Cook, B.A. and H.G. Pieper. The impact of the nursing home on clinical attitudes toward working with the elderly. *Gerontol. Geriatrics Ed.* 5(4):53-59,1986.

Eisenstat, R A. and R.D. Felner. Organizational Mediators of the Quality of Care: Job Stressors and Motivators in Human Service Settings. In B.A. Farber, ed., *Stress and Burnout in the Human Service Professions.* New York: Pergamon Press, 1983.

Gray Toft, P. and J.G. Anderson. The nursing stress scale: development of an instrument. *J. Behav. Assessment* 3:11-23, 1981a.

Institute of Medicine. *Improving the Quality of Care in Nursing Homes.* Washington, DC: National Academy Press, 1986.

Johnson-Pawlson, J. and M. Goodwin. Total approach to nurse aide training. *Provider* 12:14-18, 1986.

Michielutte, R. and R.A. Diseker. Health care providers' perceptions of the elderly and level of interest in geriatrics as a speciality. *Gerontol. Geriatrics Ed.* 5(2):65-85, 1985.

National Center for Health Statistics. *Employees in Nursing Homes in the United States: 1977 National Nursing Home Survey.* DDHS Publication No. PHS 81-1820. Hyattsville, MD: U.S. Department of Health and Human Services, 1981.

National Citizens' Coalition for Nursing Home Reform. *OBRA Status Report.* Washington, DC: National Citizens' Coalition, 1990.

Nuessel, F.H. The language of ageism. *The Gerontologist* 22:273-276, 1982.

Rountree, B.H. and G.J. Deckhard. Nursing in long-term care: dispelling a myth. *J. Long-Term Care Admin.* 14:15-19, 1986.

Smyer, M.A. Nursing homes as a setting for psychological practice. *Am. Psychologist* 44:1307-1314, 1989.

Smyer, M.A. The Nursing Home Community. In M.A. Smyer, M.D. Cohn, and D. Brannon, eds., *Mental Health Consultation in Nursing Homes*. New York: New York University Press, 1988.

Tellis-Nayak, V. and M. Tellis-Nayak. Quality of care and the burden of two cultures: when the world of the nurse's aides enters the world of the nursing home. *The Gerontologist* 29:307-313, 1989.

Toner, J.A. Instrument Development: Attitudes Toward Working with Old People. Unpublished doctoral dissertation, Teachers College, Columbia University, 1980.

U.S. Senate Special Committee on Aging. *Aging America: Trends and Projections*. Washington, DC: U.S. Department of Health and Human Services, 1985-86.

Vesperi, M. The Reluctant Consumer: Nursing Home Residents in the Post-Bergman Era. In J. Sokolovsky, ed., *Growing Old in Different Societies: Cross-Cultural Perspectives*. Belmont, CA: Wadsworth, 1983.

Waxman, H.M., E.A. Carner and G. Berkenstock. Job turnover and job satisfaction among nursing home aides. *The Gerontologist* 24:503-509, 1984.

7

# Is the Nursing Home Right
# for You?

*Roberta K. Sutker, MSW*

## THE APPLICATION PROCESS

"Nursing home"—what do these two words mean? If we take them literally, we should think of a residence in which one finds care and attention. However, when it is suggested to a caregiver that a loved one may need the services of a nursing home, feelings of anxiety, fear, guilt, apprehension and sadness are often evoked. It is important that the nursing home staff acknowledge these negative feelings and help the caregivers and potential residents deal with these emotions and to help them look at taking up residence in a nursing home as one aspect in the process of providing long-term care to older people.

Because the community is able to provide services that allow older people to stay independent longer, nursing home residents are now generally older, sicker and more frail than they were in the past. They are likely to be suffering from one or more disabling, chronic disease and often lack the economic means to deal with their condition outside of an institution.

Nursing home placement can result from a planned arrangement by the individual older person, by the family or by the caregivers; or emergency placement may be made directly from the hospital or the home.

When one enters a nursing home for the first time, it can be an overwhelming and often frightening experience to observe old people who are noticeably sick, feeble and incapacitated. For this reason, anyone going through a nursing home for the first time ought to be accompanied by a trained expert who can answer questions. Although all of those responsible for the care and treatment of older persons either before or after admission to a nursing home should be aware of their social needs, a major role belongs to the social worker. By training, skill and commitment to the profession, the effort to identify and implement social needs are clearly in the social worker's domain. It is the social worker's task to extend help in support of personal, social and family functioning and to enable the older person and family members to use their individual, unique strengths to further these goals.

The placement of an elderly relative in a nursing home is often a family's last resort. They have usually exhausted all other alternatives, often endured severe personal, social and economic stress in the process, and made the final decision with great reluctance. When long-term care is being considered, the degree of stress may vary, but feelings are mixed and family relationship patterns are vividly revealed. The older person may be in a state of anxiety and fear and he may also have feelings of abandonment and rejection, despite a warm and healthy family relationship.

The family, on the other hand, may be feeling guilt, conflict and shame, and if they themselves are elderly, they may also experience anxieties about growing old themselves. The family must also face the fact that this may be the final home for the older loved one, and this carries overtones of the ultimate separation.

Many questions arise before placement: What is the waiting period before admission? When can I meet with someone and see the facility? How do I tell my relative about this major change? How much will it cost? Will you take Medicaid? What if we have no money? Can I tell you about my particular problem? At Daughters of Israel Geriatric Center in West Orange, New Jersey, we do not try to answer all of these questions by phone. We suggest that an application be mailed out and once it is completed and returned to the social service department, a preadmission interview with a skilled social worker will be scheduled.

Filling out the application is the beginning of a life-reviewing process, which often provides a vehicle for family members to discuss thoughts and feelings that may never before have been verbalized. The social worker is sensitive to the realities that unresolved issues from the past may be stirred up and that families have a great need to resolve these issues now or they may never be resolved.

When social workers meets with families and the applicants, they will be ready to explain the application process. Questions about personal history are asked to assist the health care team to gain insight into the makeup of the applicant. The social worker will also elicit information on what the applicant and the family expect from the nursing home as well as discuss various aspects of institutional life. For example, at Daughters of Israel Geriatric Center our units are divided so that residents with similar medical and mental capabilities room together. Since most of the facility is divided into semi-private rooms, learning to live with an unknown roommate is an important consideration. Because we are a community-based, nonprofit agency, a committee appointed by the Board of Governors reviews all applications. This process allows these men and women to learn more about the types of applicants that are seeking admission, their needs, and how the community can help. The family and the applicant usually feel some relief after the application is accepted and the applicant is placed on a waiting list. During the waiting period, the social worker keeps in touch with the applicant and family.

## PREADMISSION

The waiting period is over when a room becomes available. The few days prior to admission are a time for signing admission papers and dealing with the emotional impact of the event. The task of reading and signing permission slips for such things as going to the beauty parlor, receiving mail and taking pictures creates a sense of getting things in order. Arranging for telephone installation, labeling clothes, opening a bank account and signing a contract create feelings of permanency. Signing forms dealing with unit moves when physical or mental changes warrant it, choosing a hospital should emergency treatment be required, and designating a family member to make decisions affecting life-and-death issues bring focus to the inevitable finality. Regardless of the degree of planning and the quality of the nursing home selected, all of these feelings must be dealt with.

Prior to admission, the new resident's main relationship has been with her family. With the introduction of a nursing home staff, the relationship is extended. The staff will now be the main contact and support system for the resident. They will have a great impact on her self-esteem and ability to cope with these new situations and feelings.

Psychosocial information about the new resident is provided to the staff by the social worker. The staff informs the resident about nursing home routines and expectations. This exchange of information and discussion prior to admission can lead understanding between staff, family, resident and social worker.

## THE FIRST DAY

The first day in a nursing home is a very emotional one for the resident. She may experience feelings of anger, frustration, sadness, depression, loneliness, confusion, anxiety, bewilderment and even fear of what the future may bring. The loss of independence, both mentally (due to confusion) and physically, can be devastating. After a long life of independence, the resident is now being told when to get up, when to eat, what she can or cannot do during the day, and where she can and cannot go. (For the purpose of this discussion we will be talking about a resident who has at least a minimal understanding of what is taking place and the ability to provide input. Those who are so confused and disoriented that they require a friend or relative to handle their affairs will be discussed later in the chapter.) This change in lifestyle can be overwhelming.

The social worker plays a major role in helping the new resident cope. Adjustment to the nursing home can take weeks or sometimes months, but the first day is critical for both the resident and the family. The social worker welcomes the resident and introduces her to the staff members who will make up her new world: nurses, recreational therapists, other social workers, dieticians and physical therapists. The resident is introduced to her roommate and informed about activities. It is important, however, not to overwhelm the resident with too much information at this time.

On the first day the new resident should be met with kindness and assurances that she is not alone and that she is still part of a community and as such should continue to live a fulfilled life with as much independence as possible. If the resident is confident that the social worker and other staff members can be counted upon, many of her fears will be alleviated.

The family of the resident will have similar fears and questions. The social worker will spend time listening and comforting them. There are many ways that a family can help the resident. The social worker will inform them that they are part of a health care system and that they play a very important role. They can be active in care plan meetings, participate on the board and lay committees, and make purchases and run errands for the resident. They can also participate in support groups, and referrals if needed can be made.

Entering a nursing home is a transition to a new period in life. The focus on the past will be balanced with new rules and the resolution of new successes and problems. This will be an ongoing process, but it begins with the first day when the resident and family are encouraged to believe that coming to a nursing home means continuing life, not ending it. The goal for every resident is to have a stimulating, purposeful day, every day.

## DAILY LIFE

What is it really like to live in a nursing home, share a room with a stranger, follow a preset schedule and still maintain some level of independence? The following represents a typical day in the life of two residents: one on an independent, more intact unit, and one in a unit where the individual is more dependent on others for her care. There are some similarities between these units.

The nursing staff makes certain that each resident is awake and up and has enough time to get ready for breakfast. Medication is given either before or after breakfast as required. Even on the more independent sections there are residents who require assistance in dressing, bathing and eating. These residents are usually awakened first. Every attempt is made to give those residents who are due one a bath prior to breakfast. (No one is permitted to bathe independently.) Breakfast trays are delivered between to all residents in the facility between 7:40 and 8:40 a.m. Residents receive assistance in eating when necessary, as well as assistance in their personal hygiene, if this is indicated.

After breakfast, those residents who are capable are left to their own devices. They are free to go to the daily sheltered workshop (a vocational rehabilitation program for residents with physical or mental handicaps that provides an opportunity to have a successful occupational experience while earning money), to a ceramics class, a lecture, a card painting class, or back to their individual rooms or the unit lounge where they socialize with other residents. The hairdresser is in the facility three days a week, and many of the female residents enjoy going there and socializing with others. Those residents who are less capable and unable to "navigate" the facility by themselves receive more direction from the staff. Recreational activities are brought to them almost daily. Morning activities usually last until close to noon. The residents then congregate in their individual dining rooms and await lunch. After lunch the morning routine is repeated. Various musical programs are available, some that all residents are comfortable attending and others that are appropriately geared to level of function. The afternoon activities usually last for about 90 minutes. Afterward residents either return or are returned to their respective sections. They then socialize until supper arrives.

Evenings are less structured. Residents are generally free to attend an activity, socialize or return to their individual rooms. Bedtime varies according to the individual unit and resident. Generally, however, all residents are in bed with lights out by 10:00 p.m. Although much of the day has a structure to it, residents are only required to adhere to their medication schedule and their meal time.

A social worker who is assigned to each unit makes "rounds" on a daily basis and speaks to the charge nurse about any issues or problems that may have arisen. The social worker touches base with the various residents on the unit. Frequently, she is asked to act as a mediator between roommates.

Consider the following example. Ms. W. and Mrs. P. share a room. Ms. W. has been in the facility for over a year and had shared a room with someone who became more frail and needed another unit. Mrs. P. also had been there for over a year, but in another section, and was very unhappy with her frail roommate. The staff felt that the two women would appreciate a change and would get along with one another. Pleasantries were exchanged and both expressed their happiness in rooming together. Their euphoria lasted for about a week, at which time each woman refused to compromise her sleep habits: one liked to go to bed late after reading or watching TV and the other wanted all lights out at 8:00 p.m. So far, efforts by the social worker to work out a compromise, beginning with the 10:00 p.m. house rule, have been unsuccessful and there is a distinct possibility that another room change will be necessary.

Another example is the case of Mrs. Z., who has begun to show marked mental deterioration, and her roommate Mrs. C., a mentally intact woman in poor physical health. Mrs. Z. is frequently found going through Mrs. C.'s things and dressing in her clothing. Mrs. C. says she understands her roommate's confusion, yet she is unable to accept it and becomes quite upset. Another room or unit change is likely. The social worker will make the necessary recommendations and continue to work with Mrs. C. to help her be more patient until her present situation can be rectified.

The social worker's contact with residents, staff and family is often documented on charts so that other personnel can be aware of significant events and occurrences related to that particular resident. Family contacts, initiated by either the social worker or the family are ongoing. These contacts can be made in person or by telephone. If families come only during the weekend, the charge nurse has the person-to-person contact and the social worker has only phone contact. At other times, the family is available only during the late afternoon, and the social worker is the sole connection with the facility. However, in both situations, the social worker and the nurse share information with one another so that family communications with the staff can be positive.


## THE FINAL STAGE


Because most people view being in a nursing home as the final stage in life for all practical purposes, the social worker must help the resident and family deal with this issue from the time of admission and throughout the resident's stay.

When it becomes apparent that a resident's health is failing and death is imminent, we begin the process of final preparation. This process includes daily talks with the ill resident, providing emotional support, coordinating and suggesting other support services, and interacting with the family.

Although we try to focus on the dying person, we are still bound by institutional limitations as well as the needs of other residents. Sometimes the dying person's physical and mental status changes to such a degree that a transfer from one unit to another is indicated. Transferring residents is always a difficult task and will only be done if absolutely essential for maintaining equilibrium on the unit. If it appears that death will occur in a matter of days, we generally keep the patient in the familiar setting of her room and unit. When a resident dies, the social worker needs to get in touch with her own individual feelings and sense of loss, and, at the same time, be available to family, fellow residents and sometimes fellow staff who need help in coping with the resident's death.

The social worker reaches out to the family, helps them express their feelings and acknowledges the difficulty of losing a loved one. Frequently, the social worker needs to talk with other residents who knew the deceased to help them cope with the loss of a friend. The residents will often handle the death with greater ease than might be expected. The attitude they often express is that "life goes on." With rare exceptions the residents tend to focus more on their own personal needs than on any specific thoughts about the recently deceased.

As social workers in a nursing home, we do not always have the luxury of exploring our own feelings of loss; instead we are charged with the constant task of filling that new empty bed with another person in need of help. However, we are obligated to our profession and all the residents we serve to take the time to appreciate in each case that it was a unique, individual person who died, not merely an aged resident.

# 8

# Recreational Therapy in Nursing Homes

*Marcie Cooper, MSW, RMT, Susan Sataloff, BS, Sharon Gallo, CMT, Lauren Birns, CMT and Fay Hortz, MTRS*

## MOVEMENT EDUCATION

Everything an individual does involves bodily movement of some type. When discussing movement in a long-term care setting, we are specifically referring to movement education. Movement education attempts to help residents become mentally as well as physically aware of movement patterns. Thus movement as it is discussed here is based on a conceptual approach to human movement. In other words, the better a resident understands a movement pattern, the easier it will be for that individual to develop specific physical skills. Through movement education, the positioning of each body segment in relation to the whole body is rediscovered with the help of the recreational therapist.

The experts in the field of movement education do not agree on one single definition of this term, but they do agree that movement education is dependent on physical factors in the environment and on the residents' ability to react intellectually and physically to these factors. Through movement education the therapist assists patients to develop their own techniques for dealing with the environmental factors of force, time, space and flow as they relate to various movement problems. Movement involves the body as a whole. Learning to manage the body leads to greater control and skill over gross movements. By the time many patients enter a nursing home environment, they have relinquished physical and intellectual control over their bodies. Residents will more often than not be in a nonlocomotor or fixed location. Movement exploration and education enable the therapist and patient to work together to acquire, expand, and integrate elements of general motor control through wide experience in movement, based on an exploratory and creative approach. Residents need to learn what their bodies are capable of and how they can manage their bodies effectively in a variety of movement situations and challenges.

In laying a foundation for the importance of movement education, the next step is to provide the medium for this process to take place. Two methods have been tried at the Daughters of Israel Center in New Jersey. The first is an exercise program geared for the immobile resident. The participants sit in either a straight-back chair or a wheelchair. A typical 30-minute session might include easy stretching and passive exercise for the feet, hands, neck and shoulder muscles. Controlled and deep breathing exercises are an instrumental part of the program done intermittently between each of the exercises. In presenting an exercise program it is important to make it both fun and challenging. Using different types of accessories, such as foam balls, scarves, wands and canes, serves to provide movement for the participants, thus fulfilling these needs. Music is often used to encourage the residents to "join in" in performing the different exercises or to help them exercise for a longer period of time. Additionally the music enables them to increase the number of repetitions with each exercise. During the exercise period discussions are held with the residents on the importance of what they are doing with their bodies and incorporating a sense of body and kinesthetic awareness. The program usually finishes with slow neck exercises and an attempt at meditation.

The second program for senior adults is aquatic therapy. This program is geared toward both the ambulatory and non-ambulatory resident. A typical session involves having participants enter the water slowly, acclimating themselves to the water temperature. Those residents who are capable start by a water walking "warmup." This is followed by holding onto the side of the wall and doing typical land exercises or calisthenics in the water. These include ankle circles, knee lifts, leg lifts, toe raises and water-resistant movements involving the hands, arms and legs. Aquatic flotation aids are used to strengthen legs through performance of a modified flutter kick. One of the positive outcomes of this program is that it could encourage some residents to start swimming again after many years of non-use of their major muscle groups. A typical result of a session in the pool is for the residents to emerge feeling relaxed and proud of their accomplishments.

## MASSAGE THERAPY FOR RESIDENTS OF LONG-TERM CARE FACILITIES

We live in a society that offers mixed messages about the meaning of human touch. Much documented research exists from well-respected individuals, such as Ashley Montagu and Margaret Mead, regarding the significance of loving touch for infants—specifically, that babies deprived of touch do not thrive as well as those who receive it. Past infancy and early childhood, human touch takes on different meanings. Is it appropriate? Is it abusive or aberrant behavior? During the adolescent and early adulthood years we are led to believe that touch has a sexual connotation, and it is usually a negative association. For the frail elderly, especially those residing in a long-term care facility, touch takes on a whole new expression. Medical procedures—sometimes invasive and painful—become a way of life, and what we call "activities of daily living"—bathing, dressing and feeding—become the only, and quite impersonal, way this ever-increasing population comes in contact with human touch.

Two of the authors became involved with a small group of nursing home residents two years ago as volunteers, providing brief massage therapy sessions. The enormously positive response from the participants generated growth and excitement on many levels. As increasing numbers of residents expressed interest in the program, the massage therapists began exploring further techniques to bring comfort and pain relief, along with the nurturing effects of caring human touch, to each individual. Professional staff members from many departments—recreation, social service, rehabilitation and nursing—began to offer guidance and support. In time, a very real, far-reaching program came to life through the efforts of an open-minded, forward-thinking administration and board of governors. These were the people with the authority to open a new door to the geriatric community in a long-term care facility. The Touch Therapy Program developed by At Ease, Inc. now operates in three such facilities in New Jersey. Funding for these programs comes from the institution itself or through grant awards. There is no cost to the participants.

Many elderly residents in long-term care facilities are physically and emotionally isolated in their declining years. Their sense of well-being and zest for life—and their health—are further affected because of the melancholic loss of their contemporaries and loved ones. The Touch Therapy Program, with the purpose of offering a nonthreatening sensory experience, can provide a positive therapeutic upswing in health and attitude. An added benefit for the residents is the choice of whether or not they wish to have a massage session at a particular time. For people who live in an institutional setting, being given choices is especially important.

In the most general sense, the objectives of the Touch Therapy Program are to encourage in each participant a feeling of comfort, relaxation and well-being. Prior to entering the program, an information and release form is obtained for each resident. This form provides pertinent medical information, physician approval and permission from the resident (or a family member, if necessary). A request for massage therapy sessions may come from a resident, a relative or significant other, or a staff professional. Every participant is approached by the massage therapist with utmost respect and care. Even the most regressed individuals can make their wishes known to the therapist through body language and nonverbal cues. Most often the initial visit is designed to introduce the prospective participant to the program. The therapists talk about their professional training, what massage sessions can and cannot offer, and what can be accomplished. Residents are asked what they would like to achieve from their sessions and perhaps a little bit about themselves. The resident who is hesitant or fearful has an opportunity to discuss these feelings. Usually, this introductory session lays the groundwork for a warm and trusting relationship.

Massage therapy is an innovative approach to caring for the growing population of infirm elderly. The sessions are brief, usually lasting 5 to 15 minutes, but the positive effects are prolonged. Massage can reduce edema, stimulate muscles, increase circulation, decrease muscle spasms and improve mobility. When appropriate, simple stretching exercises are demonstrated and practiced with the resident. We have been gratified to note that several touch therapy participants who had withdrawn from their rehabilitation therapy, feeling frustrated and defeated, returned to their scheduled treatments with renewed energy and commitment.

While the positive physical contributions of massage therapy sessions are clearly evident to the participants and their caregivers, the enhancement of the recipient's emotional and mental well-being cannot go unnoticed. The offer of a nurturing touch, a kind word and a caring ear can stimulate the most remarkable reactions. The authors and their student interns have been awed by the loving kindness, the heartfelt gratitude and the depth of trust shown by participants. Almost everyone, regardless of physical or mental condition, is able to express some feeling of joy for the experience of nurturing and caring touch.

A woman who came to the United States from Siberia as an adult spoke only in Russian to the nursing home staff. At times she was withdrawn, or was suddenly hostile and agitated. After several sessions of touch therapy, she revealed to the massage therapist, in English, that she had forgotten most of her knowledge of the English language after having suffered a stroke. She felt terribly frustrated in her attempts to express herself. Slowly, she began to remember some simple phrases in English. We continue to offer encouragement and patience.

A man diagnosed with advanced Alzheimer's disease had not uttered a word for months. After much gentle coaxing and encouragement, he allowed the massage therapist to stroke his hands and fingers. And one day he looked up into the face of the masseuse and said, "Gee, this feels so good."

When people outside the field of geriatric care ask us, "How can you do such depressing work?" "How can you keep going back when so many of your patients die?" we wonder how it is that so many people neglect their elders, close their eyes, and make believe this very real population is invisible. And we try to explain that the services we provide, so far from being depressing, are actually is uplifting, rewarding, and so very necessary.

In his essay "Success," Ralph Waldo Emerson says, "To know one life has breathed easier because you have lived, is to have succeeded." Those of us who offer ourselves with loving touch to others in the twilight years of their lives know this feeling of success time and again.

## PLANNING A PARTY

A party is any deviation from the usual routine for nursing home residents that brings people together. Planned to fill those unoccupied hours of the day when due to lack of other responsibilities residents are likely to just "sit," parties are major social events. They should be looked upon as one of the many vehicles to prevent social isolation in the nursing home.

All such special events should be included in the weekly or monthly schedules posted or distributed for residents. Although residents like to know in advance when something special will take place, an impromptu celebration can also bring pleasure and relieve monotony when properly presented. Simple things can make an ordinary day special. Making it happen is often a matter of using imagination and ingenuity, but most of all careful planning.

In arranging resident "get togethers," all other happenings at the nursing home must be considered. These include special medical, nursing or dietary schedules, shift changes, sheltered workshop hours and any other group activities arranged for the intended day. Because mornings and early afternoons are considered peak energy hours for residents, evening and late afternoon programs may require additional structure and the use of more assistance from staff and volunteers.

In creating an enjoyable event for residents it is essential to think ahead. Among the many aspects to consider are the following:

1.  *Planning.* Factors include location (outdoors, indoors), furniture arrangement, appropriate space for wheelchairs, equipment needed (microphone, piano, record player, etc.), special features (dressing room for entertainers, birthday cake and candles, special holiday decorations), and length of time needed for the event. Carnivals or other large-scale programs that involve the nursing home residents and families or the community require additional planning well ahead of time.

2.  *Entertainment.* Music is an important ingredient for any nursing home party. Some residents still love to dance and with a little encouragement will take to the floor. Be sure your floor plan includes enough space for a dance floor. Dancing in couples can reinforce positive feelings, since dancing provides a tactile, close, one-to-one relationship with another person. If movies are to be shown, be sure a large-size screen is available and make certain that the soundtrack is clear. Test the equipment before the residents arrive.

3.  *Food.* When all else fails, residents looking for something different to eat will come to an event. Finger foods, calclulated to meet dietary restrictions of the guests, are most successful. If a program is set up auditorium style, residents will have to eat on their laps, so keep it simple. Serve only one item at a time. Volunteers or additional staff members are often needed to help serve and to assist some residents in eating.

4.  *Spreading the word.* How will the residents learn about the party? Announce it in the weekly residents' schedule, put up posters, send notices to residents' rooms, announce it on the intercom, and send invitations to family members.

5.  *Transportation.* How will residents get to the party? Can they walk independently or will they need assistance? How many volunteers

will be needed as transporters? How will the residents get back to their rooms when the party is over?

6. *Volunteers.* How many volunteers will be needed? How many family members can be called on? Who will contact them and when?

To have a successful event in the nursing home, long-range plans, attention to details and some thought about possible problems should be undertaken well in advance. Whenever possible, the activity director should be a "floater" at the program, free to help where needed, make last-minute changes, solve problems, rearrange things, reassure and make it all a special program for the residents.

Throwing a party, a holiday celebration or providing any event that is enjoyable for the residents is usually a matter of imagination, creativity, resourcefulness and utilization of the many skills of recreation directors. Remember, a party is a deviation from the usual routine, so make it different, make it enjoyable and make it fun.

## GAMES: EXERCISES FOR THE MIND

The aging process makes us well aware that we can't store up or save muscle power until the day we need or want it—only use develops it. Our minds also work well only if we use them constantly. The nursing home resident needs to find ways to exercise all aspects of mind and body—and games are good exercise. Social isolation has been described as one of the psychosocial dilemmas facing the aging. The physical ills that are normal to aging can create or worsen a state of social isolation for nursing home residents. Games can help reduce this isolation.

To lead such a program in the nursing home takes a person with special abilities, energy, enthusiasm, and a knowledge of techniques that will motivate and encourage residents to take part. Adapted equipment and carefully arranged space are basic ingredients for successful programming. The leader must be able to switch techniques and methods as required to make the activity fit the special needs of the group and encourage maintenance or restoration of normal activity.

There can be no doubt that bingo is a favorite of many nursing home residents, despite the fact that many professionals tend to scorn the game. Bingo is more than a game of chance. It can be adapted in many ways to meet the needs of residents with different handicaps. As bingo was originally designed to be played, at least four actions are put to use. The player must (1) hear a number, (2) remember the number, (3) recognize the printed number and (4) respond with an appropriate action to that information, exercising hearing, memory, concentration, sight and ability to respond to external stimuli. During all of this, residents are enjoying themselves and having fun, not even realizing that they are exercising many senses. Bingo can be adapted so that the confused resident can also exercise while experiencing satisfaction. With assistance from staff or volunteers, the resident can be made responsible for as many of the actions in the game as his limitations allow. He can hear the number and repeat it to the volunteer, who then does the rest. Or the resident can be encouraged to hear the number and locate that number on the card, with the assistant placing the marker. Residents with hearing loss can be shown the number and then be responsible for placing the marker in the appropriate space. Participating on any of these levels can make bingo a satisfying, enjoyable and worthwhile activity for the nursing home resident.

For residents with hearing loss, limited vision and problems in manual dexterity, modifications in equipment may be required. A good sound system is a good beginning. Oversized cards with clearly printed numbers, a larger chart on which numbers can be written as they are called, and marker covers that are easy for frail, stiff fingers to pick up are often needed.

Table games also can be used in activity programs for residents. When possible, it is best to start with something familiar. Chess and checkers are games of strategy that exercise problem-solving abilities. Dominoes offers an opportunity for number recognition and improving fine motor skills. Parchesi and Monopoly provide practice in color recognition, counting and addition, while the player never realizes he is exercising. Other games, such as Lotto and Concentration and some simple card games, exercise the power of observation and memory. It is essential that games be adapted for and geared to adults.

Games are designed to be fun, and that factor should never be ignored. Paul Hahn reminds us in his book, *Recreation: A Medical Point of View,* that fun is the goal of recreation, but not its purpose: "Fun is the sign health is the goal."

## THERAPEUTIC RECREATION

Since 1969, the most broadly accepted definition of therapeutic recreation is "a process which utilizes recreation services for purposive intervention in some physical, emotional and/or social behavior to bring about a desired change in that behavior and to promote the growth and development of the individual."

Therapeutic recreators, then, are people who use recreation as a medium to assist disabled people to change certain physical, emotional or social characteristics so that they may live their leisure lifestyles as well and as independently as possible. Because these individuals are functioning at different and unique levels of ability, therapeutic recreators use recreation in many ways to help them realize their potentials for leisure enjoyment.

Therapeutic recreators are concerned with eliminating or minimizing disability, but are also concerned with the quality of the person's total existence. This includes not only the physical and emotional self, but the environment in which the person must live. They accomplish their task by using recreation as indicated through the immediate and long-term goals of the disabled person and his or her functional level. Therapeutic recreators may work within treatment or community settings to achieve these goals.

## The Treatment Setting

In the treatment setting (acute care hospitals, physical rehabilitation centers, prisons, skilled care facilities, mental health centers, institutions for the mentally retarded) the general goal is to progressively move the person toward maximal functioning. Some individuals may be functioning at so low a level that the therapeutic recreator works with the treatment team to increase basic physical or emotional operation before any sort of recreation skill-building program is initiated. This may mean spending time developing a personal relationship by talking, playing games to increase limb range or motion and strength, or taking specially planned walks to improve tolerance of open spaces.

When working with individuals who are doing well enough to focus on developing a quality leisure lifestyle, the therapeutic recreator puts together everything he has been able to find out about them to determine what needs to be accomplished toward that goal. The services provided by the therapeutic recreator may include leisure counseling, leisure skill development or adaptation of skills already possessed. The client may explore his personal motivations and desires in leisure, learn how to identify community resources, learn a new craft or work on using a new method for swimming.

When working with individuals who are able to handle their leisure fairly responsibly and independently, the role of the therapeutic recreator becomes more that of a facilitator who assists people in planning opportunities to use their abilities for participation in the leisure lifestyles they choose. These services may involve posting community recreation resources, planning or facilitating outings, scheduling requested activities, or simply providing directions to the nearest theater.

# 9

# Depression in Nursing Homes: Recent Studies of Prevalence

*Peter S. Cross, MPhil*

## BACKGROUND

Under federal law (Omnibus Reconciliation Act of 1987, Subtitle C) each state, acting as federal agent, is legally responsible for devising ways of determining (1) whether new admissions to and current residents of nursing homes are "mentally ill" and, if so, (2) whether they require "the level of services provided by a nursing facility...or an institution for mental diseases" and (3) whether they require "active treatment for mental illness." Yet data indicating the size and scope of mental illness in nursing homes is not readily available. This dearth of information inhibits a careful and full development of policy toward those suffering from mental illnesses in nursing homes. This chapter aims to draw together information on the prevalence of depression in nursing homes.

## MENTAL ILLNESS: SOME DISTINCTIONS

The term "mental disorders," broadly defined, includes any clinically significant behavioral or psychological syndrome or pattern associated with a painful symptom or impairment in functioning. Specific types of such disorders together with their diagnostic criteria are listed and described in the *Diagnostic and Statistical Manual of Mental Disorders* (third edition revised, or DSM-III-R) of the American Psychiatric Association. These criteria are of special importance here in that they have official status administratively in the financing and regulation of psychiatric care in the United States. In the nursing home reform legislation of 1987, for example, the term "mental illness" was explicitly defined as those disorders listed in the DSM-III save for Alzheimer's disease and related disorders. The term "active treatment" is not further defined in the statute but is left to be defined by rules and regulations.

However, several sets of distinctions need to be kept in mind. The long-held distinction between physical and mental illness is no longer thought to have much scientific basis. The significance of this distinction is now largely administrative; disorders listed in the DSM-III-R are "mental" in that they are congruent with those listed (in part by way of history and convention) in the chapter on mental disorders of the International Classification of Diseases. For example, no one maintains that "primary degenerative dementia of the Alzheimer type" is a only mental disorder, but rather that it is also a physical disorder. The same individual might be properly diagnosed as having either, both, or neither of these. As a practical matter, most individuals fitting the definition of the one would as well fit the other.

Some DSM-III-R disorders are, in fact, syndromes ("a group of recognizable symptoms that occur together and constitute a recognizable condition"). But "syndrome" is the more general term and may encompass several or many disorders. For example, the syndrome of dementia is characteristic of many specific disorders, such as multi-infarct dementia and primary degenerative dementia; a depressive syndrome may be found in major depression, dysthymic disorder, or in an adjustment disorder with depressed mood. Since "syndrome" is the more general term, establishing the existence of a syndrome is usually simpler and more straightforward (relying usually only on the current constellation of symptoms) than establishing the existence of a listed disorder (which might require knowledge of detailed history, other psychiatric symptoms, or special medical investigations).

## STUDIES OF DEPRESSION IN NURSING HOMES

Studies seeking to determine the prevalence of depression among the elderly in nursing homes follow any of two broad approaches. In the first, patients are directly interviewed; in the second, the psychiatric status of patients is assessed indirectly by interviewing nursing home staff or reviewing their statements in nursing home records. The two approaches are not wholly distinct and may be used in conjunction. In this chapter we treat these different sources of information separately mainly to weigh the congruence of the results each method renders.

## Studies Based on Direct Examination

In a study by Rovner and co-workers (1986), a research psychiatrist and a research geriatrician each independently examined 50 residents randomly selected from the 180 residents of a proprietary intermediate care facility (ICF) in Maryland. The psychiatric examination was based on the Geriatric Mental State Interview and the Mini-Mental State Examination (MMSE), a brief screening test for dementia. A staff member was interviewed as well about each resident and diagnoses were made following DSM-III criteria.

Parmelee and co-workers (1989) examined all current residents and all new admissions to a large voluntary facility in Philadelphia. Two screening measures of depression were used: (1) residents were examined using an adaptation of the Schedule for Affective Disorders and Schizophrenia and scored on this basis as possible DSM-III major depression, other depression, or as having no significant depressive symptoms; and (2) the Geriatric Depression Scale was administered. Those found depressed were referred to the facility's psychology/psychiatry department for evaluations and an independent clinical diagnosis was agreed upon. Clinical diagnosis of depression was shown to agree fairly well with the screening measures.

The Katz (1989) study was done at a voluntary ICF in Philadelphia. The 51 (of a random 102) residents found not to be moderately or severely demented were examined (and re-examined at six months) using the same screening measures employed by Parmelee. Subjects with symptoms consistent with major depression on the screening measures were clinically evaluated by a psychiatrist a few weeks later.

The study by Chandler and Chandler (1988) is similar in method. The sample consisted of the 65 residents of a proprietary ICF in Iowa City. Patient charts were reviewed; patients were examined by a psychiatrist and medical, neurologic and DSM-III diagnoses rendered.

Kafonek and associates (1989) reported on 65 patients admitted to the ICF and skilled nursing facility (SNF) levels of an academic nursing home in Baltimore. They were selected from 169 consecutive admissions who were still alive and at that facility a month after admission and who consented to participation. Family and psychiatric history, medical history and a brief physical examination were obtained. The MMSE and the Geriatric Depression Scale were administered independently of a psychiatric interview and assignment of a diagnosis of syndromes of dementia, delirium or depression.

Teeter and co-workers (1976) randomly selected 100 patients from two proprietary skilled nursing homes in a midwest metropolitan area, of whom (after attrition, refusals and transfers) 74 were studied. Each subject was given a semi-structured interview including the Short Portable Mental Status Questionnaire (a dementia screen). A relative and a nursing home staff member were interviewed about each patient. All interviews were conducted by a social worker. Medical records were reviewed, and psychiatric diagnoses were rendered by a psychiatrist based on review of all the information available.

Gurland and co-workers (1979) studied a two-stage probability sample of 162 elderly in 22 long-stay institutions in New York City. Subjects were assessed by brief semi-structured interviews that included a brief dementia and depression screening scale.

German and colleagues (1986) reported on the nursing home sample of the Baltimore Ecological Catchment Area (ECA) Study. All nursing residents in catchment area nursing homes for more than a year were included as well as all ECA residents admitted to nursing homes outside the catchment area in the past year. This amounted to 350 subjects in over 25 nursing homes. Assessment consisted of the Diagnostic Interview Schedule (DIS), a highly structured psychiatric examination, intended for administration by non-professionals, which claims to yield equivalents to most DSM-III diagnoses. This interview included the MMSE to determine whether or not the subject suffered from "cognitive impairment."

The study of Bland and associates (1988) has been included despite its Canadian focus. It is of special interest since it attempts to follow the methods of the ECA studies (i.e., the DIS interview including the MMSE) and because it reports on a nursing home sample drawn from a large nursing home/auxiliary hospital in Edmonton, Alberta. All 562 residents were in the sample and of these 34 percent could be given the complete DIS and an additional 13 percent the MMSE.

## Studies Based on Nursing Home Staff Reports

The National Nursing Home Survey studies are by far the largest of the staff report studies. These studies are the only source of detailed national information on nursing home patients. Conducted at irregular intervals (most notably in 1973-74, in 1977 and in 1985), these studies all follow a common multistage probability procedure to sample institutions and a small number (5 or so) of residents in each institution. Information about each resident is obtained from a staff informant who may refer to institutional records. Since the 1977 survey a special sample of discharged residents has also been studied. Starting with the 1985 survey a next-of-kin of the sampled resident was interviewed where available. (Other parts of the survey cover characteristics of the institution, its staff and finances.) Detailed tabulations are published and data tapes are available several years after completion of the survey.

Zimmer and co-workers (1984) drew a random sample of the routine utilization review records of each of 42 SNFs in upper New York State and selected for study those who required "constant or active consideration" in their care plan for a list of behavioral problems (e.g., confusion, agitation, depression, abusiveness).

## WHAT THE STUDIES SHOW

### Prevalence of Depression: The Staff View

In the 1977 National Nursing Home Survey the staff informant was asked whether each (sampled) resident was "depressed or withdrawn." Thirty-five percent of residents were so reported, and over half of these were reported by staff to require extra nursing time as a consequence (National Center for Health Statistics 1979). A similar result is reported in the 1973-74 NNHS survey.

Results from the pretest of the 1985 NNHS survey (Burns et al. 1988) found 25 percent of all patients to be "depressed" (it is not specified whether this was staff nurse opinion or from medical records, or both) with a rate of 52 percent in those with organic brain syndromes and 8 percent in the remainder. Fourteen percent of the whole sample were prescribed antidepressant medication.

Publications from the 1985 Survey include a tabulation from the question: "According to _____'s medical record does he/she currently have any of the following conditions?" The list of possible responses includes "depressive disorders," which was checked by the staff informant for 13.8 percent of all residents (16.2 percent of all those under 65; 13.4 percent of those 65 and over). Thus, results from the last two national surveys and the recent pretest are broadly consistent in placing the prevalence of depression in the 12 to 25 percent range.

There are, however, a number of reasons that one might suspect these findings. The relationship of these staff reports with clinically diagnosed depression is unknown. "Depression," after all, has rather broad everyday use and diverse meanings. Without some external validation it is difficult to know what to make of these staff reports. Are they including as "depressed" those suffering from minor states of unhappiness, those with states of depressed mood so transient or minor that no particular intervention would be warranted? Or, on the other hand, are such staff reports really underestimates of the problem? In a variety of other settings, including hospitals (Kitchell 1982; Kline 1976), primary care medical sites (Hankin and Oktay 1979) and even psychiatric hospitals (Gurland et al. 1972), it has been shown that depressions often remain unnoticed or underdiagnosed.

The accuracy of staff assessment of depression is unknown. Staff assessments, at least in these published reports, are reported in such general terms that their implication for needed interventions is unclear.

**Prevalence of Depression: Direct Examination Studies**

The studies directly examining nursing home residents may play a complementary role. Unlike the surveys based on staff reports, these studies tend to be quite small in scale, often limited to a single nursing home. While no real argument can be made that they are somehow representative, such studies tend to scrutinize depression in greater detail. The procedures for assessing depression, the diagnostic schema followed, and the kind and level of depression found are often specified.

Teeter and associates (1976) found 26 percent of patients to a have a primary psychiatric diagnosis of depression (a fifth of these were psychotic depressions) and 18 percent to have secondary depressions. Of the 37 patients with depressions, only three had such a diagnosis in their medical records.

Rovner and co-workers (1986) found 12 percent to suffer from DSM-III-R major depression and a further 18 percent to suffer secondary depression. Gurland found that 38 percent of those not severely demented suffered from a syndrome of depressive symptoms. Chandler, whose focus was primarily on neurologic diagnoses (including dementias) rendered the DSM-III diagnosis of organic affective disorder (which requires, among other things, a full depressive syndrome) in 9 percent. Katz, who limited his sample to those without dementia, found symptoms of major depression in 20 percent and dysphoria in an additional 31 percent. Parmelee found possible major depression in 9 percent and minor depression in 15 percent.

There are many points of comparison within this set of studies. Taking first the diagnoses comparable to a primary diagnosis of DSM-III-R major depression: the results fall in a fairly narrow range from 4 percent (Teeter, using a DSM-II close equivalent) or 5 percent (Bland) to 12 percent (Rovner).

A second point of comparison across these studies is the presence of a syndrome of symptoms necessary (but not in themselves sufficient) to establish diagnosis of major depression. Rates here range from a low of 9 percent (Parmelee) to 20 percent (Katz) or 21 percent (Kafonek).

Taking the whole range of "diagnosed" depression (i.e., sufficient to be listed in some form in DSM-III-R): figures range from a low of 21 percent (Parmelee) to 30 percent (Rovner) and 38 percent (Gurland) to the higher figures of 44 percent (Teeter) and 51 percent (Katz).

Such evidence of the high prevalence of depressions is confirmed by studies documenting the high prescription rate of antidepressant medications in nursing home populations (14 percent in the 1985 NNHS pretest; 12 percent in New York City in 1976).

## CONCLUSIONS AND IMPLICATIONS

The view among nursing home staff that a quarter or more of nursing home residents are depressed is strongly confirmed by more rigorous studies in which residents are systematically evaluated and diagnosed. The evidence suggests current DSM-III-R diagnoses of major depression are present in perhaps 5 to 12 percent of nursing home residents. This is a level of depression that almost invariably would be seen (at least outside the nursing home setting) as clearly warranting thorough psychiatric assessment and often intervention either directly by physicians or psychiatrists or by other mental health professionals under their close supervision.

Correct assessment and intervention would often require psychiatric examination and diagnosis, a careful review of current physical condition, an evaluation of the suitability of psychotropic drugs or other treatment, and careful monitoring of response to drugs or other treatment.

Depressions falling short of full-criteria DSM-III-R major depression are even more prevalent. The studies surveyed suggest that the rates of such lesser depressions—but such that may still be listed in DSM-III—range from 15 percent (Parmelee) to 31 percent (Katz) with the other estimates (Rovner, 22 percent; Teeter, 22 percent for depressive neurosis, or 18 percent for secondary depression) falling within this range.

Though at some point along a spectrum of severity these "non-major" depressions likely do merge with rather ordinary states of unhappiness, it is important to note that such depressions are, in fact, a common (if not the most common) focus of psychiatric and mental health services *outside* of nursing homes. Put another way, the fact that such depressions are not listed as "major" does not imply that specialist mental health services are not needed; standards of everyday mental health service practice outside of nursing homes take such depressions as a common focus of mental health treatment.

Nationally, provision of social work services is at a level of one full-time social worker for every 165 beds (National Center for Health Statistics 1989), so that one social worker would have responsibility for 165 patients at any one time, and well over 100 new patients each year.

Given these levels of staffing, the report from the 1977 National Nursing Home Survey that only 7 percent of residents had received counseling by a social worker in the past month is not surprising. Other mental health professionals play a still smaller role with only 1.4 percent of residents receiving counseling from them in the past month (National Center for Health Statistics 1979). These figures changed little, it seems, between the 1977 survey and the 1985 pretest reported by Burns (1988), who found that only 2 percent of all residents had seen a mental health specialist in the past month. For those with an organic brain syndrome, this rate was also 2 percent; even among those with mental disorders other than organic brain syndrome, this rate was only 5 percent. Psychiatric referrals are uncommon if we are to judge from Zimmer's (1984) study in upper New York State. Among those in his sample suffering from serious behavioral disturbance, less than 15 percent had a psychiatric referral at any time during their current admission.

The only national surveys of nursing homes suggest that nursing home staffs perceive 14 to 25 percent of residents to be depressed. Smaller scale studies based on direct examination of nursing home residents are fairly consistent in suggesting that 5 to 12 percent of residents suffer from a DSM-III-R major depressive disorder, and an additional 15 to 30 percent suffer from other DSM-III-R disorders in which a syndrome of depressive symptoms is present.

## REFERENCES

American Psychiatric Association. *Diagnostic and Statistical Manual of Mental Disorders*, 3rd Rev. Ed. Washington, DC: American Psychiatric Association, 1987.

Beardsley, R.S., D.B. Larson, J.S. Lyons, G.L. Gottlieb, P. Rabins and B. Rovner. Minireview: health services research in nursing homes: a systematic review of three clinical geriatric journals. *J. Gerontol.* 44:M30-35, 1989.

Bland R.C., S.C. Newman and H. Orn. Prevalence of psychiatric disorders in the elderly in Edmonton. *Acta Psychiat. Scand. Suppl.* 338:57-63, 1988.

Burns B., D.B. Larson and W.E. Johnson. Mental disorder among nursing home patients: preliminary findings from the national nursing home survey pretest. *Int. J. Geriatric Psychiatry* 3:27-35, 1988.

Chandler, J.D. and J.E. Chandler. The prevalence of neuropsychiatric disorders in a nursing home population. *J. Geriat. Psychiat. Neurol.* 1:71-76, 1988.

German, P.S., S. Shapiro and M. Kramer. Nursing Home Study of the Eastern Baltimore Epidemiological Catchment Area Study. In M.S. Harper and B.D. Lebowitz, eds., *Mental Illness in Nursing Homes: Agenda for Research*. Rockville, MD: National Institute of Mental Health, 1986.

Gurland, B., J.L. Fleiss, J.E. Barrett, Jr., et al. The Mislabeling of Depressed Patients in New York State Hospitals. In J. Zubin and F.A. Freyhan, eds., *Disorders of Mood*. Baltimore: Johns Hopkins University Press, 1972.

Gurland, B.J. et al. A cross-national comparison of the institutionalized elderly in the cities of New York and London. *Psychol. Med.* 9:781-788, 1979.

Hankin, J. and J.S. Oktay. *Mental Disorder and Primary Medical Care: An Analytical Review of the Literature.* Washington, DC: U.S. Government Printing Office, 1979.

Kafonek, S. et al. Instruments for screening for depression and dementia in a long-term care facility. *J. Am. Geriat. Soc.* 37:29-34, 1989.

Katz, I.A., E. Lesher, M. Kleban, V. Jethanandani and P. Parmelee. Clinical features of depression in the nursing home. *Int. Psychogeriat.* 1:5-15, 1989.

Kitchell, M.A. et al. Screening for depression in hospitalized geriatric medical patients. *J. Am. Geriat. Soc.* 30:174-177, 1982.

Kline, N. Incidence, prevalence and recognition of depressive illness. *Dis. Nerv. Sys.* 37:10ff, 1976.

Mann, A.H., R. Jenkins, P. Cross and B.J. Gurland. A comparison of the prescriptions received by the elderly in long-term care in New York and London. *Psychol. Med.* 14:891-897, 1984.

National Center for Health Statistics. The National Nursing Home Survey, 1977.

Summary for the United States. *Vital and Health Statistics,* Series 13, No. 43, 1979.

National Center for Health Statistics. Discharges from Nursing Homes: Preliminary Data from the 1985 National Nursing Home Survey. *Advance Data from Vital and Health Statistics,* No. 142, 1987.

National Center for Health Statistics. Use of Nursing Homes by the Elderly: Preliminary Data for the 1985 National Nursing Home Survey. *Advance Data from Vital and Health Statistics,* No. 135, 1987.

National Center for Health Statistics. The National Nursing Home Survey, 1985. Summary for the United States. *Vital and Health Statistics,* Series 13, No. 97, 1989.

Parmelee, P.A., I.A. Katz and M.P. Lawton. Depression among institutionalized aged: assessment and prevalence estimation. *J. Gerontol.* 44:M22-29, 1989.

Rovner, B.W., et al. Prevalence of mental illness in a community nursing home. *Am. J. Psychiatry* 143(11):1446-1449, 1986.

Teeter, R.B., F.K. Garetz, W.R. Miller, et al. Psychiatric disturbances of aged patients in skilled nursing homes. *Am. J. Psychiatry* 133(12):1430-1434, 1976.

Zimmer, J., N. Watson and A. Treat. Behavioral problems among patients in skilled nursing facilities. *Am. J. Public Health* 74:1118-1121, 1984.

# 10

# Problem-Solving in Long-Term Care: A Systematic Approach to Promoting Adaptive Behavior

*Patricia A. Miller, MEd, OTR*

Throughout the life cycle, people solve problems in a variety of ways, sometimes independently, but often with the guidance of trusted others. When older adults experience multiple problems, the assistance of others may be imperative for them to remain fully functional in everyday living.

This chapter is designed to offer guidelines and techniques on how to identify and solve seemingly unsolvable problems. When working with older persons, family caregivers or colleagues, service providers often feel overwhelmed by the innumerable problems that come to their attention. What do we do when we're taken into the confidence of a family member who states, "I'm exhausted and I can't handle this responsibility any longer?" When a daughter exclaims, "I love my mother, but I do not want to quit my job to take care of her." What do we say to the elderly man who lives with his children when he complains, "No one will let me do anything in this house or cares about what I think" What do we do when we're asked to help decide whether or not Mother should be placed in a nursing home and how might we help this woman adjust to a new environment if a change is indicated?

All of these complaints, requests and questions need responses and actions that can lead toward promoting optimal well-being in the persons involved. Some health care providers do not feel qualified or trained to deal with the highly emotional issues that are part of everyday life when working in long-term care. Others do step in and make recommendations based on their knowledge, resources and best judgment. These recommendations sometimes result in positive change. However, too frequently the recommended solutions are given verbally, but are never translated into action. In other instances, the recommended solutions are rejected outright.

The approach to problem-solving as it is about to be described is not new. It is known in a variety of forms to students of organizational psychology and to people in management positions. What is new is its application to long-term care practice. This approach can be used by educators, service providers, interdisciplinary teams, and family and self-help groups to identify and solve problems in a systematic and reasoned way while defusing emotions that hinder communication.

First, this chapter includes a conceptual framework for applying systematic problem-solving in long-term care settings for individuals and groups in need. Second, the vital distinction between problem-solving and decision-making assists the reader to understand the adaptive and mal-adaptive ways individuals respond to a problem-solving task. Third, the reader is introduced to the six steps of problem-solving. This involves defining each step and describing the methods necessary to engage the participants in the processes involved in achieving successful completion of each phase.

Two specific examples follow in which the systematic problem-solving method is used for an individual patient problem in a family context, and then as a teaching strategy to begin to identify and resolve a larger system-wide problem in a state agency serving the elderly. These two diverse examples demonstrate the versatile application of this problem-solving method and serve to stimulate thinking about applications to other long-term care settings.

## A CONCEPTUAL FRAMEWORK FOR PROBLEM-SOLVING

The clinical practice of occupational therapists has long been guided by the theoretical constructs of Mary Reilly, who views the health of human beings in terms of adaptation to their environment rather than in free-dom from pathology (Van Deusen 1988). Reilly's occupational behavior paradigm includes assessing the function/dysfunction continuum of individuals in terms of the balance of play, work, chores and rest in their daily activity, with emphasis on support from the environment in changing maladaptive to adaptive behavior. According to Reilly (1962) "the goal of occupational therapy is for patients/clients to engage actively with their life role tasks." Reilly's statement that "occupational therapy is designed to help patients influence the state of their own health" guides the practice of this author in the participative model of problem-solving described in this chapter.

Haley's model of "problem-solving therapy" is congruent with Reilly's conceptual framework in that the social or environmental context of human problems is emphasized rather than focusing on individual diagnoses and symptoms. "Shifting one's thinking from the individual unit to a social unit of two or more persons has consequences for the health care provider. Not only must the therapist think in different ways about human dilemmas, but he or she must consider himself or herself as a member of the social unit that contains the problem" (Haley 1978, p.2).

Haley's concept can be understood easily in terms of the ageism seen among health professionals in assessing and treating the elderly. Older patients and their adult children feel defeated when seeking assistance from some health professionals. "You're old, what can you expect?" and "Learn to live with your pain or memory problems" are frequent refrains. How can older people master their environment and develop adaptive skills after disease or injury if health care providers convey attitudes of unconcern or hopelessness instead of modeling problem-solving behavior? To what extent we are part of the problem is a reasonable question. "If therapy is to end properly, it must begin properly by negotiating a solvable problem and discovering the social situation that makes the problem necessary. The act of therapy begins with the way the problem is examined. The act of intervening brings out problems and the relationship patterns that are to be changed" (Haley 1978, p.9).

## PROBLEM-SOLVING AND DECISION-MAKING: A VITAL DISTINCTION

In order to solve problems effectively, it is important to understand the difference between problem-solving and decision-making. Too often people in stressful or crisis situations make decisions prematurely, without defining the true nature of the problem or considering alternative solutions. This can lead to unfortunate and sometimes irreversible consequences. There is the decision-maker who jumps right in before having the facts, and there is the person who must have more and more information before a decision can be made even when there is already abundant data. Discharge will be cited as one example to illustrate this dilemma. Disposition to a nursing home is obtained for a female patient who appears to be frail but dependent in self-care activities and the woman herself states that she knows she can manage in her apartment with the help of her devoted daughter who lives nearby, and her neighbors. Was this disposition premature? Were more facts needed? Another scenario involves keeping a patient in the hospital for an extended period of time, where she becomes increasingly depressed, in order to gather enough data to ascertain an appropriate placement. Does the discharge planner need assistance in problem-solving and reaching a reasonable decision?

The essence of problem-solving is an appreciation of the fact that one is wrestling with the unknown (Levenstein 1972a). "Whenever one cannot go from the given situation to the desired situation simply by action, then there has to be a recourse to thinking" (Duncker 1945, p.1). A systematic and reasoned approach to problem-solving incorporates four or more basic steps. "While problem-solving occurs when the alternative courses of action are unknown, decision-making is essentially a choice among known alternatives" (Levenstein 1972b, p.61). Decision-making, therefore, is one of the later steps in the problem-solving process occurring after the problem has been defined and possible solutions have been explored.

## SIX STEPS TO SYSTEMATIC PROBLEM-SOLVING

### Step 1: Defining the Problem

"A problem exists when a goal is unreachable or if there is a discrepancy between the way things are and the way things ought to be" (*Health Systems Clerkship Study Guide and Resource Manual* 1980). In order to define the problem accurately, it is necessary to ask as many questions as possible of each person involved. Not everyone sees the problem in the same way, and if one is too hasty, the problem defined might not be the real problem at all. Questions that begin with who, when and where are useful in eliciting facts, while questions that begin with what, how or why are likely to be most effective in stimulating thinking about solutions (Levenstein 1972a). In order to define the problem completely and accurately, identification of manifest and latent content is essential. An understanding of the complexity of any problem precedes consideration of solutions.

**Step 2: Brainstorming Solutions**

Generating ideas from all participants while postponing judgment is the process of brainstorming. All suggestions regarding ways to solve the problem are encouraged without discussion, criticism or premature rejection of possible solutions. The potential solutions may be written on a blackboard or on a sheet of paper as they are suggested so that no ideas are overlooked and all ideas can be considered when the brainstorming is completed.

**Step 3: Choosing a Solution**

It is necessary to review all ideas that are generated in the brainstorming session and discuss the possible solutions with all the individuals involved. This may take more than one meeting in order to engage the patient/consumer, family, staff and appropriate others. The merits of each solution need to be evaluated according to three criteria: (1) how much time will it take, (2) what will it cost and (3) how enthusiastic are the participants about implementing any one of the solutions. Choosing one or more solutions is then arrived at by group consensus. This is the appropriate point in the problem-solving process for reasoned decisions to be made.

**Step 4: Planning Ways to Implement the Solution**

Delegation of responsibilities for carrying out the suggested solution is essential before acting on it. One has to decide with all the individuals involved who will do what, when and where. A designated recorder documents the commitments individuals have agreed to undertake in order to alleviate the situation. A time and place should be arranged when the results of these activities can be discussed and evaluated.

**Step 5: Carrying Out the Plan**

An appropriate time to carry out the plan should be established, and the suggestions developed in steps 3 and 4 put into practice. It should be noted that difficulties that impede progress toward a solution often arise when carrying out the plan. In that case the individuals are encouraged to reconvene in order to assess ongoing and new developments.

### Step 6: Evaluating the Solution

Within the agreed-upon time it should be determined whether or not the plan of action is working. If it is not completely satisfactory to all persons involved, and if modifications are indicated, the five problem-solving steps listed above will have to be reintroduced. In that case the question should be asked: Is the problem still the same or should it be redefined? All the facts should be considered before redefining the problem. A new brainstorming session for exploring alternative solutions should be held with all the parties present.

The evaluation process, which involves repeating the six steps of problem-solving, takes time and a commitment to seeking a solution that will be most satisfactory to all parties. This requires negotiation, compromise and, most important, a willingness to communicate one's own feelings in a candid manner while listening empathically to the needs and wishes expressed by others.

The two examples that follow will illustrate some of the aforementioned principles and potential applications of systematic problem-solving in long-term care.

### EXAMPLE 1:
### Application of Systematic Problem-Solving (SPS) with a Family to Alleviate Depression

### The Case of Mr. S.

Mr. S. is a 73-year-old man with a history of cardiovascular disease and a cerebral thrombosis with partial paralysis of the right side. He was referred to a home care agency for nursing and occupational therapy services. The physician's orders were: check vital signs, increase independence in activities of daily living and relieve depression of recent onset.

The reason for this referral was Mr. S.'s daughter's concern about her father's change in behavior. She was particularly worried because there were recent occasions when her father preferred to spend the day in his pajamas rather than get dressed. When the change of behavior was questioned, Mr. S. responded, "What difference does it make?" Mr. S.'s gradual withdrawal from his daughter and grandson, with whom he lived, caused his daughter to call their physician to request help.

Six months prior to these events, Mr. S. had been hospitalized because of a cerebrovascular accident. Initially, active motion in the right upper extremity was very limited and he walked with a four-prong cane and supervision. He was dependent in most areas of self-care. The patient was shown self-assistive exercises that he was to perform daily to improve mobility in affected extremities. One-handed activities were introduced that renewed Mr. S.'s avocational interest in simple carpentry. This stimulated Mr. S.'s interest in self-care.

Gradual independence in self-care activities and improved physical ability were encouraged and achieved. Mr. S.'s affected right arm continued to be used as a functional assist. He was discharged back to the home of his working daughter and teenage grandson with the knowledge that he was able to manage at home without assistance.

### Step 1: Defining the Problem

In the course of a lengthy initial home visit by an occupational therapist, Mr. S. voiced as his chief complaint: "No one will let me do anything in this house or cares about what I think." The following questions asked by the occupational therapist elicited further information from Mr. S. and his family, making it possible to change Mr. S.'s complaint into a problem statement that was mutually agreed upon, a necessary prerequisite to exploring solutions.

| Questions Asked by Therapist | Answers by Mr. S. |
|---|---|
| Who won't let you do anything? | My daughter and grandson. |
| What would you like to do? | Repairs around the house. Before my stroke, I used to take care of everything. I even built a desk for my grandson. |
| When did you do all these things? | Six months ago. I've lived with my daughter ever since her divorce, three years ago. I've been the man around the house, but not anymore. |

| | |
|---|---|
| Why don't you do these things | She doesn't trust me (referring to daughter) and my grandson is too busy to pay attention. |
| Where did you do these things? | Down in the basement. My workbench and tools are all there. The stairs are steep. My daughter says I'll fall. Maybe she's right. |
| How do things get done around the house now? | Now, everything is a mess. The doorknob keeps falling off the front door and a new ceiling is needed in the bathroom because of a leak. The tub tile needs caulking. I could go on. |
| *Questions Asked by Therapist*<br>What is your concern, Mrs. D.? | *Answers by Mr. S.'s Family*<br>My father is not a well man and lately he seems older and weaker. He doesn't seem to want to talk to us either. |
| Can you pinpoint when he became less communicative and began to seem more frail? | I'm not sure. Dad wanted to repair our bathroom tile about a month ago. He asked my son, Tom, to buy some caulking and he never did. Tom and I don't think Dad can handle a job like that. He might slip and fall. My father was very angry when I told him I would call in a tile man. Dad doesn't realize that I'm trying to protect him. |
| Who helps with all the things that need to be done around the house? | That's a good question. We're all very busy. I work long hours and Tom, well, you must know how full a teenager's life can be. |

| | |
|---|---|
| When do you and Tom and your dad find time to talk to each other? | We've been going our separate ways a lot lately—and I guess Dad has been left out. He's not that strong. I'm not sure it's safe for him to do all the things we do. We like to eat out and it's hard for him to get in and out of the car. |
| Tom, what changes do you see in your grandfather lately? | My grandfather taught me how to do a lot of things. He's Mr. Fixit and I take after him, but he's very quiet now and Mom doesn't want him to have another stroke so he doesn't do very much. |
| How do you feel about that? | I don't know. It must be hard to live the way he does. I really don't know what to talk to him about anymore. |

Defining the Problem in Terms of Need

After all the persons involved have been encouraged to answer questions and express the problem from their point of view, the problem can be defined in terms of need: what exists now and what is desired (Bolton 1979)? It is easier to brainstorm solutions when the actual state of affairs is contrasted to the desired solution.

Example of Problem Statement

How might Mr. S., who feels unwanted and unneeded by his family, regain his status as a contributing family member while maintaining his health and safety?

*Step 2: Brainstorming Solutions*

After involving all members of Mr. S.'s family in defining the problem, brainstorming took place and several ideas were generated.

1.  Schedule a medical checkup for Mr. S., which will help allay anxiety

about his health status and serve to assist Mr. S. and his family in setting realistic plans for his daily activities.

2. Move some of the tools Mr. S. uses most frequently upstairs so that they are accessible and he doesn't have to use the basement.
3. Put a handrail on both sides of the basement stairs so that Mr. S. can go up and down safely.
4. Establish a regular family time to talk about everyone's needs and activities to counteract the tendency of each family member to pursue his own activities without involvement of the others.

*Step 3: Choosing a Solution*

Through the brainstorming process, Mr. S.'s family was able to begin to communicate their fears and concerns to each other. Of all the ideas generated, a medical checkup for Mr. S. was considered the top priority. Tom said that if the doctor agreed that his grandfather could go up and down stairs, then he would build a handrail for the basement stairs. The family also agreed that their lives had become too hectic and that they would spend more time together.

*Step 4: Planning Ways to Carry Out the Solutions*

Mr. S. stated that he would call to make an appointment for a checkup with his physician. His daughter agreed to take a half-day off from work to take her father to his appointment. Tom reiterated that he would build the handrail, with Mr. S.'s help, for the basement stairs.

*Step 5: Carrying Out the Plan*

Mr. S. received a satisfactory report from his physical examination. He and his daughter were reassured that it was safe for Mr. S. to do repairs around the house if he had all the necessary equipment with him while he was doing the activity. He was also told to pace himself by taking rest breaks. Mr. S.'s mood and energy level improved simultaneously. His daughter began to realize that her dad needed to feel productive and she wanted and needed his help. Tom and Mr. S. began caulking the bathroom tile together.

*Step 6: Evaluating the Solutions*

Upon visiting Mr. S. six weeks after the initial meeting, he stated, "Things are going pretty well. I can't do everything the way I used to, but my grandson is a great partner. We're working on Saturday mornings to get the house back into shape." Mr. S. explained that Tom and he decided not to build the handrail for the basement because they had other things to do that were more important. "My daughter put all my tools in the kitchen to make it easier for me. I called a locksmith to fix the doorknob," he stated. "After all, I'm not a young guy. I can't do everything I used to do, you know."

*Comments*

Communication patterns in families vary greatly. Some people find it easier than others to be open and honest when conflict arises. This problem-solving process enabled Mr. S.'s family to share their fears and concerns in a systematic way that led to conflict resolution. Each family member, but particularly Mr. S., felt better knowing that his feelings were understood. Mr. S.'s need to continue to pursue meaningful occupations was vital to his adaptation. Although it is rare to have problems solved to everyone's satisfaction, the process of problem-solving enables people to compromise and adjust to change while maintaining self-esteem. When individuals feel understood, it is easier to accept limitations and acknowledge strengths. In this case example, a systematic approach to problem-solving provided a participative model for facilitating adaptive skills in later life.

**EXAMPLE 2:**
**Systematic Problem-Solving (SPS) as a**
**Teaching Strategy with Service Providers**

**Rationale for SPS as a Teaching Strategy**

Through the process of SPS, service providers become aware of their own resources and abilities. The approach builds on their experiences, gives recognition for their efforts, encourages peer support and provides the incentive to seek assistance in solving problems that at first may appear too difficult to solve. This teaching strategy has particular value for use with service providers of the elderly. The proportion of persons with health problems increases with age, and the elderly as a group are more likely than younger persons to have multiple and chronic, but sometimes severely disabling conditions (Burnside 1984).

It is a fact, too, that most agencies and institutions do not have the personnel to meet the complex needs of their older adult clients. This formula of too few staff for too many people with multiple needs can lead to feelings of frustration, discouragement and a sense of impotence among providers.

At the completion of an SPS training session participants should feel that their problems have been identified, understood as complex but not unsolvable, and they should be motivated to implement some of the recommended solutions for more effective work with the elderly.

### SPS with a State Department of Community Affairs

In answer to a request by the Department of Community Affairs of the New Jersey State Division on Aging, the Columbia University Center for Geriatrics and Gerontology provided a workshop to assist coordinators of congregate housing to motivate tenants to accept services. The congregate housing service (CHS) programs are located in specially designed subsidized housing projects for the elderly. The supportive services include the provision of meals, housekeeping and personal assistance based on the specific needs of participants who are impaired or socially isolated.

Numerous requests for assistance had been received from coordinators who found that those people most in need of services were frequently refusing the services offered. The author's SPS workshop is discussed below.

*Step 1: Defining the Problem*

One of the first issues that arose in the discussion among coordinators was the difficulty they had in accepting the reasons for tenants' refusal of services. Were the reasons given by tenants the real reasons? Understanding the resistance to accepting services in terms of the meanings behind the tenants' words, as well as the words themselves, was emphasized by the workshop leader.

Reik (1972) refers to the process of effective listening as listening with the third ear. This may be understood in terms of the tenant's *latent* message. Latent reasons for refusal of services refer to those services that are dormant, present without being explicit, and sometimes hidden. This can be contrasted to the *manifest* content of a person's message, i.e., those reasons that are clearly evident, visible or explicitly stated.

Through effective listening, the coordinator interacts with the tenants in a manner that establishes what the tenant really means. This involves listening for both the manifest and the latent content of each tenant's message.

In order to define the problem of refusal to accept congregate housing services completely and accurately, the coordinators began to identify the manifest and latent reasons for their refusals. Among the *manifest* reasons stated by the tenants were the following:

1. I can prepare food for myself for less money.
2. I don't like the food they serve here.
3. I'm on a special diet and need special food.
4. I'm not sick and do not need the program.
5. I don't trust strangers to help me.

Among the *latent* reasons for refusal hypothesized by the coordinators were these:

1. Tenants may reject meals because they do not reflect their customary tastes.
2. Tenants may have financial resources but be afraid to spend any money.
3. Tenants may not want others to observe their limitations or disabilities.
4. Tenants may be depressed and feel that nothing is worthwhile.
5. Tenants may be frightened of the "newcomer" or "outsider" role in the group situation.
6. Tenants want to appear independent to themselves and others.

Problem Statements Generated by the Coordinators

As with many problems in long-term care, the reasons for refusal to accept congregate housing services were multifactorial. Included below are three problem statements generated by the coordinators as they considered both the manifest and latent messages received from tenants.

1. Tenants fear that acceptance of congregate housing services will mean that family members will relinquish their responsibility, which may mean loss of regular contact with their families.
2. Tenants are too depressed to accept any assistance. The depression may be acute or chronic due to a variety of causes. Loss of a spouse was the most frequently expressed cause of depression.
3. Tenants with memory problems or other mental/emotional symp-

toms are difficult to maintain as active members of the program. They require constant reminders to participate, and the staff does not have the time to supervise these tenants on a regular basis.

*Step 2 : Brainstorming Solutions*

Several contributing solutions were proposed by the coordinators:

1. Acquaint tenants with CHS gradually so that they will know what services are available on any given day without feeling coerced.
2. Gather as much information as possible about each tenant prior to the first visit, e.g., medical history, diet, recent death in the family, special fears. This information may help the coordinator establish a rapport, be empathic and understand the specific resistances to accepting services.
3. Establish good communication with each tenant, showing interest in a supportive and consistent way. For example, explore tenants' interests, e.g., talk about the latest books they may be reading or recent news items. Clues from their apartment may be used to spark conversation, such as family photos and collections.
4. Establish a trusting relationship: be available, leave your telephone number, show tenants where your office is located, visit with tenants frequently. After a positive rapport has been established and the need for services identified, a straightforward approach that enables the older person to admit real needs should be encouraged. In addition, establish trust with tenants' families and invite their cooperation in helping tenants to accept the services.
5. Increase visibility of available services. Make a variety of opportunities available to join the CHS, such as an information flyer, newsletter or additional follow-up visits to tenants' apartments.
6. In order to assist tenants to make a change in their lives that involves accepting services, the following ideas were suggested: (a) offer services on a trial basis, (b) learn tenants' favorite foods and invite them to a meal when these dishes will be served, (c) explain costs in terms of one meal per day instead of monthly charges, and (d) provide an initial "free" luncheon.
7. If a tenant presents a problem that is too difficult to handle alone, the coordinator should make use of all available resources, such as consultation with the supervisor, the building superintendent, co-workers, other tenants, and the tenant's family.

*Conclusion*

Through systematic problem-solving, the coordinators were able to identify some of their problems in motivating older persons to accept congregate housing services and to devise solutions to mitigate or eliminate their
resistance. Two workshops related to this topic heightened the
participants' awareness of the complexity of the problems and of the
solutions. The first two steps in the problem-solving process—defining
the problem and brainstorming solutions—were addressed. In order to
truly solve the problem of motivating tenants to accept CHS, the next four
steps of SPS have to be taken.

Some of the recommended solutions to the problems are of an
interpersonal nature and, with varying degrees of success, may be implemented immediately. Other suggested solutions are of a policy nature,
requiring administrative exploration as to the feasibility of their practical-
ity and value. Therefore, choosing the solutions, planning ways to implement them, implementing the plans and, within a reasonable time period,
evaluating the solutions, must follow the first two steps of SPS.

It is hoped that these problem-solving workshops, by building on
the coordinators' knowledge and experiences, have further facilitated
their ability to respond creatively to the challenge of motivating tenants
to accept congregate housing services. The most salient point made by
several coordinators about the value of SPS was that the process enabled
them to see the individual differences among older people, and that one
must assess each person and situation separately to avoid generalizing
about the needs of older people.

The systematic problem-solving technique described in this chapter
is applicable to both community and institutional service systems and is
especially effective when used by a team (Miller and Toner 1991). It is
useful in helping individuals and families find solutions to impasses in
interpersonal relationships and daily living; it is also beneficial in teaching
people to identify problems in working relationships and to devise solutions for more effective interactions, policies and procedures; and it can
be used as a teaching strategy for solving problems in practice.

## REFERENCES

Bolton, R. *People Skills.* Englewood Cliffs, NJ: Prentice-Hall, 1979.
Burnside, I. *Working with the Elderly: Group Process and Technique.* Belmont, CA:
    Wadsworth Health Sciences, 1984.

Center for Interdisciplinary Education in Allied Health. *Health Systems Clerkship Study Guide and Resource Manual.* Lexington, KY: University of Kentucky, 1980.

Duncker, K. On problem-solving. *Psychol. Monographs* 58(5), 1945.

Haley, J. *Problem-Solving Therapy.* San Francisco: Jossey-Bass, 1978.

Levenstein, A. Problem-solving Through Group Action. In A.C. Bennett, ed., *Improving the Effectiveness of Hospital Management.* New York: Metromedia Analearn Publications, 1972a.

Levenstein, A. The Art of Decision-Making. In A.C. Bennett, ed., *Improving the Effectiveness of Hospital Management.* New York: Metromedia Analearn Publications, 1972b.

Miller, P. and J. Toner. The Making of a Geriatric Team. In W. Myers, ed., *New Techniques in the Psychotherapy of Older Patients.* Washington, DC: American Psychiatric Press, 1991.

Reik, T. *Listening with the Third Ear.* New York: Pyramid, 1972.

Reilly, M. Occupational therapy can be one of the great ideas of 20th century medicine. *Am. J. Occup. Ther.* 16:1-9, 1962.

Van Deusen, J. Mary Reilly. In B.R. Miller, K. Sieg, F.M. Ludwig, S.D. Shortridge, and J. Van Deusen, eds., *Six Perspectives on Theory for the Practice of Occupational Therapy.* Rockville, MD: Aspen Publications, 1988.

# 11

# Key Psychosocial Aspects in the Medical Management of Chronic Illness

*Terry Kinzel, MD, FACP*

## CLINICAL DECISION-MAKING

The most important aspect of providing good medical care to those with chronic illness is sound clinical decision-making (Cassel 1982; Cassem 1978). A somewhat irreverent contrast between acute and long-term care will help set the context for exploring the differences between the two. Acute care patients are expected to get well or die; in long-term care, while patients do in fact die, more often there is a prolonged time when the patient neither gets well nor dies, but suffers exacerbations and remissions of chronic (frequently multiple) illnesses. To understand the difference is critical. To not understand it is to put the chronically ill patient at risk for both overtreatment and undertreatment. These issues will be discussed in more detail below.

### Decision-Making: Acute Illness

In the acute care setting, the patient presents with a potentially reversible condition. In this context it is appropriate to place emphasis on an accurate diagnosis of the cause and aggressive treatment to resolve the problem. In pursuit of these ends, it is often reasonable to tolerate a significant amount of discomfort and risk. At the same time a lesser emphasis is placed on symptom control per se, although it is never excusable to ignore symptoms in the pursuit of diagnosis and treatment.

**Decision-Making: Chronic Illness**

Chronic illnesses are, by definition, not curable. Thus, no matter how vigorously we pursue diagnosis and treatment, the patient will be left with residual, usually progressive disease. Here it is appropriate to shift the emphasis to function and symptom management rather than cure of disease. Less discomfort and risk should be tolerated in diagnosis and treatment. Particularly in the advanced phases of chronic illness, if the physician is not able to make this shift, the patient is at risk for overtreatment. A simple example might be the pursuit of an elevated alkaline phosphatase in a person with advanced Alzheimer's disease. Conversely, patients with chronic disease are at risk for undertreatment as well. Since the pace of their illness tends to be slower, they may be considered "less interesting" by some physicians and consequently their problems are less attended to. This is compounded by the fact that the symptoms are frequently vague or nonspecific and multiple simultaneous illnesses make diagnosis difficult. For example, in a patient with Alzheimer's disease the onset of incontinence may be part of the disease process that would be difficult to treat. Conversely, it could be due to something as easy to correct as a bladder infection (the symptoms of which the patient may not be able to describe) or the inappropriate use of restraints. The key is to carefully evaluate the whole patient, realistically appraise the usefulness of each treatment in a chronic illness, and maintain a high level of attention over time, seeking easily treatable aspects of the patient's condition to maximize function and minimize symptoms.

**Decision-Making: Terminal Illness**

Care of terminally ill patients is one area where no effort should be spared in the relief of symptoms (Angell 1982). Also, very little is to be tolerated in the way of discomfort or risk in diagnosis and treatment. That is not to excuse superficial assessment or thinking. There is also no excuse for not diagnosing and treating, for example, a urinary tract infection in a patient with advanced cancer.

Having acknowledged that even in terminal illness, accurate diagnosis and effective treatment of some acute complicating illnesses remains important, clearly, in this setting, the emphasis should be on the relief of symptoms. In a patient who is dying and suffering with pain, addiction is not a concern; the amount of narcotic is not a concern; what peers say is not a concern. What is a concern is that analgesics are used effectively and in a way that minimizes their side effects. In patients in the final stages of suffocating from emphysema, that the maximum recommended dose of beta agonist is exceeded or that it may cause an arrhythmia is less of a concern than that everything possible is used to attempt to relieve the patient's suffering (Portenoy 1987; Kinzel 1988; Saunders 1978).

## THE LIMITED TREATMENT PLAN AND ADVANCED DIRECTIVES

The most potent tool available to the physician in the approach to good decision-making in patients who are chronically or terminally ill is the limited treatment plan. This allows the physician, along with nursing and other health care staff, to work with the patient and family to clearly identify what goals are important and what diagnostic tests and treatments are appropriate to meet these goals. The use of a well-developed limited treatment plan helps the physician to understand what is important to the patient, to provide the care that will best achieve this, and to avoid "meddlesome" medicine.

Frequently, advanced directives and instruments such as "living wills" are thought of in the rather limited scope of allowing the patient to forgo heroic measures in the case of catastrophic illness. Aside from the fact that "heroic" may encompass a great range of interpretations, this narrow understanding of advanced directives fails to unleash much of their inherent power. When used most effectively, they allow physicians to help patients understand what medicine can and cannot do, what the risks and benefits of various options are, and how patients might best accomplish their goals. Conversely, advanced directives allow patients the opportunity to inform the physician about what is important to them. This expanded understanding of advanced directives helps to emphasize the caveat that "do not resuscitate" does not mean "do not treat." The issue is not simply the use of resuscitation or respirators, but an understanding of which of the whole range of treatments available are likely to achieve the patient's goals (Graham 1986; Cohen-Cole 1986). Once the limited treatment plan is in place, the health care team must be clear that the patient will not be abandoned—literally and psychologically, as is discussed in greater detail below.

The final caveat regarding the limited treatment plan and advanced directives is that they are not writ in stone. They are living documents that need ongoing reappraisal. Patients' goals and wishes may change as the disease process changes or as their understanding changes or simply from a change of mind. In these instances, the treatment plan must be reappraised and changed as appropriate.

## PSYCHOSOCIAL ISSUES IN THE MANAGEMENT OF ANXIETY IN CHRONIC AND TERMINAL ILLNESSES

Anxiety is a common problem in patients with advanced, progressive illness seen in the long-term care setting. When patients were not known by staff before they became ill it is not uncommon for staff to attribute patients dependency and anxiety to their personality. Most often, this is not the case. Key factors contributing to anxiety in this setting include the fear of abandonment, loss of control and inadequate relief of symptoms.

### Fear of Abandonment

The dramatic rise in the costs of health care, the changing patterns of care with early discharges, and an overburdened, inadequately financed long-term care system provide a very real basis for patient fears. Less obvious is the change in the relationship between the patient and the physician when the patient moves from the acute care "get well or die" setting into chronic care. We are taught to cure disease and save lives. In chronic and terminal illness where incurable disease and death is the rule rather than the exception, many of our best physicians are at a loss as to how to relate to the patient. The patient's uncured illness becomes a "scarlet letter" constantly reminding us of our failure. Our response is frequently unacknowledged guilt and sense of helplessness. In an effort to escape we may visit the patient as infrequently and as briefly as possible. Conversely, we may launch into futile and often painful treatments to avoid acknowledging our helplessness. When these things occur, the patient rightly feels abandoned.

Techniques to help patients avoid feelings of abandonment include walking all the way into the patient's room; always making hands-on contact, even if you are not looking for masses or listening for murmurs; and always sitting down, usually on the bed, but at least in a bedside chair—this tells the patient that the business to be attended to is in his room. It is also useful to frequently review the medications and treatments with the patient, and, if possible, make some minor change that allows the patient (and the physician) to feel that the magic of therapeutics is still alive (Kinzel 1988). Finally, it is a good idea for physicians to review the limited treatment plan to remind themselves that cure is not usually the goal, so that success or failure is not judged against the unattainable standard of cure, but against the success in helping patients attain their goals.

## Loss of Control

Progressive illness in the long-term care setting is invariably accompanied by loss of control for the patient. Even in the best institutions, the most basic functions of a person's life—eating, bathing, sleeping, toileting—are often influenced by the needs and schedules of the institution. The more disabled the individual, the greater the dependency, the greater the loss of control. Sometimes the only control patients have left is to decide whether or not they will eat. These behaviors may be very frustrating to the direct care staff, but once staff recognizes that they are the result of loss of control, the frustration is lessened. Often the physician can take steps to lessen a patient's loss of control. How often is a salt-restricted diet actually critical in the death of a cancer patient? Is the fact that the patient's cholesterol is high really a reason to forbid eggs (Kinzel 1991)?

## Inadequate Relief of Symptoms

The inadequate relief of symptoms, especially pain, in chronic and terminal illness may contribute greatly to anxiety. Effective approaches to the relief of symptoms in this setting are well described in the hospice literature. Accurate assessment of symptoms accompanied by appropriate use of analgesics and other therapeutics unrestrained by the conventions of acute care may often provide a degree of symptom relief. Unfortunately, too often this is not the case. Even physicians skilled in palliative care, if not using a limited treatment plan, may miss opportunities to relieve symptoms. Effective relief of symptoms is a potent tool in the relief of anxiety.

## CONCLUSION

While all the issues discussed in this chapter apply to persons with chronic illness regardless of the setting, there are several additional issues that become prominent in the nursing home setting. The first of these, from the patient's perspective, is the sense of finality. Many elderly persons view the nursing home as the final step before death. To them, Dante's admonition upon entering Hell—"Abandon all hope, ye who enter here"—seems all too true. With the changes in medical practice since the onset of DRG reimbursement, the nursing home has become a place of active rehabilitation for many patients, and indeed at the Nursing Home Care Unit of the Veterans Affairs Medical Center in Iron Mountain, Michigan, fully 40 percent of our admissions are discharged to a setting requiring less care, many of them to their homes. Nevertheless, to many the nursing home is the last stop and it is important to take this aspect of care into consideration.

A second issue of particular importance in the nursing home concerns finances. At this time in the United States, Medicare and private insurance provide minimal support for the very great cost of nursing home care. Thus the burden for most falls to Medicaid, in many cases contributing to the impoverishment of the family before eligibility is achieved. Over the past decade, as the federal government followed by one state after another has abandoned any pretense of providing equitable access to health care, this dilemma has become much worse and has contributed to further suffering.

Finally, the issue of abandonment is particularly acute in the decision-making process. The spouse or other caregiver is often accused of abandoning the patient, by the patient or other relatives (who, it should be noted, almost never contribute to care themselves), when placement in a nursing home is considered. In my experience, most caregivers use their personal resources to the maximum before seeking nursing home placement and it is rare for a caregiver to "dump" a patient. Thus the effort here needs to address both the feeling of abandonment by the patient and the feelings of guilt experienced by the caregiver.

A great deal of suffering occurs in patients with progressive, chronic illnesses. Careful attention to the key psychosocial aspects of medical care in this setting can help minimize this suffering. This includes defining the important differences in medical decision-making in the acute, chronic and terminal settings; developing and using a limited treatment plan; understanding advanced directives; and attention to relief of the fear of abandonment, loss of control and relief of symptoms. Where cure is not possible, the quality of compassion and mercy is paramount.

## REFERENCES

Angell, M. The quality of mercy. *N. Engl. J. Med.* 306:98, 1982.

Cassell, E.J. The nature of suffering and the goals of medicine. *N. Engl. J.Med.* 306:639, 1982.

Cassem, N. Treatment Decisions in Irreversible Illness. In T. Hackett, and N. Cassem, eds., *Massachusetts General Hospital Psychiatry.* St. Louis: C.V. Mosby, 1978.

Cohen-Cole, S. A practical guide for helping patients cope with their emotions. *Quality Life Cardiovasc. Care* 3:53, 1986.

Graham, J.O. and R.W. Perrett. Truth telling and fatal illness. *N.Z. Med. J.* 99:759, 1986.

Kinzel, T. Symptom control in geriatric patients with terminal cancer: pain, nausea, and vomiting. *Geriatrics* 43(6):83, 1988.

Kinzel, T. Relief of emotional symptoms in elderly patients with terminal cancer. *Geriatrics* 43(7):61, 1988.

Kinzel, T. Managing lung disease in late life. *Geriatrics* 46(1):54, 1991.

Portenoy, R.K. Optimal pain control in elderly cancer patients. *Geriatrics* 45(5):33, 1987.

Saunders, C.M. The Philosophy of Terminal Care. In C.M. Saunders, ed., *The Management of Terminal Disease.* New York: Edward Arnold, 1978.

# 12

# The Relationship Between Grieving and the Alzheimer's Family

*Sister Robert Clare Swarts*

This may seem like a very strange approach to this topic, but the more I deal with the families of Alzheimer's victims, the more similarity I see to the stages of dying described so aptly by Elisabeth Kübler-Ross. When Kübler-Ross identified these stages, she did so by describing distinct phases through which a dying individual with a terminal illness passes before death. The family of a person diagnosed as having Alzheimer's disease passes through very similar stages. I find that drawing this parallel and identifying the stages is a tremendous help to me in assisting these families.

I direct a medical day care program for Alzheimer's patients. I am also the assistant administrator of the nursing home where the day care program is housed. This enables me to work closely with individuals and families from the early to the late stages of Alzheimer's disease.

It is often believed that the actual death of a loved one is when the family begins to go through the stages of grieving. Sometimes this is true. Alzheimer's disease is unique in many ways, but especially so in one particular aspect. The family that loses a loved one to death experiences a loss, a void in their lives; they suffer through the stages of grief and eventually adjust to life without that person. The victim of Alzheimer's disease does not leave physically; the body remains but a person that the family has known and loved is gradually fading, slowly (but sometimes rapidly) changing. The family's adaptation is not to go on with life but to adjust constantly to a disease process that is changing their lives.

As a person experiences the onset of Alzheimer's disease (AD) and becomes forgetful, restless or uninterested in things that used to be of great interest, the family begins to notice the changes but they often perceive this as merely aging. As the confusion becomes more pronounced and can't be ignored any longer the *denial stage* begins. It is at this time that confusion is evident and is more pronounced than the usual forgetfulness that everyone experiences with aging. The family will become aware of it if, for example, the spouse becomes ill or dies and the other family members have an opportunity to observe the AD victim more closely. Frequently they will realize that the spouse was covering up for the confused partner. Sometimes hospitalization will call attention to this condition.

At the point that the family realizes there is a problem they begin to seek medical advice. Often the family physician will deal with the problem by prescribing medication. Frequently a physician will tell a family, "It's senility or dementia; there's nothing you can do." This causes most families to become very frustrated. They deny that their loved one is deteriorating; they cannot accept the behavior being exhibited and yet they know something is happening. At this point they are looking for a cure.

Imagine, for example, a father who is a strong family head and provider, who is loved and admired by his wife, children and grandchildren. Physically this man looks the same as always and he seems to be in good health. Suddenly he starts refusing to take a shower. The whole family becomes upset. Everyone pushes him, insisting that he get washed. He in turn displays anger and continues to refuse. It is difficult to help the family members realize that the AD victim just doesn't remember how to take a shower. The wife may find that he goes into the bathroom and just stands there; he doesn't get washed. In this stage we can help the family to understand that he is confused by choices. Standing in a shower where there are several knobs to turn will frustrate him. He doesn't know which to turn so he will walk away. We can assist by guiding the family to set everything up, lay out the towels and soap, turn on the water to the appropriate temperature and then lead him to the shower. This eliminates the choices and frustration for him and he will take the shower.

This is just one simple illustration of what a family trying to cope with early Alzheimer's disease has to deal with. It is so difficult to accept the fact that the victim can no longer remember what happened recently or how to do simple, routine things. Suddenly the most basic activities, performed countless times before, can be monumental sources of stress and frustration for both the victim and the caregiver.

Anger is the second stage and it is exhibited in a variety of ways by families. The Alzheimer's victim is often in a different era of his life on different days. Each day by asking a few simple questions at day care we can get an idea of where that person is in time that day. After hearing a compliment on a dress or scarf, a woman might say, "Thank you; my mother dressed me today." This is a clue for us that today she is a little girl; she lives with her mother. Today we deal with her on that level. Insisting that her daughter dressed her today will frustrate and anger her. She may deny that she ever married and that she has had children.

In the *anger stage* the family is disconcerted and will sometimes lash out at the doctor, criticizing the treatment prescribed. They may go to several doctors looking for a cure. If parents are living together the children may criticize the well parent, thinking that the sick parent is not being handled properly. When the victim does something inappropriate the family members may react by yelling or even striking him. Frustration for everyone is the main characteristic of this stage.

In the anger stage the family comes to realize that something has to be done and they begin to look at alternatives. It is usually at this point that they will investigate day care as an option. Family members will call and inquire about the program. They may come in for a tour and even take an application. Incidents are related that show obvious anger. Often they feel that on some level the victim is actually cognizant and deliberately behaves inappropriately. Families believe that the behavior is calculated to frustrate them. An example is the confused person who gets lost. The family simply can't believe that their loved one, who has lived in the same home for 40 years, in the same neighborhood and town, can get lost and be unable to get home again or even recall the correct address.

When I see a family in this stage I know that I can make some suggestions and can let them know that they are not going through this alone, that many other families are having the same experiences. There is consolation in knowing that their family member is not so unusual and that there are people who understand what they are going through. They leave impressed with the program, but I know I will probably not hear from them for a few months. They feel better and convince themselves that they can handle this a while longer. It is consoling to them that when they need help they know there is somewhere to go.

In the *bargaining stage* the victim has deteriorated to a point where the family realizes that caregiving is a 24-hour-a-day job. It is not safe to leave the person alone, eating is a problem, a great deal of patience is needed and the caregivers are overwhelmed. Usually at this time there is some family member who realizes that the victim is not going to get well. They have perhaps already seen him move through a few different plateaus, and having read some information on Alzheimer's, they know what the future will hold.

The bargaining begins with the family member deciding on appropriate care and recognizing that the primary caregiver needs some type of respite from continually caring for the AD victim. Often day care is seen as a way to keep the person at home and avoid the nursing home. It is most often at this stage that the application taken a few months previously is submitted and the person begins to come to day care on a regular basis.

It always amazes families that their relative likes and responds to day care. Over and over I have heard, "I'll try it but my father was never a club person," or "My mother was never a joiner and never liked craft things." The vast majority of clients respond very positively to day care. The reason is that the atmosphere in day care is calm and quiet. We accept the clients as they are. We do not put pressure on them to be as they used to be or to remember what they should but can't remember. Frequently after a client has been coming to the day care program two times per week, the family will call and ask to increase the frequency because the client is getting ready and waiting for the transport van on days when he is not scheduled to attend.

At this time of bargaining when the caregivers have become adjusted to a day care program, they really come to rely on that span of free time. They appreciate having the few hours of independence to get some errands done or get in some extra visiting or rest. It is important to realize that these stages may occur rapidly or over a period of time, again depending on personalities, tolerance levels, progress of the disease and family circumstances.

Eventually the disease progresses to a point where the family realizes that the disease is not going to be cured and is going to progress. They see the deterioration and can no longer deny it. With this deterioration comes depression. The children will often ask: Is this hereditary? Is this how I'm going to end up? I have come to believe that one of the most devastating experiences for anyone, regardless of age, is when your own parent or spouse doesn't know you or recognize you any more. The amount of support that families need to deal with this is tremendous. Many people never arrive at a point of acceptance. Some will say, "As far as I'm concerned my father left us four years ago." In many respects this is true. There may be a physical resemblance to the person they know as parent, provider, lover, mentor or role model, but the resemblance stops there. Even the grandchildren who had a wonderful relationship with a grandparent need help to understand and accept. When you take on the care of the Alzheimer's afflicted, in a very real sense you take on the care of the entire family because all are suffering and all have needs.

Acceptance is the final stage Kübler-Ross describes for the dying. She speaks of it as a time when depression is left behind and the person is resigned and begins to put things in order. Once again I can see a similarity with the families of Alzheimer's victims. In the *acceptance stage* of this progressing disease the family comes to realize that they can no longer handle the care of the victim on a 24-hour basis and that placement in a skilled nursing facility is the best solution. This is never an easy decision. It literally is agony and many families never quite forgive themselves even though they know it is best.

Usually family members react to placement in one of two ways. Some family members have such difficulty accepting placement in a nursing home that they just can't bear to visit. Coping with the deterioration of their loved one and seeing others in more advanced stages are just too much for them. Adjusting to the fact that they could not handle the care of a loved one, they feel such guilt that they can't forgive themselves. Other family members are able to cope and find it easier to visit more frequently.

Often the nursing home staff gets to know one or two family members very well and see them as devoted to the resident. Basically, frequent visitors are those who feel "this is my family member and regardless of what condition he is in I am obligated to him." At the time of death it is sometimes found that there are two or three other family members that the staff never knew about or saw only occasionally. This other group feels: this is not the person I loved and I can't stand to see him this way.

We try to help the staff understand that every situation is different; you must not judge family members too harshly. Everyone handles the circumstances differently and copes differently.

I am reminded of one resident who had two daughters. One was a nurse by profession and was a frequent visitor. The other visited only a few times a year. It was obvious that the second daughter found it very difficult to see her mother so confused. Before she left each time she would come to my office and leave a substantial donation. She would tell me how grateful she was to have her mother at our nursing home and to have her cared for so lovingly. She would express how badly she felt that she could not care for her mother herself but that she just could not stand seeing her the way she was. She needed to know that I did not think she was a terrible daughter because she did not visit often.

A big part of caring for Alzheimer's patients is caring for the family as a whole, assisting the whole family because all of them are suffering.

The identification of the process that family members are going through as well as what the actual victim is experiencing is very important. Offering assistance by providing information, education, referrals, or just listening is also of value. Providing support groups for family members or care givers,   as well as day care programs and long-term nursing home care, is a tremendous service and comfort.

# 13

# Group Therapy with the Elderly

*Lynn M. Tepper, EdD*

## BACKGROUND

The past twenty years have witnessed rapid growth in the number of older Americans. The discipline of gerontology has become a focus of extensive concern as a subject of study and specialization within the fields of medicine, social work, psychology, nursing, dentistry, occupational and physical therapy, and public health. Business and industry have taken notice of this population as worthy consumers of supplies and services. The educational system has opened its doors to older students in search of enrichment for reasons such as retirement planning, self-improvement, socialization and the attainment of a high school, college or graduate degree.

The term "new old" has been used to describe this group, as they differ from previous generations of the elderly in a number of ways. Increased longevity is one of the most obvious changes, with the numbers of persons living to be 75 and older approaching 10 million in 1990, as compared to fewer than 1 million in 1900. While the number of people over 65 has increased eightfold since 1900, the number of people living past 85 has increased more than twentyfold! In addition to the great leap in longevity for this group, they are also better educated, are financially more secure, have a higher standard of living as a result, are healthier than previous generations of older people, and are able to retain most of their usual activity levels into old age.

Prior to this increased interest in older people, health providers and social scientists often avoided this group for many reasons. Their training may not have prepared them adequately to meet the often complex needs of this population. Inaccurate negative stereotypes may have discouraged working with them. Many practitioners would rather work with younger people who could make more active contributions to society. Older people could also have represented their "future selves," a sign of their own mortality. A realistic view of this population does acknowledge more complex medical, social and psychiatric problems, and a lower rate of cure for many medical concerns. The good news, however, is that many of these attitudes and beliefs of mental health providers appear to have improved, due to educational interventions, research and changes in public opinion. The sheer numbers in this group have forced care providers to become aware of their needs, as have public policy initiatives that promote service to this population.

## RATIONALE

The "new old" are more inclined to view mental health as being part of their total health picture. Considering the facts that this population grew up when movies and documentaries such as *The Snake Pit* were popular, that conditions in many state hospitals were disgraceful, and that only the truly mentally ill had recourse to psychiatrists and psychologists, this group has certainly come a long way in modifying or changing their views of mental health services.

This combination of factors—larger numbers of older people, their increased longevity, their more complex psychosocial and medical conditions, and their recognition of the importance of mental health intervention—points to the fact that there are and will continue to be unprecedented demands on all parts of the mental health community. These demands will expand to other professionals who now view mental health as an essential part of the older person's total health care picture. This further suggests that the elderly will become even greater participants in group therapy, both in residential care facilities and in the community.

Practitioners of group work will need to expand their knowledge in many directions in order to work with effectively with the elderly. Those who have trained within the past decade are at a distinct advantage, as the possibilities for education in gerontology have increased during this period. Those trained earlier may feel the need to continue their education so as to expand their knowledge about this population and the new types of therapeutic group interventions available to them. A good place to start would be to learn about normal aging, including information about physical changes and their implications, psychological and social theories and changes, minority issues, family patterns, living environments, death and dying, long-term care program planning, and policy issues that often determine service delivery.

A very brief introductory review of some of the psychosocial theories that support the need for group therapy with the older population is necessary before discussing group therapy approaches.

One of the earliest and most controversial theories of aging, known as the disengagement theory, emerged as a result of the Kansas City Study (1960), which examined the psychosocial lives of a large elderly population. This theory held that social disengagement is an inevitable, gradual process for a majority of the elderly and that it is in the best interest and mutually satisfying to both the individual and society. The emergence of this theory brought forth much controversy, especially from those who did not see this process as intrinsic or inevitable for all individuals. One of the theories emerging from those with strong differing positions was the activity theory of aging. It held that a high level of activity (mental, social and physical) is necessary and promotes successful aging. Those differing with both of these views promoted a third theory, sometimes referred to as the substitution theory of aging, which drew from both the disengagement and activity theories. It held that in fact many activities may require some degree of disengagement in later life, but the maintenance of the accustomed level of activity is critical. This requires that the individual substitute new roles and new activities for those given up because of physical limitations, social role changes or losses. Another theory that has also gained much acceptance is the continuity theory of aging. It maintains that once we reach adulthood we develop habits, commitments and preferences that have become ingrained in our personalities. As we age there is a continuity of this personality that becomes even more prominent in later adulthood. It allows the individual to adapt to the aging process. A consideration of all processes—physical, psychological, social and situational—must be acknowledged in order to provide us with insight into the individual's behavior. An excellent review of these theories was elaborated upon by Reigel in Birren and Shaie's *Handbook of the Psychology of Aging* (1977).

Havighurst (1975) updated his developmental task theory to later maturity by developing a list of developmental tasks that are appropriate to this population. These tasks include:

1. Deciding where and how to live out one's remaining years.
2. Continuing supportive, close relationships with spouse or significant other.
3. Finding a satisfactory, safe living place.
4. Adjusting living standards.
5. Maintaining a maximum level of health.
6. Maintaining contact with children, grandchildren and other relatives.
7. Maintaining interest in people and civic affairs.
8. Pursuing new interests but maintaining former ones.
9. Finding meaning in life after retirement.
10. Working out a philosophy of life and living.
11. Adjusting to the death of a spouse or of friends and other loved ones.

These theories and approaches to understanding the psychosocial lives of older people highlight some of the factors issues that should be considered in order to promote mental health and treat dysfunction. They also can represent goals for practitioners who are running groups.

## THE INSTITUTIONALIZED ELDERLY

Recent surveys report that over one million persons over age 65 are residing in long-term care facilities. This represents only 5 percent of the country's older population, but a number that has grown faster than any other age group. In the past, older adult residents have been one of the most underserved groups of adults. This group can, however, benefit significantly from a variety of mental health interventions. Some nursing homes have begun to develop sophisticated mental health programs for depressed, socially isolated and mentally impaired residents and they have been very beneficial.

Life in the best of institutions has the ability to influence a person's state of mind. A syndrome characterized by apathy, lack of initiative, lack of expressive feelings, resentment, loss of interest in the future and the deterioration of personal habits has been referred to as "institutional neurosis" (Zusman 1967). Institutional life can often foster dependence on others, an isolated existence, withdrawal from the mainstream of life, lowered self-esteem and an extreme sense of loss. Considering that over half of all nursing home residents have some form of senile dementia, this large population represents a group who may benefit from group work, especially those who are mildly to moderately impaired. A description of techniques used with institutionalized elderly will be followed by some general considerations for approaching group work with older adults.

Often the first question that arises is: What makes group work with the elderly different from group work with younger populations? The differences between group work with the elderly and with other populations are distinct. Group work with the elderly usually involves a more direct approach (Corey and Corey 1977), and leaders must take a more active role in providing information, answering questions and sharing themselves with the group. Leaders should be very supportive, encouraging and empathetic because of the special and complex problems and conditions found in this population. There is often more physical contact, such as hugging and touching, in group work with the elderly, and groups usually contain more women than men. The preoccupation with loss is a common emotional theme in older age groups, so the goals of group work often are to alleviate this general anxiety by assisting members in solving immediate problems (Burnside 1984). Often reminiscence is a predominant part of the group process. Generally, group psychotherapy with the elderly emphasizes staying mentally healthy and avoiding dysfunction rather than achieving personality change or gaining insight into behavior related to childhood experiences. Other issues such as sensory losses and physical limitations need to be addressed. Remember that it is important to speak slowly and clearly, to have the group sit close together, to keep groups small and address access barriers. The energy levels of the group participants will influence the length of the sessions. Defensive behavior occurs in groups of all ages, but the elderly are more prone to use their age and health conditions as excuses for not attending. Some group therapists telephone members or visit them when this happens, but the dependency that often results from this behavior is an issue that the therapist must address. Communication between group leaders and members, their families and staff must be handled carefully, especially when members may be forgetful or somewhat disoriented.

Group work with the elderly covers a wide territory. Weiner, Brok and Snadowsky (1987) differentiate between group work with the community elderly and group work in institutions, using practical approaches in both settings. Burnside (1984) identifies four levels of group work and the type of leader required for each. The four group methods commonly used with the elderly are reality orientation, remotivation, reminiscing and group psychotherapy. These broad categories can be expanded to include health teaching; bibliotherapy; scribotherapy; topic-specific groups such as those focusing on music, poetry, art and current events; and member-specific groups such as those for caregivers, widows and families of the recently institutionalized.

The term "psychotherapy group" includes group work with both elderly psychotic and demented elderly *and* the well or frail elderly. To fit the description of "therapeutic," all of the groups mentioned above can be considered beneficial in this sense. It assists all who are experiencing problems in adjusting to losses or changes in their lives; it reduces the sense of isolation that may be experienced; it helps develop new or familiar roles; and it provides a support system that contributes to better self-esteem (Finkel 1982).

The discussion below gives brief descriptions of the main categories of group methods used primarily with older persons living in long-term care facilities, but they can be adapted for use with the community elderly as well.

**Reality Orientation**

Reality orientation was developed for use with the moderately confused client and consists of exercises designed to relearn what has been forgotten due to dementia, stroke or head trauma. The individual is often disoriented as to time, place or person in varying degrees. This approach consists of providing the client with accurate information, on a consistent basis, 24 hours a day, every day. Repetition is used, and correct answers are reinforced. Individuals in these groups relearn information including who they are, where they are, the date and time, the weather and other information that will assist in orienting them to their environment. This is accomplished well in small (3- to 5-member) groups, for not more than 30 minutes at a time. The leader may use a reality orientation board, a clock, calendar, color boards and various word-letter games. Reality orientation is accomplished both in long-term care institutions and in the community where day treatment programs exist.

**Sensory Training Groups**

Sensory training groups have been found effective for use with highly regressed residents who are experiencing sensory, verbal, movement and intellectual deficits, who are having difficulties recognizing and identifying their surroundings. Most of these people also have few if any social contacts, and lead very limited lives. These groups are usually small (6 to 8 persons) and are conducted daily in the same place in order to eliminate further confusion. Members are stimulated by the socialization as well as the stimulation of their senses. Common, everyday objects are used to remind participants of smells, tastes, sounds and tactile experiences that were once very familiar to them. They can exchange stories and discuss what they are experiencing, and are thereby stimulated by this new level of activity.

## Remotivation Groups

Remotivation groups are used with withdrawn or apathetic clients for the purpose of remotivating them to take an interest in their environment and to reawaken the pre-existing elements of their personalities. They assist clients in thinking about topics related to the real world and help them relate to and communicate with other people (Barnes et al. 1973). Topics of discussion should be noncontroversial—holidays, current events, food and other aspects of daily life work well. These groups take place in institutional settings and in the community, and can be used effectively with patients who are mildly demented, depressed, withdrawn or experiencing losses that have isolated them from others. These experiences often function as the first step for motivating residents to participate in other therapeutic programs.

## Reminiscence Groups

Reminiscence groups are run for the purpose of exploring memories and coming to terms with one's life. Such groups often develop naturally with older clients because reminiscence is a universal mental process that increases considerably when one is nearing the end of life. They assist older persons in coming to terms with life as it has been lived, and this helps prepare them for the acceptance of death. Butler (1961) views reminiscence as part of the "life review process," manifested in activities such as nostalgia, story-telling, mirror-gazing and reconsidering or restructuring past experiences, often with great detail. These memories usually serve a therapeutic purpose, often with positive results such as righting wrongs, re-evaluating old relationships, changing attitudes toward family and friends, fostering a sense of pride in one's accomplishments, and ultimately leading to a sense of personal acceptance and serenity. Sad feelings may also emerge, but sharing these memories with others in a group can assist with acceptance and result in gaining support from others. These groups can be run in community settings such as senior centers, adult day-care facilities, churches and synagogues, as well as in institutions.

## Topic-Specific Groups

Topic-specific groups often use the modality of activities and recreation therapy to optimize residents' functioning and improve their quality of life. A wide variety of activities can be accomplished individually as well as in small or large groups. Choosing the activity is also therapeutic and adds to the beneficial outcome of participation. They take as many forms as there are topics to be discussed or activities to be held. *Art therapy* groups can be used with both cognitively and physically impaired elderly, and the well elderly residing in the community. Such groups can be used to relieve boredom and isolation and to develop a sense of creativity. Activities can range from interpreting drawings to producing items for a show or crafts fair. *Poetry groups* can be used for similar purposes, with an emphasis on verbal creativity, discussion, interpretation, or just listening to the reading of poetry. Both bibliotherapy and scribotherapy offer individuals the opportunity for self-expression and self-discovery. *Bibliotherapy* (reading aloud) can encourage problem-solving if materials are appropriate, and *scribotherapy* (writing therapy) can foster self-revelation, self-esteem, increased social interaction and constructive reminiscence.

## Pet Therapy Groups

Pet therapy groups have become popular in recent years and have been known to improve both the mental and physical health of older people. The presence of pets often triggers memories, promotes social interaction, and enhances self-esteem and a sense of control. Pets can also be used in remotivation groups to stimulate participation in discussion and increase responsiveness.

## THE COMMUNITY ELDERLY

Older people living in the community account for approximately 95 percent of the population over age 65. Many function well with few limitations, but a significant number are less fortunate, experiencing many chronic illnesses and some of the resultant psychosocial losses. It is estimated that anywhere from 10 to 15 percent of this population would benefit from some of the same mental health programs as those living in long-term care facilities. The "older old," those over age 75, are the fastest growing group of older people, and their increasing frailty has influenced mental health programming at senior centers, nutrition sites, adult day care centers and respite programs. The younger or minimally impaired older adult would also benefit from reminiscence groups as well as the topic-specific activity groups described above.

### Health-Related Groups

Health-related groups are both educational and supportive. Older people are often in need of more information about various conditions and health maintenance than is offered by their physicians. The goals of these groups vary. All provide information, but some evolve into support groups of individuals with similar afflictions. Coping with the limitations that illness often imposes can also be a goal of these groups. Crisis resolution may result, as can overcoming feelings of isolation or depression. Health groups can be held in community settings such as senior centers, nutrition sites and hospitals, or in residential or institutional settings such as senior housing, retirement communities and nursing homes.

Groups can focus on specific developmental tasks or crises that arise in the lives of older people. *Caregiver groups* offer support to those who care for impaired elderly relatives or friends. They can also be educational, as members share their own approaches to managing persons in need of care. Similarly, *widowhood groups* offer support to the bereaved and resocialization for those who have become socially isolated. These groups usually take place in community settings, but can also take place in residential care facilities. Within practice settings, clients over a specific age can become members of a group, such as an "octogenarian club," that meets periodically to focus on topics related to that age group. These groups have goals of socialization, reduced loneliness, intellectual stimulation and increased self-esteem, and have been known to contribute to the increased mental health of their members (Butler and Lewis 1982).

## Psychotherapy Groups

Psychotherapy groups, sometimes distinguished from groups that are medically therapeutic, are differentiated by clinicians by the intensity of their psychodynamic approaches. They emphasize insight, interpersonal relationships and personality development (Weiner et al. 1984). These groups are usually led by a therapist trained in group work within the disciplines of psychology, psychiatry, nursing, the ministry or social work. Traditional group psychotherapy for this population has its benefits and its limitations. This age group may have some difficulty expressing personal problems in a group setting. Defensive behavior, by this time, can become well established, which may discourage the extent to which this approach is beneficial. Other limitations include some practical aspects such as transportation, environmental access barriers, energy level and group discontinuity due to excessive absenteeism.

The benefits of group psychotherapy should not be overlooked. Many older people do not have access to groups and therefore cannot reap the benefits of group participation, which assist them in working through problems, gaining personal insight into their behavior and recognizing that their problems may not be unique to them but shared by many of their age. It often establishes new relationships with others, including both group members and the group leader. Many long-term care facilities have instituted supportive group therapy for their residents to help them deal with some of the effects of institutionalization, such as feelings of loneliness, isolation and inferiority, and adjusting to institutional life. Group therapy tends to be less expensive than individual therapy at a time when income may be limited. Staff-time limitations may also necessitate group programming. The multitude of age-related crises during this period of life often necessitates intervention and supportive assistance, and access to friends and relatives may be limited. Group members may be chosen on the basis of diagnosis or a mixture of diagnoses. However, it is advisable not to mix cognitively impaired clients and those with normal intellectual functioning, since those who are mentally alert may be threatened with fears of becoming "senile." Group psychotherapy may be beneficial to the elderly, but extreme care must be taken to assess the benefits for each potential group member.

## SUMMARY

A wide range of group therapy options exists for the elderly, both in institutions and in the community. A great deal of personal commitment is required by group leaders, but the rewards are great, even though the changes may be less dramatic than with younger populations. A majority of elderly individuals continue to be very responsive to these approaches, and the economic and staff-time benefits cannot be overlooked. This discussion has not focused on a description of the state of the art of group therapy for the elderly, but rather has attempted to provide the reader with general information on techniques and approaches that should prove helpful in the establishment of groups to assist older people with the numerous adaptations they face.

## REFERENCES

Barnes, E.K., A. Sack and H. Shore. Guidelines to treatment approaches. *Gerontologist* 13:513-527, 1973.

Burnside, I. *Working with the Elderly: Group Processes and Techniques.* Monterey, CA: Wadsworth Publishers, 1984.

Butler, R.M. Re-awakening interest. *Nursing Homes* 10:8-19, 1961.

Butler, R.M. and M.I. Lewis. *Aging and Mental Health,* 3rd Ed. St. Louis: C.V. Mosby, 1982.

Corey, G. and M. Corey. *Groups: Process and Practice.* Monterey, CA: Brooks/Cole, 1977.

Erikson, E. *Childhood and Society,* 2nd Ed. New York: W.W. Norton, 1963.

Finkel, S. Experiences of a private practice psychiatrist working with the elderly in the community. *Int. J. Mental Health* 8:3-4, 1982.

Goldfarb, A. Group Therapy with the Old and Aged. In H. Kaplan and B. Sadok, eds., *Comprehensive Group Therapy.* Baltimore: Williams & Wilkins, 1971.

Havighurst, R. A Social-Psychological Perspective on Aging. In W. Sze, ed., *Human Life Cycle.* New York: Aronson Press, 1975.

Reigel, K. History of Psychological Gerontology. In J. Birren and K.W. Shaie, eds., *Handbook of the Psychology of Aging.* New York: Van Nostrand Reinhold, 1977.

Weiner, M., A. Brock and A. Snadowsky. *Working with the Aged: Practical Approaches in the Institution and in the Community,* 2nd Ed. East Norwalk, CT: Appleton & Lange, 1987.

Zusman, J. Some explanations of the changed appearance of institutionalized patients. *Int. J. Psychiatry* 4:216-237, 1967.

# 14

# Dilemmas in the Care of Chronically and Terminally Ill Patients

*Seymour Herschberg, MD, FACP*

Developments in medical technology interacting with changes in the expectations of individual patients, their families or society on the one hand and realistic goals on the other have brought to the surface ethical issues for the physician with respect to terminally or chronically ill patients. The complexity of these challenges is further increased by the burgeoning costs of health care, the expanding base of elderly patients who consume a disproportionate amount of health services and the fiscal crises in health care today.

The cost issues need to be addressed by society as a whole. Denial of needed resources by a physician for purely economic reasons is not likely to be defensible in the event of an adverse outcome (Blumstein 1981). The allocation of fiscal resources among health care and competing arenas such as environmental protection and national defense is beyond the scope of this chapter and, therefore, the financial dilemmas will not be addressed in this discussion.

The fundamental legal issues with regard to the relationship between the physician and the elderly patient—or any patient for that matter—are discussed by Kapp (1985). He notes that there is a rapidly developing literature concerning the ethical and legal rights of older individuals within the health care system, addressing the individual's right to consent to or refuse therapy. His essay deals with the ethical and legal responsibilities of the physician toward the individual who desires the delivery of health care services; that is, the ethical and legal rights of the individual to access the desired health care services and the corresponding obligations of the physician to actuate and fulfill the individual's access rights. Although the focus of this book is on issues related primarily to the elderly, and Kapp writes in terms of the elderly, this chapter uses terminology applicable to all age groups as there is no inherent difference in the rights of an individual consequent to age alone.

A detailed narration of Kapp's paper would not be productive here, but a brief listing of his points seems appropriate. First, society has an ethical obligation to ensure equitable access to health care for all, but this ethical precept has never been codified into a legally enforceable right, though these benefits have invariably emerged to some degree as a condition or by-product of a governmental health care funding scheme. Second, most physicians in the field of geriatrics sincerely desire to provide services to the elderly, serving the patient by free choice. And third, once this voluntary physician-patient relationship is formed there are certain well-recognized, legally enforceable duties—fiduciary and contractual—that have evolved.

Kapp elaborates that the fiduciary or trust quality of the relationship obligates the physician to always act in the "best interests" of the patient, and the contractual aspect involves an expressed or implied promise to behave in a similar fashion. The traditional professional liability principles are fully applicable. He then discusses the standards of care with reference to the specialized knowledge of the data base available for the elderly. This latter point is germane to this discussion. Another point of relevance is the legal responsibility to positively interact with all other relevant health or human service professionals who are seeking to serve that individual. He states, "Interprofessional cooperation on behalf of the older patient/client is not only clinically and ethically desirable, but, at least arguably, legally enforceable as well."

Wanzer and co-workers have published on the physician responsibility toward hopelessly ill patients. The original publication appeared in 1984 and a followup in 1989. The latter paper notes that some of the practices that were controversial at the time of the earlier publication have now become accepted and routine. Several of the issues discussed are relevant to this chapter and will be further elaborated.

Do-not-resuscitate (DNR) orders, nonexistent in the early 1980s, are now commonplace. This is particularly germane in light of the studies indicating little benefit from routine resuscitation efforts in elderly debilitated individuals (Applebaum et al. 1990; Miles 1990). In tandem with this development has been the concurrence of many physicians and ethicists that there is little difference between nasogastric or intravenous hydration and other life-sustaining measures. Consequently, it is regarded as permissible to withdraw nutrition and hydration from certain dying, hopelessly ill or permanently unconscious patients. The public and the courts have generally accepted this principle.

Health professionals and the public have developed an increased sensitivity to the desires of terminally ill individuals, resulting in more open discussion of issues. Increased awareness has resulted in new laws legitimizing advance directives and designated proxies. The right of the patient to refuse medical treatment has been upheld in numerous court decisions (New York Society for the Right to Die 1988a), though as a general rule the early decisions involved terminally ill patients expected to die whether or not treatment was continued, and the treatment at issue was often regarded as intrusive or burdensome (e.g., dialysis or mechanical ventilation). More recent decisions support the patient's right to die whether or not terminally ill or suffering, such as an individual in the persistent vegetative state (New York Society for the Right to Die 1988b). These concepts regarding the rights of patients have spread into long-term care. In 1987, the California Department of Health promulgated guidelines for the removal of life support, including tube feeding, in that state's long-term care facilities. Despite these precedents there remains a gap between theory and practice; many physicians are reluctant to withhold aggressive therapy, even in the hopelessly ill. This is evident in a study by Wolff and associates (1985).

Wolff studied treatment decisions in a skilled nursing facility, noting discordance of nurses' treatment preferences and physician treatment decisions. The study involved collection of data from charts and from questionnaires completed by nurses and family members. Though very few decisions were made to treat life-threatening illness in the nursing home setting, physician decisions to hospitalize patients appeared to conflict frequently with attitudes expressed by the five head nurses of the facility. This area of disagreement was regarded as being of importance because, in the nursing home setting, the nurses are the professionals charged with identifying a patient's deterioration and thereby initiating the transfer process.

The Wolff study was conducted in a 200-bed, nonprofit facility in which 150 residents required total care and 125 had some form of intellectual or psychiatric impairment. One hundred residents—chosen by alternate room site—were studied along with half (N=20) of those residents who had died during the preceding year. The average age was 84, with a median of 85 for those alive and 87 for those deceased. Twelve and a half percent were men and 87.5 percent were women. Eighteen percent had chronic neurologic disorders and 80 percent of these were progressive. Sixteen percent were incontinent of only urine, 1 percent of only stool and 47 percent of both. Six percent had noncutaneous malignancy and it was suspected in an additional 4 percent.

Charts were reviewed to ascertain each instance of acute illness during the preceding year for which referral to a hospital was either made or considered, the latter information taken from physicians' or nurses' notes. Types of chronic impairment and the involved organ systems were also noted along with age, sex, mental status, functional status and the patient's legal guardian or conservator. Documentation of consultation with residents and their family members relative to the decision to hospitalize was sought as well as documentation of discussions and conclusions pertaining to treatment status (i.e., type of institution, initiation of new treatment, designation of resuscitation status and compliance with the wishes of the residents or their families).

Family members were asked to recall the previously ascertained instances of acute illness and to indicate by whom they were notified, when they were notified of the decision to hospitalize, and whether they agreed with the decision in terms of locus and intensity of therapy. Due to difficulties in recall of details this inquiry was restricted to the two most recent episodes.

The head nurses—who had been personally familiar with the individual subjects—were asked to complete a series of hierarchically arranged questionnaires. In the first the patient was described as being in progressively poorer chronic medical condition and the nurse asked to indicate whether or not hospitalization would be appropriate for the given situation (e.g., fever, unresponsiveness, seizure, gastrointestinal bleed, etc., to cardiac arrest). In the second a hierarchy of procedures was listed and the respondent asked to indicate whether or not a given procedure was appropriate for that patient as he or she currently functioned. The same decisions were requested for assumed immobility and for assumed permanent unresponsiveness. A numerical score was devised based upon the first "yes" response, with lower scores representing therapeutic intervention at less severe states.

Sixty-four of the 100 living subjects experienced 174 episodes requiring referral to hospital for diagnosis or treatment, and there were 37 such nonterminal episodes in 11 of the 20 who subsequently died. In 30 percent of these episodes there was no recorded chart documentation of relevant discussions with family members. In each of these episodes the families indicated that they had been notified after the transfer had been made. Spouses were rarely consulted while offspring were frequently consulted, likely due to the fact that the overwhelming majority of the facility's residents were widows. The family's reaction to the treatment decision was recorded only 22 percent of the time, being undocumented in 78 percent. Three instances of family disagreement were noted in the chart, 6.5 percent of those documented, and four additional instances of disagreement were reported by family members. In only seven instances was a decision made to keep the patient in the nursing home and on only four occasions was there a decision not to institute new therapy.

Though there may be some weaknesses in this study due to lack of documentation or poor recall, nurses as a group displayed a more conservative treatment orientation than was apparent in the actual treatment activities. Considering current circumstances the nurses deemed that 37 percent of the patients should not be hospitalized. This increased to 46 percent with the hypothetical addition of immobility and to 87 percent if unresponsive. Even though gastrointestinal bleeding provided the most compelling impetus for hospitalization, transfusion was considered too aggressive for 55 percent of the patients at their current level of function, increasing to 72 percent if immobile and 95 percent if unresponsive. The scores for treatment aggressiveness likewise declined with hypothetically decreasing functional status such that, based on current status or immobilization, the nurses would provide intravenous fluids and medication, but not transfusion, and that if unresponsive the patient should not even receive intravenous infusions.

On the other hand, for only 31 of the living patients could the nurses conceive of an instance in which termination of treatment would be appropriate, though dialysis was considered inappropriate for 97 percent of cases at current functional status, while bronchoscopy, endoscopy and intubation were considered appropriate in 82 percent.

It is of some interest to further review the 37 living patients whom the nurses would not have hospitalized under the most compelling circumstances. Twenty-eight (76 percent) of these had been hospitalized. Of these instances, 11 (30 percent) were for falls and acute musculoskeletal trauma, including two for orthopedic surgery and five for precautionary x-rays only. Nine of 36 whom the nurses would not have hospitalized for gastrointestinal bleeding were hospitalized for such an event. Of the 14 patients for whom the nurses favored no new therapy all had chronic neurologic failure, 9 were incontinent, 10 were sometimes agitated, 5 were sometimes assaultive, 8 were verbally abusive and 12 were depressed.

In discussing these results, Wolff's group pointed out that some findings were reassuring; that is, there was relative concordance of treatment decisions with family wishes and the family reports of appropriate notification by the staff. They expressed concern, however, about the contrast between actual (physician) practice and the nurses' conception as to the appropriate intensity of care. This was believed, by the authors, to reflect a prevalent ethical disquiet on the part of the health professionals who provide most of the daily supervision—the nurses. It was not known whether the involved physicians felt similar conflicts, but the authors believed that the fact that one-third of the transfer decisions had been made before consultation with the family implied that physicians opt in favor of more aggressive treatment and that the families subsequently concur in such a presumption. Other interpretations are also possible: that the physicians knew family wishes from contacts not documented in the chart and that the nurses were less sensitive to or knowledgeable about the families' wishes. However, it is not appropriate to second guess the authors.

Wolff's group noted that since the head nurses were queried retrospectively, it is quite possible that they would have acted as had the nurse on duty; that is, they would have notified the physician and accepted the decision without documenting disagreement. They further stated that their data do not demonstrate that the considered preferences of the senior nurses were at variance with many of the actions taken. The rationale for this latter statement is not clear unless it pertains to the fact that the nurses would have hospitalized more than 63 percent of the patients, or it may refer to the fact that there was a greater concurrence with the treatments as opposed to the issue of hospitalization. In this context it should be noted that the opposition of the nurses to hospitalization per se was generally limited to those situations, such as falls and trauma, where hospitalizations were usually precautionary. On the other hand, the nurses tended to concur with hospitalization when there was a perceived need for bedside monitoring, as with gastrointestinal bleeding. The lower preference for intervention in the presence of immobility or unresponsiveness was thought to demonstrate the nurses' consideration of quality of life in their decision-making.

The results were discussed with the nursing staff, who concurred that their feelings were accurately reflected and that they had not, in fact, expressed disagreement with the decisions despite the implications of the questionnaire. The nurses further expressed the belief that many unnecessary hospitalizations occur, after diagnostic workup is complete, because of a lack of knowledge on the part of emergency room personnel as to the interventions possible and the quality of personnel available in the skilled nursing facility.

The authors noted, anecdotally, that adult children of intellectually impaired patients appear hesitant to request that technological intervention be limited, and that the physicians had felt uncomfortable at times with the intensity of treatment toward which they felt impelled.

How does all this relate to the theme of this chapter? It is relevant in that the Wolff study demonstrates the real and potential psychosocial conflicts for patients and their families, physicians, nurses and other caregivers when dealing with acute situations in the long-term care setting (compare Seckler et al. 1991; Finucane and Denman 1989; Danis et al. 1991).

Are there any solutions? Before suggesting solutions, some additional background material needs to be presented. As one reads the popular medical press and the professional literature, several things are evident. These include, but may not be limited to, the following: (1) medical care is labor intensive (as well as technologically costly); (2) more intensive care is more costly and hospital care is more costly than skilled nursing care, which in turn is more costly than custodial care; (3) nursing facilities have a relative lack of acute supportive services (e.g. x-ray and laboratory) and have lower staffing ratios, which make it difficult to deal with acute situations requiring these resources; (4) more and more, the members of the public as individuals want to have the benefits of all the latest resources, but at the same time more elderly individuals with chronic illnesses and diminished quality of life are willing to forgo measures that are of little use and that may cause the individual to lose a sense of dignity.

Several years ago, I was Chief of Extended Care Services at a medical school-affiliated Veterans Administration Medical Center. We had nearly 400 extended care beds, approximately half of which were skilled nursing beds. Though not technically part of the hospital, the units were physically connected to it, and the laboratory and x-ray facilities of the hospital were readily available. There were four full-time primary care physicians in addition to myself, and we had the benefit of available coverage by the resident staff during nights, weekends and holidays.

How does this translate into a solution? What might be done to resolve the conflicts discussed? First is a broad-based public education program relating to patient rights, the limitations of technology, and the concept of inappropriate interventions. Second is a campaign to have individuals and their physicians discuss prospectively the individual's desired level of care in potential future circumstances. These wishes should then be set out in a living will or a durable power of attorney.

The third step is for extended care facilities to upgrade their abilities to care for a reasonable amount of acute situations in a cost-effective manner that would provide the necessary care at lower cost than in hospitals. Some avenues to explore are contracts with nearby laboratories (hospital or independent) to provide for the necessary evaluations in a timely manner. A short taxi ride is more likely to be less costly than the cost of an additional day in the hospital. As for radiologic services, it might prove cost-effective to purchase a portable x-ray machine and have a part-time technician or an available on-call arrangement with the technicians and radiologists of a nearby hospital or radiology group practice.

If the facility is located within walking distance of an institution with an appropriate resident training program, night and weekend coverage might be arranged either in conjunction with the training program or as a service to a facility likely to refer patients. Alternatively, licensed residents might be on-call from home, utilizing a fixed stipend per night or a fee-per-patient visit, or a combination of these. It might also be feasible to require physicians who have a patient in the facility or who regularly care for patients in the facility to share an on-call rotation. All of these, save possibly the obligation of the private attending physicians, would generate costs that would have to be acknowledged and reimbursed by our health care system. Nevertheless, such arrangements would almost certainly be cost-effective, would provide quality care and would avoid many of the conflicts described in this chapter.

## REFERENCES

Applebaum, G.E., J.E. King and T.E. Finucane. The outcome of CPR initiated in nursing homes. *J. Am. Geriatrics Soc.* 38:197-200, 1990.

Blumstein, J. Rationing medical resources: a constitutional, legal and policy analysis. *Texas Law Rev.* 59:1345, 1981.

California Dept. of Health Services. Guidelines Regarding Withdrawal or Withholding of Life-sustaining Procedure(s) in Long-term Care Facilities. Sacramento, August 7, 1987.

Danis, M., L.I. Southerland, J.M. Garrett, et al. A prospective study of advance directives for life-sustaining care. *N. Engl. J. Med.* 324:882-888, 1991.

Finucane, T.E. and S.J. Denman. Deciding about resuscitation in a nursing home: theory and practice. *J. Am. Geriatrics Soc.* 37:684-688, 1989.

Kapp, M.B. Legal and ethical standards in geriatric medicine. *J. Am. Geriatrics Soc.* 33:179, 1985.

Miles, S.H. Resuscitating the nursing home resident: futility and pseudofutility. *J. Am. Geriatrics Soc.* 38:1037-1038, 1990.

New York Society for the Right to Die. Adult Right to Die Case Citations. New York, 1988a.

New York Society for the Right to Die. Right to Die Court Decisions: Artificial Feeding. New York, 1988b.

Seckler, A.B., D.E. Meier, M. Mulvihill and B.E. Cammer Paris. Substituted judgement: how accurate are proxy predictions? *Ann. Intern. Med.* 115:92-98, 1991.

Wanzer, S.H., S.J. Adelstein, R.E. Cranford, et al. The physician's responsibility toward hopelessly ill patients. *N. Engl. J. Med.* 310:955, 1984.

Wanzer, S.H., D.D. Federman, S.J. Abelstein, et al. The physician's responsibility toward hopelessly ill patients. *N. Engl. J. Med.* 320:844, 1989.

Wolff, M.L., S. Smolen and L. Ferrara. Treatment decisions in a skilled-nursing facility: discordance with nurses' preferences. *J. Am. Geriatrics Soc.* 33:440, 1985.

# 15

# The Impact of Recent Mental Health Legislation on Long-Term Care

*D. Peter Birkett, MD*

There are many different OBRAs. The acronym stands for Omnibus Budget Reconciliation Act, and several of these have been passed. These acts often cover various pieces of legislation. The one that is usually meant in the nursing home industry is that of 1987, often called "OBRA '87."

Did OBRA '87 change anything? Has it accomplished its stated purpose, according to its sponsor, Congressman Henry Waxman, to "stop dumping the mentally ill in nursing homes"?

The Omnibus Budget Reconciliation Act was enacted in the face of evidence that nursing homes were really miniature mental hospitals. The process of transfer of the mentally ill to nursing homes had been stimulated by the passage of the Mental Health Act of 1972. The Mental Health Act provided federal funding for programs that were supposed to help the mentally ill who had been in state hospitals. Federally funded community mental health centers were set up and the states also tried to stop admitting anyone to their state-funded hospitals.

As the population of state mental hospitals in the United States went down, the population of nursing homes went up. The nursing home population increased 20-fold in the 20 years from 1955 to 1975, and the state hospital population fell by three quarters during the same time.

It seemed that patients were being transferred for the purpose of shifting the financial burden from the state-financed mental hospitals to federal funding via Medicaid in the nursing homes. In 1975 approximately half of the aged chronically ill patients discharged from state hospitals were referred to nursing homes. Between 1950 and 1970 the mean age for inpatients in the state facilities was over 50, and by 1975 it was approximately 40. The proportion of patients with senile/organic disorders in the state hospitals was 18 percent in 1950 and 1 percent in 1975 (Redlich and Keilert 1978).

It was not long before the policy of putting the mentally ill in nursing homes began to be questioned. In fact, after 1975 many nursing homes stopped admitting patients from state hospitals because they found that the state hospitals refused to take them back when they became acutely psychotic.

Schmidt and co-workers (1977) were among the first to be alarmed by the supposed shift of the mentally ill to the nursing homes. The title of their paper was "The mentally ill in nursing homes, new back wards in the community," which suggests their theme. They used Medicaid data from Utah nursing homes and found from these records that a third of the residents had a psychiatric diagnosis and that more than half of these were psychotic. Rovner and associates (1986) concluded that the nursing home was "in reality a long-term psychiatric facility without its having the usual trained personnel and treatment approaches found in psychiatric hospitals."

Estimates of the number of mentally ill in nursing homes continued to vary considerably, from as "low" as 30 percent to as high as 85 percent (Beardsley 1989). This question of the tendency to increased numbers in recent years was investigated by Linn (1989), who found it was probably a true increase.

Such studies certainly showed that there was much mental disorder in the nursing homes. However, there was also evidence against the "dumping" hypothesis. The kinds of mental disorders that filled the nursing homes were not the same kinds as had filled the mental hospitals. The nursing home patients were largely demented or depressed, whereas the mental hospital patients had been schizophrenic.

Could some of the allegedly demented nursing home residents be former schizophrenics? Certainly there are a large group of nursing home patients who are labeled as demented and who simply do not communicate enough for any diagnosis to be established. Some surveys may be including these patients as demented and missing ex-schizophrenics.

Surveys of the present populations of state hospitals do not suggest that they got rid of their elderly or physically frail. Their present inpatient population is largely composed of the very old. It looks more as if they reduced their censuses (and the burden on state budgets) by discharging or turning away young and physically fit psychotics.

Most of the elderly remaining in the state hospitals had been admitted at young ages with a diagnosis of paranoid schizophrenia. Those who enter the state hospitals in old age with a paranoid diagnosis often respond to treatment and are discharged (Goodman and Siegel 1986).

In the face of this kind of evidence, the 1987 Omnibus Budget Reconciliation Act made further rules against putting the mentally ill in nursing homes. The law was framed in such a way as to suggest that it might be intended to improve treatment of the mentally ill by specifying that they could only be admitted to an institution that provided active care. What most observers took this to mean was that the mentally ill (or mentally retarded) could not be admitted to nursing homes. The law seemed to say, however, that the demented could be admitted to nursing homes, and also that the mentally ill could be admitted if mental illness was not their primary diagnosis.

There was much ambiguity and delay. It was not until 1989 that anyone was able to find out from the federal government what was intended by the OBRA regulations. HCFA (the Health Care Financing Administration) insisted that this gave the states ample time to develop alternative care plans, and the states insisted they had been told nothing about it. Thus there was further delay and uncertainty while the various states interpreted the federal regulations and passed them on down the line.

There was another stay of execution before HCFA implemented its new Requirements for Long-Term Care Facilities and began inspections to ensure that facilities were in compliance, with the withholding of federal money via Medicaid if they were not. If the new regulations were to have been fully enforced, then HCFA would have got the mentally ill out of the nursing homes. This was to have been accomplished by means of PASARR (Pre-admission Screening and Annual Resident Review). PASARR is a document that is supposed to determine whether the patient needs active psychiatric treatment. Essentially the federal law now says that patients suffering from a mental illness other than dementia cannot now be admitted to nursing homes except under certain narrowly defined conditions.

There are many exemptions in PASARR that may allow the continued placement of the mentally ill in nursing homes, for example, the presence of a medical illness. This "medical override" can come into effect if the patient is terminally ill or comatose, or is convalescent from a recoverable condition following hospitalization, or has severe lung or heart disease or certain progressive neurological diseases. There is also an exemption for dementia due to Alzheimer's disease and related conditions, but if the diagnosis of dementia is made, it has to be substantiated by investigations and consultations.

It is extremely difficult to diagnose dementia in the mentally retarded. For this reason Alzheimer's disease is not given any specific mention in the sections of PASARR on mental retardation (*Federal Register* 1989). The prohibition against admission to a nursing home presumably applies to the mentally retarded even if "dementia" is also diagnosed. However the "ICF-MR" category has been retained so that Medicaid can fund care for the mentally retarded in certain institutions. There was no actual prohibition on nursing homes taking such patients. It was merely mandated that the patients were to get active treatment and that Medicaid was not going to pay for it. In other words, it was basically going to be up to the nursing homes to see that they did not "get stuck" with psychiatric patients.

The states became bound by OBRA to conduct screening as of the beginning of 1989, even though HCFA had not given them exact direction as to how to do so. The states had to work on enforcing regulations that HCFA could later on tell them were not the right ones. Even in 1992 this was still to some extent the case. The start-up date for the OBRA requirements was October 1, 1990, and the implementation rules were the work of the Health Care Financing Administration (HCFA) in the Department of Health and Human Services. The so-called Final Rule was issued on September 26, 1991; it said that the states had 90 days to submit plan amendments and that the final regulations were to be effective on April 1, 1992. A definition of "serious mental illness," to be "defined by the secretary in consultation of (sic) the National Institutes of Health," remains to be promulgated.

There have been several modifications of the original regulations. The term "active treatment" for mental illness has been replaced by "specialized services." "Rehabilitative services" for mental illness are to be provided by the nursing facility (NF), but "we believe that specialized services can only be ordinarily delivered in the NF setting with difficulty because the overall level of services in NFs is not as intense as needed to address these needs. If the state's PASARR program determines that an individual with mental illness or mental retardation may enter or continue to reside in the NF, even though he or she needs specialized services and the individual does so, then the state must provide or arrange for the provision of additional services to raise the level of intensity of services to the level needed by the resident."

According to the *Federal Register*, "We have changed the references in those sections from psychosocial to mental and psychosocial...the concept of mental status appears to include the mental dysfunction present in a sad or anxious mood as well as overt behavioral manifestations such as wandering, verbal abuse, and physical abuse. The concept of psychosocial well-being appears to relate to how people feel about themselves and their lives. This includes involvement in life around them, having satisfactory relationships with others as well as self-respect and a sense of satisfaction with life."

Did OBRA '87 have the impact that was intended? Has anything improved? The National Coalition for Nursing Homes Reform, Dr. Gail Wilensky, administrator of HCFA, and HHS Secretary Sullivan are reported to be pleased. Congressman Waxman is also pleased but has complained about too many deadlines missed and unwarranted delays.

In some areas there has been definite change. OBRA took a strong stand against antipsychotic drugs. It specified that "Residents who have not used antipsychotic drugs and (sic) are not given these drugs unless antipsychotic drug therapy is necessary to treat a specific condition" and that "residents who use antipsychotic drugs receive gradual dose reductions, drug holidays or behavioral programming unless clinically contraindicated in an effort to discontinue these drugs." (The specific requirement for drug holidays has been dropped.)

The nursing homes are finding it inconvenient to use psychotropic medications because there are so many forms to fill out. HCFA guidelines for the surveyors implementing OBRA prohibit the use of psychotropic drugs "for the purpose of discipline or convenience and not required to treat the resident's medical symptoms." One response to this has been that when the patient is to be given Haldol or Thorazine, a mental health professional is called in. Such mental health consultations are used as a formality to justify the use of the psychotropic drugs. The regulations have resulted in an increase in the involvement of mental health professionals in nursing homes, and it is going to be up to mental health professionals to see that this makes a genuine contribution to the patient's welfare.

There has been reduction in the use of physical restraints, though there is still ambiguity as to whether side rails constitute restraints. The HCFA Interpretive Guidelines for surveyors define a physical restraint as "any manual method or physical or mechanical device, material or equipment attached or adjacent to the resident's body that the resident cannot move easily which restricts freedom of movement or normal access to one's body." Restraints cannot be ordered whenever desired. The physician must justify their use and alternatives must be considered.

These restraints on restraints would perhaps have come about even without OBRA. There are several reasons for this. One has been a libertarian movement to unbind the elderly originating from Pennsylvania. There have also been several legal decisions suggesting that restraints can generate litigation rather than protect against it: the three Louisiana cases of *Booty v. Kenwood Nursing Home* (1985), *Field v. Senior Citizen Center* (1988), and *McGillivray Ray v. Rapides Iberia Management Enterprises* (1986), and also the Alabama case of *Ruby Davis v. Montrose Bay Care Center* (1989). Another factor has been an increase in the sophistication and availability of electronic devices to warn about wandering and climbing out of bed. The nursing home is still in a quandary with the patient who is wobbly on her feet, insists on getting up and then falls, but it is rather comforting to be able to put the blame on the government.

Documentation of dementia has improved. This may represent a trend that was already in progress with the proliferation of the CAT scan. In fact there is a widespread but erroneous impression that a CAT scan and a neurological consultation are mandatory. This would be useful for those involved in research, but may be an unnecessary imposition and expense in the very elderly.

On the whole the dreaded increase in paperwork has not been as bad as was feared. The new regulations have made things more uniform from state to state. We in New York have felt only a slight increase. The new Minimum Data Set (MDS), for example, has not been as awful a piece of paperwork as was feared. It no longer has to be completed within four days of admission, but rather within two weeks. However, some commentators have found that the form is time-consuming and contains many antiquated ideas (Morley 1991).

If one understands and agrees with the spirit and intent of the new regulations, the paperwork becomes easier. It is possible to see the reasoning behind it. The new MDS is just a way of giving a comprehensive picture of the patient. It used to be possible for a patient to be in a nursing home with a recorded diagnosis of congestive heart failure when the real problems were incontinence and inability to walk. Records of this sort needed a lot of work to bring them into line with OBRA.

What sort of defects have the surveyors been finding in the nursing homes inspected? According to the American Health Care Association, the leading areas of deficiency have been comprehensive care plans, food, use of restraints and maintenance of an accident-free environment. The HCFA reports that the most cited areas have been residents' rights, restraint use and physical environment (*Provider,* June 1991, p. 6).

The presence of registered nurses has increased, although this was already adequate in New York State. At least one RN must be on duty 8 hours a day, and at least one LPN 24 hours a day.

The states are circumventing the requirements about keeping out the mentally ill. In some cases this is done openly by state requirements that are in contravention of OBRA, and in others by interpretations that bend the rules. OBRA has failed to reduce the number of mentally ill in nursing homes, because of the Alzheimer's exemption and because of action by the states to prevent elderly admissions to state hospitals. There seems to be as much mental disturbance in the nursing homes as ever, but staffs are becoming more aware of it as a treatable entity.

Schizophrenic patients in nursing homes are not usually regarded by the staff as particularly difficult. One schizophrenic under my care in a nursing home was sent there from a general hospital. She is delusional and mutters to herself, but is fully ambulant, dresses and feeds herself, and is not incontinent. In fact, one of our concerns has become that she does not need an intense enough level of care to justify our reimbursement for her. A major problem is that the most severe behavior disturbances in nursing homes are associated with organic brain damage rather than functional psychosis. The dementia exemption has proved a wide open door. The nursing homes continue to contain the grossly psychotic, and the state shows no inclination to provide services for them. Even if the provision that the state must provide services were to be enforced, the services would be provided for the less severely disturbed patients. State hospitals are citing OBRA as justification for refusing to admit even the most disturbed of dementia patients.

This is anecdotal, of course, but there is also statistical evidence that OBRA '87 did not reduce mental illness in the nursing homes. On the most conservative of the estimates reviewed above, about a fifth of those in nursing homes were mentally ill. Removing these should have reduced the nursing home census considerably. In fact, the number of nursing homes has increased to 15,607, and the number of nursing home patients to 1,563,941, but the ratio of nursing home beds to population over 65 remains 53.3. Wisconsin has the highest ratio (93.5) and Hawaii the lowest (18.9) (*Marion Merrell Dow Managed Care Digest* 1991). These figures may conceal a subtle demographic shift, but they could mean that a lot of things have not changed.

REFERENCES

Beardsley, R.S., D.B. Larson, B.J. Burns, W.T. Thompson and D.B. Kamerow. Prescribing of psychotropics in elderly nursing home patients. *J. Am. Geriatric Soc.* 37:327-330, 1989.
Birkett, D.P. *Psychiatry in the Nursing Home.* New York: Haworth Press, 1991.

Gallo, J.J., P.R. Katz, S.A. Levenson and J.E. Scherger. Can the new rules really improve nursing home care? *Patient Care* 25:57-64, 1991.

Burns, B.J., D.B. Larson, I.D. Goldstrom, et al. Mental disorder among nursing home patients: preliminary findings from the National Nursing Home Survey Pretest. *Int. J. Geriatric Psych.* 3:27-35, 1988.

*Federal Register.* Medicare and Medicaid requirements for long-term care facilities. Final Rule (September 26, 1991).

Goodman, A.B. and S. Siegel. Elderly schizophrenic inpatients in the wake of deinstitutionalization. *Am. J. Psychiatry* 143:204-207, 1986.

Harsch, H.H. Nursing homes 1989. *Psychiatric News* 24(14):29, 1989.

HHS sued over new regs on nursing home screening. *Psychiatric News* 24(10), May 1988.

Hollingshead, A.B. and Redlich, F.C. *Social Class and Mental Illness.* New York: John Wiley and Sons, 1958.

Lathrop, L., S. Corcoran and M. Ryden. Description and analysis of preadmission screening. *Public Health Nurs.* 6:23-27, 1989.

Linn, M.W., L. Gurel, W.O. Williford, et al. Nursing home care as an alternative to psychiatric hospitalization. *Arch. Gen. Psychiatry* 42: 544-551, 1985.

*Marion Merrell Dow Managed Care Digest,* Long-Term Care Edition. Kansas City: Marion Merrell Dow, 1991.

Morley, J.E. OBRA '87: the good, the bad, and the ugly. *Geriatric Medicine Today.* 10:17, 1991.

National Center for Health Statistics. *The National Nursing Home Survey, 1977: Summary for the United States.* Vital and Health Statistics, Serial 13, No. 43. Washington DC: U.S. Government Printing Office, 1977.

Redlich, F. and S.R. Kellert. Trends in American mental health. *Am. J. Psychiatry* 135:22-28, 1978.

Rovner, B.W., S. Kafonek, L. Filipp, M.J. Lucas and M.F. Folstein. Prevalence of mental illness in a community nursing home. *Am. J. Psychiatry* 143:1446-1449, 1986.

Schmidt, L., A.M. Reinhardt, R.L. Kane, et al. The mentally ill in nursing homes: new back wards in the community. *Arch. Gen. Psychiatry* 34:687-691, 1977.

Teeter, R.B., F.K. Garetz and W.R. Miller. Psychiatric disturbances of aged patients in skilled nursing homes. *Am. J. Psychiatry* 133:1430-1434, 1976.

Talbott, J.A. Nursing homes are not the answer. *Hosp. Community Psychiatry* 39:115, 1988.

Weissert, W.B. and C.M. Cready. Determinants of hospital-to-nursing home placement delays. *Health Service Res.* 23:619-647, 1988.

# 16

# Ethical Considerations in Long-Term Care

*Theresa L. Martico-Greenfield, MPH, Ellen Olson, MD and Eileen Chichin, DSW, RN*

Increasingly, ethical issues are assuming prominence in the day-to-day lives of those who live and work in long-term care settings. Among the most common problems that require resolution are decisions involving the need for therapeutic or diagnostic intervention, cardiopulmonary resuscitation, choice of health care agent and maintenance of nutrition and hydration. Many facilities, like their acute care counterparts, have established ethics committees whose primary responsibilities are to review problems and make recommendations on how to resolve them (Brown, Miles and Aroskar 1987; Glaser, Zweibel and Cassel 1988; Miller and Cugliari 1990).

A somewhat different approach has been taken by The Jewish Home and Hospital for Aged in New York City in its Kathy and Alan C. Greenberg Center on Ethics in Geriatrics and Long-Term Care. Developed as a result of the Home's long-standing interest in ethics and formalized in 1990, the Center uses a three-pronged model that addresses education, direct service and research in ethics and long-term care.

The Jewish Home and Hospital for Aged, the teaching nursing home affiliate of Mount Sinai Medical Center, has numerous programs that serve more than 3000 well and frail elderly on any given day. Among these are three long-term care facilities and three types of senior housing. In addition there is a short-stay inpatient rehabilitation unit, adult day care (for frail elderly, for Alzheimer's patients and for the visually impaired elderly), long-term home health care, geriatric outreach and an Alzheimer's at-home respite program. Each of these groups and settings presents its own ethical dilemmas and to date the three-pronged approach of education, practice and research has encouraged the optimum resolution of issues.

## EDUCATION AND DIRECT PRACTICE:
## THE USE OF "ETHICS ROUNDS"

In an effort to create a mechanism that could educate staff, residents and families in the area of ethics, The Jewish Home and Hospital for Aged developed ethics rounds in 1985. Similar to clinical grand rounds in structure and format, ethics rounds function both as an educational tool and a method to provide direct service to those residents whose cases are involved. Its usual format includes a case presentation by the health care team and a formal presentation by an invited expert on the topic or issue illustrated by the case. Ethics rounds are open to all staff, including nurses, physicians, social workers, administrators, dietitians, rehabilitation therapists and nurses aides. Often elderly individuals whose cases are being discussed and their families are asked to participate if they wish. Key to the success of the rounds is interdisciplinary exchange, which serves to clarify issues and suggest options for intervention. Although decisions are not made in the course of ethics rounds, the staff caring for the resident whose case is presented may be influenced by the interchange. Thus, when a decision *is* made, the elderly individual (when able), his or her family, and the members of the primary health care team usually take into consideration the input offered at ethics rounds.

Ethics rounds have been found to be beneficial to all involved. Their clinical case format is an excellent mechanism for educating a wide range of staff members. The process of interdisciplinary exchange enhances awareness of value systems of different disciplines. As far as residents and family members are concerned, ethics rounds make a symbolic statement of the institution's respect for the autonomy and well-being of residents and their families.

Problematic to a small number of staff members is the inability to derive a definitive answer to the questions raised at ethics rounds. On the positive side, it can be argued that the process of rounds, rather than the outcome, is the most valuable characteristic of this technique. In the words of Libow and his colleagues (1992), "One of the most powerful contributions that ethics rounds may make to learning at our institution is to create a minute microcosm in which this purposeful ambiguity is allowed to prevail."


## DECISIONS NEAR THE END OF LIFE


The Jewish Home and Hospital's second effort in the area of bioethics education was undertaken collaboratively with the Education Development Center (EDC), an international nonprofit research and development organization that applies educational strategies to address a wide range of health, education and social problems, and the Hastings Center, which is known for its research, education, consultation and publications in the field of bioethics.

In 1989, The Jewish Home and Hospital was among nine acute and long-term care institutions invited to collaborate in the design and development of a three-part curriculum entitled "Decisions Near the End of Life." The curriculum was developed by EDC and Hastings with support from the W.K. Kellogg Foundation.

The "Decisions" program included a training seminar for staff who would serve as faculty for The Jewish Home and Hospital, a pre- and post-program questionnaire that assessed knowledge and attitudes about ethical issues and a three-tiered curriculum.

Since the fall of 1989, approximately 600 professional Jewish Home and Hospital staff members have participated. The first two tiers of the "Decisions" curriculum consisted of an overview, a session on legal implications and four in-depth modules that were taught in groups of 15 to 20 participants. The four modules focused on the issues of planning with patients, learning to weigh the burdens and benefits of treatment, working with the decisionally incapable and problem-solving in difficult cases.

The third tier of the "Decisions" curriculum is ongoing. It utilizes working groups to analyze facility-specific issues and develop policies and practice approaches to address these. In addition, it stimulates ideas for research and provides a basis for planning educational programs for those not reached by the efforts already undertaken.

At this time The Jewish Home and Hospital for Aged is directing efforts toward adapting the "Decisions" curriculum for paraprofessional staff. In long-term care settings, both institutional and community-based, it is clear that those with the greatest amount of contact with elderly clients are the paraprofessionals—nurses aides, orderlies, technicians, home health aides and personal care workers. However, little if anything has been done to address the needs of these workers with respect to recognizing and addressing bioethical issues.

To begin to address the needs of paraprofessional staff members at The Jewish Home and Hospital, a small number of nurses aides were invited to participate in focus groups. In meetings with members of the nursing administration and the coordinator of the Center on Ethics, these paraprofessional staff members discussed their ethical concerns and their feelings about the ethical dilemmas they faced. Following this, a questionnaire was developed to assess the knowledge and attitudes about ethics among the entire paraprofessional nursing staff. After participating in an educational program especially geared to their needs, the nurses aides will again be asked to fill out a questionnaire designed to determine if the educational program in ethics has changed their knowledge or attitudes about these issues.

## THE ETHICS CONSULT TEAM

The Patient Self-Determination Act contained in OBRA 1990 mandates that long-term care facilities establish a mechanism for the resolution of ethical dilemmas. Rather than use the ethics committee model from acute care, The Jewish Home and Hospital for Aged has developed an ethics consult team with members from administration, medicine, nursing, social work and other disciplines as required. Unlike most ethics committees, the team does not "take over" cases from the primary team and is not invested with decision-making authority. Instead the ethics consult team works with the primary team responsible for the care of the individual. Together they apply ethical principles, law and sound medical approaches as well as client and family input to resolve issues.

Perhaps the best way to illustrate how the ethics consult team functions is to present an actual case, the case of Ms. M.

Ms. M. was admitted to The Jewish Home and Hospital for Aged from the hospital in October 1991 at the age of 91 after suffering two strokes that left her paralyzed on her left side and unable to speak. While she was at the hospital a nasogastric feeding tube was inserted. She also had bronchitis. She was conscious and alert but not able to recognize people or respond to questions. Ms. M. had been an active participant in The Jewish Home and Hospital's Geriatric Outreach Program for several years prior to her hospitalization.

Three days after her admission, we learned that Ms. M. had a living will that had been prepared prior to the onset of her health problems.

Her living will clearly stated that if she were to be in an irreversible physical or mental condition with no reasonable expectation of recovery and if she were to be conscious but unable to make decisions and express her wishes, she did not want CPR, mechanical respiration, tube feeding or antibiotics given to her.

This situation arose on a Saturday and presented a difficult problem. Treatments that were obviously contrary to Ms. M's wishes had been initiated by the hospital from which she had come (tube feeding and antibiotics) and were, therefore, continued when she was admitted to The Jewish Home and Hospital.

The work of the ethics consult team began when the weekend administrator phoned the assistant administrator for guidance. A series of steps were needed to answer the following questions:

1. Did Ms. M. have the capacity to make health care decisions?
2. If not, did Ms. M. have a health care proxy or any other surrogate?
3. Why were antibiotics and tube feeding begun in the hospital?
4. What were Ms. M's present diagnosis and prognosis?
5. Pending the answers to the above, what steps should be taken to abide by Ms. M's wishes?

The assistant administrator and the weekend administrator proceeded to contact members of the ethics consult team as well as others who could be helpful in answering these questions. The Jewish Home and Hospital's covering physician completed a thorough examination of Ms. M., reviewed the most recent laboratory results and concluded that she was not able to make decisions, was awake and alert but aphasic and had bronchopneumonia. In addition to this, the weekend administrator attempted to elicit a response from Ms. M. on two occasions during the day to determine her level of capacity. Ms. M. was not able to respond in any way that indicated understanding of what was being said or asked.

Ms. M.'s social worker from the Geriatric Outreach Program was contacted to determine what Ms. M.'s functioning and responsiveness had been upon admission and in the hospital. The social worker, who had known Ms. M. for five years and had witnessed her living will, told us that Ms. M. had been unresponsive for more than four weeks.

During this time the administrator and the directors of medicine and nursing were also telephoned for guidance. By mid-afternoon, the team had determined that Ms. M. could no longer participate in decision-making, had no legally designated health care agent, had a validly executed living will and that there was enough medical information to discuss the situation with Ms. M.'s cousin (Mr. G.), her closest next-of-kin. The assistant administrator spoke with Mr. G. at length. He confirmed that Ms. M. would not want the antibiotics continued under the circumstances at hand. He also believed that she would not want the tube feeding to continue. Both treatments had been instituted at the hospital despite Ms. M.'s living will and without any prior discussion with her family. Mr. G. expressed that he did not feel able to challenge these decisions at the time.

Thereafter, Ms. M.'s antibiotic therapy was discontinued according to her wishes and a plan for comfort care was put in place. The ethics consult team believed further review of the tube feeding was required, especially since they had not had the benefit of hearing the primary health care team's assessment and perceptions. (On this weekend the unit head nurse, doctor and social worker were all off duty.)

Mr. G. wrote a statement expressing what he believed to be his cousin's wishes, as well as a description of how the feeding tube came to be initiated in the hospital. The ethics team requested this since living wills do not always *solely* provide "clear and convincing" evidence by legal standards. In addition, in New York State there is no legislation that makes living wills legal documents, although a body of case law does exist. (This technical aspect may, in fact, have been the hospital's justification for not following Ms. M.'s living will.) To establish clear and convincing evidence The Jewish Home and Hospital for Aged sought a preponderance of consistent evidence of Ms. M.'s wishes.

The ethics consult team met with the primary health care team on the following Monday morning to review the weekend's events and to discuss the next steps regarding Ms. M.'s feeding tube. Mr. G. joined the team for this discussion. On this particular day the ethics consult team included the assistant administrator, the Director and Associate Director of Nursing, the Director and Assistant Director of Medicine, the Ethics Coordinator, the Director of Medical Education and Ms. M.'s social worker from the Geriatric Outreach Program. What followed was an intense, thorough, poignant dialogue between the ethics team, the primary health care team and Mr. G. Ms. M.'s life, values and beliefs were discussed. The ethics team described how and when Ms. M.'s capacity for decision-making was reviewed, how living wills are used and how family members' information is considered. It was agreed that Ms. M. would want the feeding tube to be discontinued, and a comprehensive care plan was developed in keeping with her wishes for comfort care.

Following this meeting the ethics consult team remained available throughtout Ms. M.'s last days to anyone from the primary team and to

Mr. G. for support, guidance, information and discussion. Several members of the team also visited with Ms. M. during this time.

Ms. M. died peacefully and comfortably with the dignity she so clearly wanted. After her death the ethics consult team met with the primary team to provide a "safe haven" where they could talk about their personal feelings as well as their feelings as caregivers. They revealed their ambivalence, sympathy, sensitivity, sadness and sense of having done the "right" thing for Ms. M., even if their own preferences were different.

Probing questions arose about how to distinguish comfort measures from treatment, how to be sure a person who can no longer make decisions would still make the same decision that was stated in a living will, how to evaluate the quality and value of a human life, how to grieve, how to act in accordance with a patient's wishes when they are in conflict with those of the team. This discussion was a valuable experience for everyone and has become part of the process for all situations considered by the ethics consult team.

In the case of Ms. M. the ethics consult team guided the primary team through the most difficult of circumstances. The issue arose during a weekend, treatments were already in place, the resident was not able to participate in decisions and there was no legally designated proxy. Together, the ethics consult team considered the evidence of Ms. M.'s wishes, her current situation, the questions remaining, new information as it was brought out, additional information that was needed, the law and ethical principles. The ethics consult team also provided the caregivers with a place to openly express their feelings, viewpoints and interpretations and to receive support.

## RESEARCH IN ETHICS

The interrelationship between practice and research is a strong one. Optimally, research should inform practice. The converse is also true. With respect to research in ethics in long-term care, The Jewish Home and Hospital is in a particularly fortunate position. Characterized as a teaching nursing home, this setting is an ideal one in which to conduct research.

Long-term care settings offer numerous opportunities for research. With respect to ethics, these issues can be as dramatic as those surrounding end-of-life decision-making, or as basic as what Caplan (1990) has referred to as "the morality of the mundane." To date, ethics research at The Jewish Home and Hospital has addressed such issues as living wills and the use of feeding tubes for severely demented individuals (Peck, Cohen and Mulvihill 1990) and living wills. In addition, data have been collected from residents (Michelson et al. 1991), their family surrogates and health care providers regarding residents' preferences for life-sustaining treatment. The interaction and cooperation between research staff and clinical staff in research efforts is most important because of the ultimate benefits for residents, community clients and families.

## ADAPTING THE MODEL TO OTHER INSTITUTIONS

This three-pronged model for bioethics has been found to be effective at The Jewish Home and Hospital for Aged. It permits staff to address ethical dilemmas as they arise, it provides ongoing education, and it utilizes research—our own and that of others—to inform practice. It is a model that we would recommend enthusiastically to other institutions with an interest in extending their efforts in ethics.

However, the application of this model and these techniques may not be appropriate in every institution. At a minimum, the use of this three-pronged model requires strong administrative support and financial backing. In addition, staff members with expertise in research or education are needed. Very often these requirements are beyond the capacity of smaller facilities. Nonetheless, there are certain aspects of this model that are easily transferable and can be adapted to almost any long-term care setting.

First, with respect to direct service, long-term care facilities may want to consider the use of an ethics consult team rather than an ethics committee to address the day-to-day ethical dilemmas that affect their residents and staff. As noted by others (Brown, Miles and Aroskar 1987), ethics committees provide a variety of useful services in numerous nursing homes around the country. From policy development and staff education to resident care consultation and case review, these committees provide a valuable service in numerous institutions. However, ethics committees typically have between 8 and 20 members (Poirier 1991). Assembling this number of individuals when an ethical dilemma arises may be a difficult and time-consuming task.

Suggested is the use of an ethics consult team instead of the typical ethics committee. An ethics consult team is less unwieldy than an ethics committee. With fewer members than an ethics committee, it has the advantage of portability. Long-term care institutions have traditionally been comfortable with the team concept, utilizing it regularly to deliver care. Key to the efficient operation of a team is using the fewest number of people needed to accomplish a task. Bringing together four or five team members, and when necessary going directly to the bedside, can accomplish the same tasks as an ethics committee, often in a more timely and personal way.

As can be seen, direct practice in ethics can be undertaken by various techniques. Similarly, ethics education can take more than one form. We have found ethics rounds and the use of the "Decisions Near the End of Life" program to be especially effective. Further, all or part of these educational tools can be used in other settings. Most institutions have the capability to invite individuals with knowledge of ethics and the skills to deal with ethical issues to speak to their staff. Local clergy and attorneys with an interest in the elderly may be appropriate speakers for ethics rounds. A "Grand Rounds" format is both a teaching tool and a problem-solving technique. Small group discussions are also effective and permit the exchange of knowledge among disciplines. There is a collective wisdom among the staff members of most institutions that can effectively solve most ethical dilemmas that may arise.

Research in ethics is probably the component of this three-pronged bioethics model that is least transferable to most smaller facilities. However, an awareness of the research that has been done with respect to ethical issues in long-term care is one of the most important ways that practitioners can enhance their practice. Facilities may want to develop some mechanism through which staff members may become aware of research findings and apply them to the work situation as needed. Where possible, a "research committee" may assume responsibility for keeping abreast of published research regarding ethical issues in long-term care. When the number and availability of staff members preclude an institution's ability to have a research committee, an individual may undertake the task of keeping appropriate staff members apprised of current research issues that may apply to older persons in long-term care settings.

In conclusion, it should be noted that ethics and long-term care are closely interrelated. With advances in technology and the ability to sustain life for prolonged periods, ethical dilemmas will continue to arise in long-term care institutions. In doing so, these dilemmas will have an impact upon the lives not only of nursing home residents, but also their families and their health care providers. Any mechanism we can develop to address ethical issues has the potential to increase the autonomy of nursing home residents, improve the care they receive and enhance the quality of their lives.

# REFERENCES

Brown, B.A., S.H. Miles and M.A. Aroskar. The prevalence and design of ethics committees in nursing homes. *J. Am. Geriatrics Soc.* 35:1028-1033, 1987.

Glaser, G., M.N. Sweibel and C.K. Cassel. The ethics committee in the nursing home: results of a national survey. *J. Am. Geriatrics Soc.* 38:150-156, 1988.

Kane, R.A. and A.L. Caplan, eds. *Everyday Ethics: Resolving Dilemmas in Nursing Home Life.* New York: Springer, 1990.

Libow, L.S., E. Olson, R. Neufeld, T. Martico-Greenfield, H. Meyers, N. Gordon, and E. Barnett. Ethics rounds at the nursing home: an alternative to an ethics committee. *J. Am. Geriatrics Soc.* 40:95-97, 1992.

Michelson, C., M. Mulvihill, M.A. Hsu and E. Olson. Eliciting medical care preferences from nursing home residents. *Gerontologist* 31(3):358-363, 1991.

Miller, T. and A.M. Cugliari. Withdrawing and withholding treatment: policies in long-term care facilities. *Gerontologist* 30:462-468, 1990.

Peck, A., C.E. Cohen and M.N. Mulvihill. Long-term enteral feeding of aged demented nursing home patients. *J. Am. Geriatrics Soc.* 38:1195-1198, 1990.

Poirier, K.M. Launching an ethics committee. *Contemp. Long-Term Care* 14(5):24, 63, 1991.

# 17

# Long-Term Care for the Chronic Mentally Ill

*George Serban, MD*

As a result of medical progress, life has been extended for many chronic conditions that otherwise might have been fatal at an earlier age. Many patients, instead of dying of intercurrent disease, now require long term care. One group includes the chronically ill, the physically impaired, the mentally ill and the mentally retarded. Another group is represented by the elderly functionally impaired who need help with caretaking. This means that at one end of the population covered by long-term care are those in need of social services, while at the other end are the chronically ill. These inclusions are in accordance with the working definition of the Health Care Financing Administration (1985), which considers long-term care representing health, social and residential services provided to chronically disabled persons over extended periods of time. These services may be provided in a variety of settings, including the client's own home. However, the main modality for offering these services is considered to be the nursing home.

In 1986 there were 1.6 million chronically ill and physically disabled residents in nursing homes. The physically disabled represented a variety of functional disorders from severe impairment of senses or locomotion to bedridden conditions.

It has been calculated that in the population aged 65 and over living in the community there are over 2,549,000, or 9.6 percent, in need of help with the activities associated with daily living, while 3,711,000 people, representing 14 percent, are in need of help with instrumental activities (Kovar et al. 1984).

In a report of the National Center for Health Statistics (1984) regarding the population over age 65, it was found that 9 percent are either unable to walk or have severe difficulty in walking; 6.5 percent have marked difficulty in walking and 2.5 percent are decidedly unable to walk. Basically, 12.6 percent of the population over 65 require help to walk.

There are other physical limitations experienced by the population over age 65, such as hearing problems (27.8 percent), vision problems (12.8 percent), vision problems even with the use of glasses (31.1 percent) and difficulty grasping small objects (10.7 percent) (McKinley 1984). In addition, their limitations may be due to a chronic disease such as arthritis (46 percent), hypertension (37 percent) and heart conditions (28 percent), according to the statistics of the Office of Technology Assessment (1985).

All these people need to receive one type or another of continuous health care until their state deteriorates to the point of requiring hospitalization or nursing care, assuming that they or their families are unable to take responsibility. Let us not forget that life expectancy of the elderly is increasing too due to the better conditions of living. People who are reaching 65 now have an average life expectancy of another 16 years (14 more years for men and 18 more for women). With increasing longevity, they are confronted with new health crises, the most frightening of which are cancer and Alzheimer's disease. It is estimated that 20 percent of the population over 80 years of age develop some form of dementia. When they become confused and cognitively impaired, many are sent to nursing homes.

The same is not true for the chronic mentally ill, such as schizophrenics, who may be severely mentally impaired and may continue to live in the community, utilizing its resources for health care or at least those for social support. These patients seem to be in a category by themselves. Many of them remain in the community either at home or in overnight shelters or single-occupancy hotels. It is interesting to note that the trend for the last two decades has been toward providing long-term care for the chronically ill, including the physically disabled and the elderly cognitively impaired, but this approach has hardly applied to the existing health policy for the mentally ill.

The mentally ill have not fully benefited from the governmental policy of long-term care due to the prevailing attitude among mental health workers and legislators who attempted to treat these patients in the community, even though many communities did not accept them. This is a result of the policy of deinstitutionalization introduced in the sixties when due to exaggerated anticipation of remission it was believed that the mentally ill could be cured by treatment with tranquilizers. It was a time when every psychiatrist working in a state hospital believed himself to be a "new Pinel" and was indiscriminately discharging chronically ill mental patients into the community. Yet the new national policy oriented toward treatment in communities was haphazardly developed and inadequately carried out. It resulted in the "revolving door" situation created by discharging mentally ill patients to communities where only poorly organized programs were available.

The Community Mental Health Act of 1963 led to the development of community psychiatry, a system of delivery of services to mental patients in their communities rather than in state hospitals or asylums. The basic idea was that of using the most advanced medical and rehabilitative resources available in the community for control or reduction of behavioral symptoms, thereby leading to an improvement of the patient's social functioning. This was supposed to be a response to long-term hospitalization with its attendant creation of new psychopathology and dependency. (It had been thought that tranquilizers could control the problematic symptoms and restore patients' functioning in the community.)

Another untested assumption based on the enthusiastic projections of social activists and radical psychiatrists was that the community was ready to accept the mentally ill and able to work together until these people were fully reintegrated. Unfortunately, the mentally ill have been unable to function by the norms of the community due to their ongoing mental conditions, and the community has been unable to tolerate the deviant behavior of the mentally ill.

The philosophy of community psychiatry has been based to a large extent on a social model of mental illness rather than a medical one. In the sixties, a strong antipsychiatry trend became popular, particularly among mental health workers and, to a lesser extent, among psychiatrists. The theories of "antipsychiatry" can be lumped together under the common belief that mental illness in general, and schizophrenia in particular, is a disease of adaptation. At one extreme were the sociological studies that attempted to link schizophrenia to environmental factors, particularly to the lower social class, but not to the exclusion of other biological factors; at the other extreme were the radical theories that mental illness did not exist. It has been suggested that mental illness was a form of alienation from society (Laing 1970) or a rebellion against social conformity (Siirala 1963), or just a different level of perceiving reality (Szasz 1970). The main idea behind these theories has been that the mentally ill can function in the community without any hindrance as long as they are left alone. Certainly, this concept has given a free signal to the social activists for promoting a simpler, more permissive atmosphere in the community for the mentally ill with the understanding that this will automatically improve their mental state.

In reality, this approach not only led to the repeated hospitalization of patients, but let them loose in the community where their lives were fraught with disaster. The net result was the changing of their status from that of inpatients to a new pseudoambulatory state (Serban 1980). Eviction, arrest, drug and alcohol abuse, and homelessness became routine aspects of life, interspersed with hospitalization. It is estimated that about 70 percent of schizophrenics living in the community have a marginal life. Their lives are unproductive and aimless, with many schizophrenics living in dilapidated hotels, private proprietary houses, shelters, or just on the street.

It is obvious that long-term care for the mentally ill is not the smooth operation envisioned by the mental health community planners. This does not really matter since the mass hospitalization of the mentally ill is a dead issue. One reason is that out of 560,000 psychiatric beds available in 1955, only about 110,000 exist now. To this should be added the increase in the number of beds in the private sector from 36,689 in 1970 to 86,009 by 1986, as well as the psychiatric inpatient services that are provided by most general hospitals. As shown by Talbot (1978), the responsibility for the care of the chronic mentally ill has gradually shifted from the state to the general hospital. This is exactly what happened in New York City.

The study of psychiatric bed utilization in the general hospitals of New York done by Salit and Marcos (1991) points to the irresponsibility of governmental and state policies toward the chronic mentally ill. The statistical analysis done for the 13-year period from 1977 to 1989 shows that the mean length of stay almost tripled from 10.5 days to 28.4 days, while the occupancy rate rose from 83 to 104 percent. Citywide occupancy, including private hospitals, increased substantially from 85 percent in 1975 to 97 percent by 1988. In addition, patients who stayed longer than 60 days represented one-third of the patients at the time of discharge to state hospitals and 8 percent of those sent to aftercare facilities, while the remainder were released directly into the community. In terms of diagnosis, 63 percent met the criteria of chronic mental illness. It is obvious that the chronic mentally ill are continuously switched within the system from one form of health care to another, and this is highly disruptive both for the patient and the community. In addition there is a serious shortage of community treatment programs due to lack of funds (Salit and Marcos

1991). Nursing homes with federal restrictions on payment for psychiatric treatment have further limited the availability of help for the mentally ill.

Those among the chronic mentally ill who do not have a concomitant disabling physical condition that would place them in a nursing home must remain in the community in whatever programs are available to them. Attendance at these programs is voluntary, which assumes that these patients have the capacity to understand the nature of their illness and the need for its continuous treatment.

The federal mental health specialists and the legislators of the community mental health program have not paid full attention to the complexity of the problem of the post-hospital adaptation of chronic schizophrenics to their communities. Their ability to maintain a socially functional state depends upon many factors, such as regular attendance at an aftercare clinic, taking the prescribed medications, participation in a rehabilitation program and a structured organization of daily life within a network of support systems. Moreover, one of the most important elements of a patient's ability to function in the community is disrupted by his limited capacity to cope with the stress of adapting to the push and pull of community living. Due to his psychological deficits, a patients's inability to handle stress is exacerbated by noncompliance with taking medication, and this is one of the main factors contributing to his rehospitalization (Serban 1980).

It is important to realize that the residual psychological deficit still present at discharge makes it difficult for a patient to meaningfully appraise the events of his daily life, thereby inducing stress that further impairs his ability to cope with community living. Indeed, it is unrealistic to expect that a chronic mentally ill patient discharged to the community will manage with the same amount of help for living in the community as that given to a chronically disabled patient. The mentally ill require continuous monitoring of their tolerance to stress events and their interaction with family members and others. Additional stress is induced by the differing expectations of the family and the discharged patient regarding his capacity to function in the community. The wider the gap between these expectations, the more troubled the patient.

Can the chronically ill mental patient be helped by the community? Certainly, provided that two conditions are met: first, the availability of competent mental health services with integrated social programs adapted to the needs of the mentally ill, and second, the willingness of the patient to participate in these social-medical programs. Both these conditions present serious problems for the chronic mentally ill. To begin with, the success of rehabilitation is determined by the degree of the patient's awareness of his difficulty in coping with the community's demands, by his degree of cognitive or emotional impairment and deviant behavior and by his willingness to seek help voluntarily. But here is the twist: most of these patients are unaware of their mental illness and tend to refuse even the minimum of treatment. This is mainly reflected in their noncompliance with taking medication after hospitalization. For instance, in a study done by the author (Serban 1980), only 151 patients out of a sample of 516 (or 29.3 percent) reported strict compliance with their recommended drug regimen after hospitalization. However, even this figure was inaccurate when checked against other significant information. In reality, only 19.8 percent had regularly followed their prescribed drug regimen.

These data are even more relevant in view of the fact that out of 216 chronic patients, 67.8 percent professed at discharge a belief in the need for compliance with medication regimens after hospitalization. None of them followed through with their commitment, and none of them gave a meaningful reason as to why they did not take medication in the post-hospitalization period. The discrepancy between their generally positive attitude toward medication and their failure to use it goes beyond lack of motivation and strongly suggests that these patients have a lack of understanding of the importance of medication for the stability of their mental functioning. In a further analysis of their noncompliance, 52.3 percent of the chronic mentally ill felt that they should be able to decide for themselves when to discontinue medication. Many felt that medication interfered with their activity. Thirty-nine percent felt that taking the medication made them different from others, and 45.2 percent felt that they were entitled to stop taking the medication since they perceived no difference in their condition while taking it and after discontinuing it. When asked whether it would be helpful if someone reminded them to take their medication, only 16.1 percent answered positively.

Even when a patient is institutionalized, the issue of refusal of medication has to be decided by the courts. The court has to determine whether the constitutional rights of the patient are being violated and whether the treatment proposed by the psychiatrist is clearly for the well-being of the patient. In the case of *Rivers v. Katz* (1986), both issues were simultaneously determined by the court. The study of Zito and co-workers (1991) of court decisions concerning refusal of medication by involuntarily admitted patients shows that this judicial approach is usually a time-consuming procedure with little actual benefit to the patient. Ninety-two percent of the applications made over patient objections were approved in favor of the psychiatrist with the net result of delay in the discharge of the patient and extra cost for the state.

Furthermore, when the same large sample of patients was asked about their attitude toward aftercare treatment programs, they were found to share the same negative views as they had toward medication compliance. Out of 516 chronic patients, 227 (44 percent) declared their lack of interest in seeking outpatient treatment, whether in the clinical setting or the psychiatric office, and another 143 (27 percent) reported irregular attendance. Yet, at the same time, 72 percent of these patients agreed that attending a mental health clinic could be beneficial to their health. The discrepancy between expressed attitude and practical behavior again proves the patients' inability to make responsible judgments about their own mental health.

It is not surprising that most of the chronic mentally ill are rehospitalized after a relatively brief stay in the community. In our previously described sample, 258 patients (50 percent) were readmitted during the two-year period of the followup. Another 20 percent attended various halfway homes or residency programs. The remainder were under the care of families or relatives. Nonuse of the prescribed medication appeared to be one of the main causes of their rehospitalization.

Often, the community does not have the financial means of taking care of the chronic mentally ill. While federal and state policies are conflicting at best, many communities reject the responsibility of taking care of patients with whom they have no direct affiliation except for having been forced to deal with them. While beneficiaries of a liberal policy of community care, the chronic mentally ill do not reap the benefit because society does not have the means to carry out unrealistic programs for community reintegration. For instance, in New York City in 1989 there were only 2528 community residence beds for the mentally ill, although the state hospital population in 1974 was 14,970 and was subsequently reduced to 3920 (Salit and Marcos 1991). In addition, single-room occupancy declined during 1980 in New York to approximately 87 percent due to real estate development. This may explain why over 20,000 chronic mentally ill persons are homeless in New York City (*New York Times,* January 12, 1992).

It is clear that many chronically ill patients would benefit by participating in long-term care programs in the community. Yet, as already documented, they do not, since the attendance of such programs is on a voluntary basis. The chronic mentally ill are not aware of their condition or motivated to attend these programs even when they are available. This resistance is helped by the existing mental health laws of the states. For instance, in the current version of the New York State Mental Health Law (1973), conditional discharge is virtually absent. The law naively assumes that at discharge the psychiatric patient, particularly the schizophrenic, is healthy enough to participate voluntarily in the aftercare programs that will insure his continued psychological well-being. It is also assumed that in cases of exacerbation of his mental condition he will be aware enough to seek immediate treatment. The reality is that most discharged schizophrenics do not do this. As a result, they are often rehospitalized or even arrested at the request of their families or neighbors.

Another study has documented that since most schizophrenics come from the lower socioeconomic strata, they show unusual resistance to structured programs, and this is another reason for their lack of compliance. Basically, however, it is the lack of awareness of the need for treatment that is responsible for the fact that only 3.9 percent of schizophrenic patients requiring hospitalization are self-admitting (Serban 1980).

At admission the most frequent symptom found among the chronically schizophrenic has been confusion (76.4 percent) followed by inappropriate behavior (51.7 percent) and depression (30.6 percent). This lack of insight into their condition makes most of the chronic mentally ill unwilling to attend any regular aftercare programs. As a result, under the pressure of community living, their mental condition deteriorates fairly rapidly, leading to the need for readmission. Alcohol and substance abuse or antisocial acts, combined with failure to take medication, accelerates their departure from the community setting.

Thus the patient, while progressively getting sicker, does not seek voluntary help, as the short-sighted law would like to assume. When his behavior becomes uncontrollable, he is either hospitalized by others or directed to an aftercare treatment center. Furthermore, the falseness of the assumption that the chronic mentally ill can be integrated into the community is shown by the fact that by one year after discharge, 89 percent of chronic schizophrenics function below the norms of the community, failing to perform their expected roles, such as self-support (Serban 1979).

The situation has become more critical with the emergence of private, for-profit psychiatric hospitals that are less involved than the general hospitals with psychiatric services for the community. According to a national study of psychiatric hospital cases done by Dorwart and co-workers in 1991, private, for-profit psychiatric hospitals offer fewer community services for the mentally ill because they are less profitable. Case management for chronic mentally ill patients, a service not covered by insurance, is offered by about 50 percent of public specialty hospitals, 39 percent of nonprofit facilities and about 7 percent of the for-profit services involved in the survey. At the same time, these hospitals are more inclined not to admit chronic mentally ill persons to their facilities.

These findings show how tenuous the position of the chronically ill is in long-term care community programs. The Mental Hygiene Law of New York State conflicts with the intention of the federal Mental Health Act of 1963 and its amendments of 1975, which established long-term community programs for the mentally ill. Most of the treatment and rehabilitation programs are underused; only about 40 percent of the chronic mentally ill attending these programs at various times.

It is an irony that people committed to state hospitals want to receive adequate treatment in the community. The right to treatment was considered a major decision in the cases of *Rause v. Cameron* (1966), *Wyatt v. Stickney* (1972) and *O'Connor v. Donaldson* (1975), yet the mentally handicapped live on the street, in shelters or in adult homes with minimal psychiatric care.

As mentioned earlier, it has been estimated that in New York City alone there are about 20,000 mentally ill homeless people. Their mental health care is infrequently monitored and generally inadequate. At best, they receive only emergency psychiatric attention.

For the mentally ill homeless, the problem is an acute one. It is also an ethical and a social one. While they are victims of community neglect, they are also socially disruptive, affecting the daily functioning of the community. As Lamb (1990) suggested, comprehensive programs run by professionally dedicated people are needed to engage the homeless in treatment programs. For the present, however, this seems to be an unrealistic goal due to budgetary restrictions and lack of cooperation by the homeless themselves. Their forced hospitalization, as Lamb suggested, will create legal problems arising from court decisions concerning their right to nontreatment.

The New York State Mental Hygiene Law, for example, seems to support the right to nontreatment for the chronic mentally ill discharged to the community. Basically, the law ignores the fact that due to their residual personality disorganization and cognitive impairment, most ex-patients are unable to pursue goals that foster good health.

The discharge of mental patients into the community without compulsory aftercare treatment programs is actually detrimental to their welfare. It minimizes their chances for attending community programs that could stabilize their condition and prolong their community stay. The lack of treatment for most chronic schizophrenics living in the community all too often results in self-medication with inappropriate drugs or alcohol. Their psychotic symptoms are compounded, making their rehabilitation that much more difficult.

The justification for the deinstitutionalization of chronically ill patients might have appeared legitimate in view of the past abuses against the mentally ill, such as their maintenance in preventive custody without adequate treatment. Certainly, in this era of psychotropic therapy, there is no need for indefinite detention of the mentally ill in state mental hospitals, but this does not presume their neglect in the community under the protection of the law.

Even assuming that there are services available in the community, will the chronic schizophrenic make use of them? If he will do so, then the question to be answered is that of the efficacy of treatment. The conditions required for even the marginal functioning of a chronic schizophrenic in the community are so demanding and costly that their implementation presupposes a real concerted effort on the part of health planners and the ex-patient. Most often this does not happen. Even when it does, we should remember that 15 to 20 percent of chronic schizophrenics with negative symptoms are resistant to most tranquilizers and require continuous supervision (Serban 1992), if not admission to a state hospital. If we add to this the present budgetary constraints at various administrative levels that have reduced services in the mental health community centers and other psychiatric community services, then we will realize that long-term care for the chronic mentally ill is still far from adequate.

Let us see how another group of chronic mentally ill persons—chronic alcoholics who develop symptoms of dementia, blackout, seizures or psychotic symptoms with or without other physical diseases—receive long-term care. Chronic alcoholics without neurological impairment exhibit signs of cognitively impaired functions from defects in abstract thinking to memory losses. In addition, general comorbidity is high among this group. It has been found that the life-time existence of copsychiatric diagnosis is about 78 percent. One breakdown by coexistent psychiatric diagnosis showed that 42 percent had antisocial personality disorders, 31 percent had phobias, 23 percent major depression, 13 percent dysthymia, 9 percent panic disorder and 8 percent schizophrenia (Ross et al. 1988). The team also found that the likelihood of a psychiatric diagnosis increases the severity of alcohol dependence.

Ultimately, long-term alcohol dependency results in brain damage. Brain imaging studies like CAT have consistently shown brain atrophy (Ron 1983). It has been associated with loss of brain weight, increased brain sulci and enlargement of cerebral ventricles. MRI studies support these findings. In addition, imaging has shown the degree of brain atrophy in Wernicke's encephalopathy related to chronic alcoholism, poor nutrition and thiamine deficiency. Losses have been noticed in mamillary bodies, which may explain the short-term memory deficit in alcoholics (Charnes et al. 1988).

From a neuropsychiatric point of view, chronic alcoholics develop organic mental disorders that require long-term care. The most common ones are the alcoholic amnestic disorder, also known as Korsakoff's psychosis, and dementia associated with alcoholism. Alcohol amnestic disorder is associated with short-term memory impairment but without general loss of intellectual functions. It has also been noticed by some researchers (Muuronen et al. 1989) that after a period of alcohol abstinence the memory and intellectual deficits are partly restored. Certainly, persons with these organic brain syndromes require long-term care in nursing homes since they are no longer accepted in state hospitals.

For the chronic alcoholic with nonorganic psychiatric disorder, the response to treatment depends upon the severity of coexistent psychiatric illness. For instance, Rounsaville and co-workers found in a 1987 study that male alcoholics with major depression or antisocial personality responded poorly to treatment. Alcoholism and major depression seem to be independent conditions; as a part of alcoholism, depression can be present in the initial period of abstinence in chronic alcoholics. This has to be differentiated from the primary depression of affective disorder (Schuckit and Monteiro 1988). At the same time major depression could coexist with alcoholism, as demonstrated in a study by Dorus and associates (1987) in which out of 50 inpatient alcoholics, 16 (32 percent) were suffering from major depression.

While most of these patients with major depression and alcohol as comorbidity can be treated in the community; some of them with severe alcoholic dependence are unable to take care of themselves, requiring continuous supervision in long-term care programs. In general, patients admitted to long-term care facilities have to meet at least one of three conditions: a nonambulatory state, incontinence or confusion. Most of the chronically alcoholic mentally ill meet the last two conditions or at least that of confusion. If in the past these patients were committed for life to the back wards of state hospitals, today some are successfully placed in adult homes or other residential community facilities or in nursing homes.

With the enactment of Medicaid and Medicare, physically and mentally disabled people have access to the long-term health care system. If the problem is considered a purely psychiatric one, however, Medicare has a lifetime limit on its benefits. As a result, Medicaid has to take over the responsibility for paying. But eligibility for Medicare requires either that the patient be demonstrably indigent or that the family contribute heavily to the long-term care program in a residential or nursing home. Under these circumstances, access to care remains a problem for those just above the poverty line. A serious problem, still unresolved, is the deductible and co-insurance policy of Medicare for those who are not classed as poor. This policy makes it quite difficult for many of the middle-class mentally ill to afford the cost of nursing home care. Nursing homes constitute the third largest governmental expenditure after hospitals and physicians. Yet, only half of the cost is supported by the government, with the rest being paid by nursing home residents or their families. As a result, nursing home services are chiefly utilized by the poor and are underutilized by the other sectors of the population.

The same problem is encountered in the community mental health services. Greater access for the older population to these services will reduce or forestall long-term hospitalization for depression, the most commonly encountered psychological problem among the elderly. A study by Steel and associates (1990) found that even for Alzheimer's disease sufferers living in the community, placement in a nursing home was accelerated by exacerbation of psychiatric symptoms or behavioral disorders rather than by the severity of cognitive impairment. Thus their stay in the community would likely be extended if psychiatric treatment were available. This might have an impact on the escalating cost of nursing homes, which has reached an annual expenditure of over $23 billion (1991).

With the aging of the population, a large segment of the elderly will require some form of long-term care. If services in the community are not available at reasonable cost, the burden for the families of the elderly who need care will only grow worse. It is estimated that by the year 2000, over 2 million people will suffer from major dementia (Cross and Gurland 1986). In view of the staggering cost of maintaining these people in long-term care, more efficient formulas will have to be found for assisting them in the community. This will require a recasting of the role of the psychiatrist as a participant in the policymaking for the delivery of mental health services. Such a recasting will be more in line with the view of the public, who see him not only as a healer, but also as a business-oriented professional. The psychiatrist is no longer viewed as the sole mental health arbiter determining the type and terms of health care provided to the patient.

If "the charismatic image" of the physician has changed in the public's eye, as Tischler (1991) suggests, then psychiatrists have to change in order to meet the challenge of the management of the mentally ill patient. To start with, they must broaden their therapeutic concept. It is no longer practical for psychiatrists to approach the patient's treatment parochially with a commitment to a particular form of treatment model. Psychiatrists must be eclectic in their therapeutic approach in order to be able to help mentally ill patients return to their previous social environment. At the same time, they must be cost-conscious in order to meet the demands of the third-party payer, who acts as a co-partner in the case management of the patient. At the same time community programs must expand their effort beyond the most motivated and functional patients, as Bachrach and co-workers (1989) have stressed. They must try to attract the unmotivated, seriously mentally ill. In order to change this situation, the health administrations of these programs have to be held accountable in terms of the services they offer to the health care consumer. This also applies to nursing homes, which, as Henderson (1992) put it, are becoming "expensive warehouses for the dying," a last stop after the residents have "spended down."

## REFERENCES

Bachrach, G.L. and H.R. Lamb. What we learned from deinstitutionalization. *Psychiatric Ann.* 19:12-21, 1989.
Charnes, M.E., L.A. Querimit and K. Henteleff. Ethanol differentially regulates G proteins in neural cells. *Biochem. Biophys. Res. Comm.* 155(1):138-143, 1988.
Cross, P.S. and B.J. Gurland. The Epidemiology of Dementing Disorders. Report prepared for the Office of Technology Assessment, U.S. Congress. Washington, DC: U.S. Government Printing Office, 1986.
Dorus, W., J. Kennedy, R.D. Gibbons, and S.D. Ravi. Symptoms and diagnosis of depression in alcoholism. *Alcoholics* 11(2):150-154, 1987.
Dorwart, A.R., M. Schlesinger, H. Davidson, S. Epstein and C. Hoover. A national study of psychiatric care. *Am. J. Psychiatry* 148(2):204-210, 1991.
Health Care Financing Administration. Medicare Program Statistics. Baltimore: Bureau of Data Management and Strategy, 1985.
Henderson, C.T. It's time to do something about nursing home care. *Am. Med. News,* January 20, 1992.
Kovar, G.M. Functional Ability and the Need for Care Issues for Measurement Research. *Vital and Health Statistics: Proceedings, 1988.* Washington, DC: National Center for Health Statistics, 1991.
Laing, R.D. *The Politics of Experience.* New York: Ballantine Books, 1970.
Lamb, H.A. Will we save the homeless mentally ill? *Am. J. Psychiatry* 147:649-651, 1990.
McKinley, B.J. Optimal Survey Research Methods for Studying Health Related Behavior of Older People. *Vital and Health Statistics: Proceedings, 1988.* Washington, DC: National Center for Health Statistics, 1991.
Mental Hygiene Law of New York State. "An act to repeal the mental hygiene law and to enact a recodified mental hygiene law." *McKinney Consolidated Law of New York,* 34A, 1971.
Muuronen, A., H. Bergman, T. Hindmarsh and I. Telakivi. Influence of improved

drinking habits on brain atrophy and cognitive performance in alcoholic patients. A 5-Year follow-up study. *Alcoholics* 13(1):137-141, 1989.

National Center for Health Statistics. *Patterns of Ambulatory Care in Internal Medicine: The National Ambulatory Care Survey, U.S., January 1980-December 1981.* Washington, DC: U.S. Department of Health and Human Services, 1984.

*New York Times.* Big shelters hold terrors for the mentally ill, January 12, 1992.

*O'Connor v. Donaldson,* 43 USL W 4929, 1975.

Office of Technology Assessment. Pub. BA 264. Washington DC: U.S. Government Printing Office, 1985.

*Rause v. Cameron,* 373 F2d 451, DC cir., 1966.

Ron, M. *The Alcoholic Brain CT Scan and Psychological Findings.* Psychological Medicine Monograph Supplement No. 3. Cambridge, England: Cambridge University Press, 1983.

Ross, H.E. and F.B. Glaser. The prevalence of psychiatric disorder in inpatients with alcohol and drug problems. *Arch. Gen. Psychiatry* 45:1023-1028, 1988.

Rounsaville, B.J., Z.S. Dolinsky, F.F. Babor and R.E. Meyer. Psychopathology as a predictor of treatment outcome in alcoholism. *Arch. Gen. Psychiatry* 44:505-513, 1987.

*Rivers v. Katz,* 67 NY2d 48J; 495 NE 2nd 337, 5O4 NYS 2nd 74, 1986.

Salit, A.S. and R.L. Marcos. Have general hospitals become chronic care institutions for mentally ill? *Am. J. Psychiatry* 148(7):892-897, 1991.

Schuckit, M.A. and M.G. Monteiro. Alcoholism, anxiety, and depression. *Br. J. Addiction* 83(12):1371-1380, 1988.

Serban, G. *Adjustment of Schizophrenics in the Community.* New York: SP Medical and Scientific Books, 1980.

Serban, G. and C.B. Gidinski. Relationship between cognitive defect, affect response and community adjustment in chronic schizophrenics. *Br. J. Psychiatry* 134:602-608, 1979.

Serban G., S. Siegel and M. Gaffney. Response of negative symptoms to neuroleptic treatment. *J. Clin. Psychiatry* 32(2), 1992.

Siirala, M. Schizophrenia: a human situation. *Am. J. Psychoanal.* 23:29-66, 1963.

Steele, C., B. Rovner, A.G. Chase and M. Folstein. Psychiatric symptoms over nursing home placement of patients with Alzheimer's disease. *Am. J. Psychiatry* 167(8):1049-1051, 1991.

Szasz, T. *The Manufacture of Madness.* New York: Harper & Row, 1970.

Talbot, J.A. *The Death of the Asylum: A Critical Study of State Hospital Management Services and Care.* New York: Grune & Stratton, 1978.

Tischler, L.G. Utilization management of mental health services by private third party. *Am. J. Psychiatry* 147(8):967-973, 1990.

*Wyatt v. Stickney,* 325 F Supp. 481, MD Ala 1971.

*Wyatt v. Stickney,* 325 F Supp. 373, 379, 385, MD Ala 1972.

Zito M.J., J.T. Craig and J. Wanderling. New York under the Rivers decision: an epidemiological study of drug treatment refusal. *Am. J. Psychiatry* 148(7):904-909, 1991.

# 18

# Cancer Pain Management in Long-Term Care

*Margaret M. Shannon, MS, RNC*

Today the 23 million Americans who are aged 65 and older make up approximately 11 percent of the population. It is projected that over the next 40 years the number of elderly will increase to 55 million and will make up more than 18 percent of the population. Approximately 50 percent of cancers occur in people over age 65, and the incidence of cancer doubles from age 60 to age 80 (Yancik 1983). These projections indicate that cancer is most likely to develop at an age when an individual's functional status is deteriorating. As care requirements increase, fewer family members and friends are available to provide support. Society needs to meet this challenge to provide care for this growing population.

Until recently, most persons with advanced cancer were cared for at home with the acute care hospital as a back-up provider when the person's symptoms became unmanageable at home. Today the acute care hospital is designed to provide "high-tech" curative services. Because of current reimbursement formulas, hospitals are less able to support persons during the dying process.

The modern hospice movement has expanded to become part of the continuum of health care, and hospice care is preferred when the objective of care changes from cure to comfort. Since hospice is a concept rather than a place, it is appropriate that the philosophy and principles of hospice care guide practice wherever there are people who are dying (McCracken and Gerdsen 1991).

Given current reimbursement systems for hospices, most of these organizations are viable only as long as 80 percent of hospice care can be provided at home. In many urban areas where people live alone, or rural areas where distance precludes adequate home services, patients with advanced cancer can receive appropriate care only within a long-term care (LTC) facility. People with cancer are admitted to LTC facilities for the same reasons as all other residents. They have a chronic disease that has resulted in dependence on others for assistance with daily living, and recurrent health problems requiring access to medical care. Personnel in LTC facilities who care for people with chronic conditions, providing comfort rather than cure, should be prepared to provide expert palliative care for people with advanced cancer.

Rehabilitation therapies and a prosthetic environment should enable each resident to function at his optimal level and to be as independent as his condition allows. Using the Minimum Data Set tool should help to uncover changes in the resident's physical and mental status. For the person with cancer, ongoing assessment of pain and the effectiveness of pain therapy are essential parts of these periodic reevaluations.

## CONTROL OF CANCER PAIN

Although pain is not universally associated with cancer, it is a dreaded symptom of the disease. The fear of pain has given rise to much of the concern about euthanasia. However, a comprehensive body of knowledge about managing the cancer patient with pain has developed over the past 15 years. When current knowledge of pain relief is applied, most cancer pain can be controlled. The World Health Organization's Expert Panel on Cancer Pain and Palliative Care issued recommendations stating that: "Governments should ensure that cancer pain relief and palliative care programmes are incorporated into their existing health care systems," and that "Governments should ensure the availability of both opioid and nonopioid analgesics" (WHO 1990).

The principal barrier to effective cancer pain management is lack of knowledge by health care professionals. This prevents patients from receiving adequate pain management with opioid drugs. An unfounded fear of addiction is a concern of many physicians, nurses and patients. In addition, government regulations often interfere with access to narcotic analgesics (Foley 1991).

## INCIDENCE OF CANCER PAIN

There is a lack of national epidemiologic data on the incidence of cancer pain. Surveys of cancer pain are difficult to interpret because the information is derived by different methods about diverse populations. In chart reviews of 667 patients with cancer admitted to one hospital over a 10-month period, pain was a symptom of 6 percent of patients with nonmetastatic cancer and 33 percent of patients with metastatic cancer. Those with metastatic prostate and breast cancer had the highest incidence of pain; the rates were 75 and 64 percent, respectively (Daut and Cleeland 1982).

When estimates of cancer pain are extrapolated from numerous studies of cancer populations around the world, the incidence of pain in all stages of the disease is 51 percent, while 74 percent of patients with advanced metastatic disease experience pain (Bonica 1990).

In a survey of over 1017 patients with advanced cancer admitted to Calvary Hospital over a one-year period, pain was a complaint on admission for 73 percent of the patients; 38 percent had severe pain. Nearly one-half of the patients with bone metastasis had severe pain (Brescia et al. 1992).

## CAUSES OF CANCER PAIN

There are four different causes of pain in persons with cancer. Pain may result from direct tumor invasion or compression of pain-sensitive structures. Cancer therapy, paraneoplastic syndromes and disorders unrelated to cancer or cancer therapy may cause pain. Invasion of bone by a primary or metastatic lesion is the most frequent cause of cancer pain. Tumors may invade nerve tissue, compressing the nerve roots, trunks or plexuses. Tumors may grow in the liver, kidney or splenic parenchyma, distending pain-sensitive structures. Visceral pain may result from tumor obstruction of the hollow organs of the gastrointestinal tract, the urinary tract or the uterus. Radiotherapy can cause nerve damage or fibrosis of surrounding tissue. Chemotherapy may result in peripheral neuropathy, dysesthesias and mucositis. Herpes infections induced by immunosuppression may be followed by painful postherpetic neuralgia (Howard-Ruben et al. 1987).

## ASSESSMENT OF CANCER PAIN

Pain is a complex, multidimensional, neurophysiologic process that is modified by individual memory, expectations and emotions. The perception of pain is an individual subjective experience. Pain is present whenever the patient says he has pain; there are no objective measures. Appropriate pain relief can be achieved only after careful assessment.

Several assessment instruments are available. The Brief Pain Inventory developed by Daut and co-workers (1983) is one example. The dimensions of the pain experience that need to be assessed are: duration, location, intensity, factors that exacerbate or relieve the pain and the effects of pain on behavior.

One method of determining the location of the pain is to ask the person to point to the location of his pain on an outline of the human body. Patients with metastatic disease often have pain at several sites.

It is important to ascertain the factors that increase the pain. Is the pain worse when the patient moves, lies down, swallows or coughs? Is the pain relieved when he assumes a certain posture? Is the pain relieved only by analgesic use?

There are two common methods of measuring pain intensity. With the verbal descriptor scale, the patient is asked to select the word that best describes the pain, ranging from no pain to excruciating pain. A visual analog scale is a 100 mm. line with two anchors: no pain at one end and the worst possible pain at the other. The patient is asked to make a mark on the line that represents the severity of his pain.

Visual analog scales also can be used to measure the effects of pain on both physical and psychosocial functioning. Some functions that can be assessed include mobility; ADL activities such as eating, dressing and toileting; appetite; sleep; interacting with others and enjoyment of leisure time. The anchors for the 100 mm. lines are no interference with carrying out the particular function and total interference with performing the function.

Another assessment tool, the Memorial Pain Assessment Card, provides rapid evaluation of subjective pain experiences: pain intensity, pain relief and mood. It can be used to monitor the effectiveness of therapy (Fishman et al. 1987).

It is important to determine whether the pain is acute or chronic. Acute pain has a distinct onset and a short duration. It is usually accompanied by signs of sympathetic nervous system activity such as increased pulse and respiratory rate and elevated blood pressure. Acute cancer-related pain can occur at any stage of the disease. With some cancers pain is an early warning symptom that should prompt attention to diagnosis and treatment. Acute pain can be caused by cancer therapy. It also can occur in advanced cancer when pathologic fractures occur. Cancer pain is sometimes classified as acute and ongoing because of continued nociceptive stimulation by uncontrolled metastatic disease (Wall 1990).

Chronic pain usually has a duration of six months or more. The patient may show no physiological signs of pain, but may show psychosocial consequences such as depression, decreased socialization, impaired ambulation and sleep disturbance (Ferrell 1991).

## DRUG TREATMENT OF CANCER PAIN

The most widely used treatment of cancer pain is the administration of systemic analgesics, sometimes in combination with adjuvant drugs. There are three classes of analgesics: nonopioid analgesics such as aspirin, acetaminophen and nonsteroidal anti-inflammatory drugs (NSAIDs); weak opioids such as codeine, and strong opioids such as morphine and hydromorphone.

A variety of drugs that have other primary indications are effective as adjuvant drugs for cancer pain. The corticosteroids such as dexamethasone relieve pain caused by nerve compression and metastasis to bone. Amitriptyline and other antidepressants, as well as anticonvulsants such as tegretal, are helpful in reducing neuropathic pain. They also potentiate narcotic analgesia, elevate mood and increase sedation.

The World Health Organization's Cancer Pain Relief Committee has recommended guidelines to assist clinicians in prescribing appropriate therapy for management of cancer pain. The WHO analgesic ladder, a simple and useful method of drug selection, consists of three steps. Adjuvants may be included with the analgesics at any step. Step 1 is a trial with nonopioid analgesics. If reevaluation reveals that pain persists, step 2, a trial with weak opioids, is begun. If pain continues, then step 3, the use of strong opioids, is initiated. There are multiple drugs in each category with idiosyncratic differences in effectiveness and toxicity. If one drug is ineffective or not well tolerated, a trial with a different drug in the same category is warranted (Portenoy 1990).

### Mechanism of Analgesic Action

A variety of analgesic drugs are needed because pain impulses can be blocked at several locations along the pain pathway. Pain is perceived when noxious stimuli affect pain receptors, initiating nerve impulses that enter the central nervous system and reach the cerebral cortex. Pain receptors are sensitized to these stimuli after a series of neurochemicals are produced and released. Nonopioid analgesics relieve pain by blocking the action of some of these neurochemicals, in particular, prostaglandins.

Opioids act by binding to opiate receptors within the brain, dampening the effectiveness of the incoming nerve impulses. Steroids act as adjuvants because they inhibit production of arachidonic acid and, therefore, block the production of leukotrienes and prostaglandins. Anticonvulsants act as adjuvants by stabilizing the cell membranes of neurons, preventing conduction of the nerve impulses (Wilkie 1990).

**Titration of Doses**

Cancer pain is best managed by analgesic drugs administered around the clock in gradually increasing doses until pain relief has been achieved. Since titration often produces tolerance to the adverse effects of opioids, such as respiratory depression and clouding of consciousness, doses can be increased gradually to levels high enough to relieve severe pain. However, arriving at the correct dose requires time, patience and understanding.

After evaluating the person's pain intensity, physical condition and prior pain therapy, the initial dose is selected and administered at intervals frequent enough to maintain an adequate plasma level. During the titration phase, "breakthrough pain" may occur near the end of the dosing interval. A supplemental dose of a rapid-acting form of the drug should be administered to the patient immediately. Following that, either the dose of the drug being titrated is increased or the time interval between doses is shortened.

Oral preparations of a drug usually can achieve the same results as parenteral preparations as long as equianalgesic doses are administered at appropriate intervals. Oral preparations are more convenient to administer and less restrictive for the patient. Controlled-release oral morphine preparations can be administered two or three times a day and produce continuous analgesia.

Table 1 lists the equianalgesic dose and plasma half-life of some representative narcotic analgesics.

*Table 1.*

Comparison of Opioids

| Opioid | Equianalgesic dose (mg.) | | Duration (hr.) | Plasma half-life (hr.) |
|--------|------|------|------|------|
|        | IM   | PO   |      |      |
| Morphine | 10 | 60 | 4-6 | 2-3.5 |
| Hydromorphone | 1.5 | 7.5 | 4-6 | 2-3 |
| Methadone | 10 | 20 | 5-7 | 17-24 |
| Levorphanol | 2 | 4 | 5-8 | 12-16 |
| Oxycodone | — | 30 | 3-5 | not known |
| Codeine | 130 | 200 | 4-6 | 3 |

Adapted from K.M. Foley, The treatment of cancer pain. *N. Engl. J. Med.* 313:84-95, 1985.

This table is used when switching from one opioid to another or from one route of administration to another. It demonstrates that a person receiving 10 mg. of morphine intramuscularly will receive the same analgesic effect if given 1.5 mg. of hydromorphone intramuscularly or 7.5 mg. of hydromorphone orally. Before changing to a different drug or modality, each drug should be administered long enough for a steady state to develop. The time for the steady state to develop depends on the half-life of the drug. Morphine which has a short half-life of 2 to 3.5 hours, will develop a steady state in 48 hours, whereas methadone, with a long half-life of 17 to 24 hours, may take up to six days to achieve a steady state (Bonica 1990).

## BREAKTHROUGH PAIN

Breakthrough pain is a transitory increase in pain to greater than moderate intensity. There are two types: those that occur spontaneously without a precipitating event and those that are precipitated by an action of the person. The treatment for breakthrough pain is administration of a "rescue dose," a supplemental dose of an analgesic drug given on an as-needed basis in combination with a fixed, around-the-clock dosing schedule.

Precipitated pains, also known as incident pains, may be either predictable or unpredictable. When breakthrough pains are predictable, such as pain induced by movement or a dressing change, the analgesic dose should be taken half an hour to an hour before the precipitating event. If the occurrence of pain is unpredictable, such as pain induced by myoclonic jerks or coughing, the "rescue dose" should be taken as soon as possible after the pain starts (Portenoy and Hagen 1989).

## PAIN, ANALGESIA AND THE ELDERLY

Given the demographic facts about the incidence of cancer, many persons with cancer in LTC facilities will be in the older age group. Variations in the perception and expression of pain by older persons as well as the action of analgesics in older persons need to be considered.

Harkins and co-workers (1984) summarized the experimental studies comparing pain sensitivity in elderly and young volunteers, and concluded that it is unclear if systematic age-related changes in pain sensibility exist. Some painful conditions, such as acute appendicitis, present similarly regardless of age. Others, such as myocardial infarction, change with age; more than half of older people do not complain of cardiac pain. Their survey of patients with chronic pain revealed no consistent age-related differences in pain intensity or interference with activities of daily living.

In a survey of patients with advanced cancer admitted to Calvary Hospital, the complaint of severe pain was inversely related to age. Severe pain was reported most often by patients under 55, and least often by those over 75 (Brescia et al. 1992).

The elderly have increased sensitivity to narcotics due to multiple factors such as changes in plasma protein binding and prolonged renal clearance of the drugs. When titrating analgesics for older persons, a narcotic with a short plasma half-life should be selected, and the initial dose should be smaller than that given to younger persons. At all ages, the optimal dose depends on the person's response. The goal for all is freedom from pain and freedom from adverse effects.

Since many residents of LTC facilities suffer from dementia, the staff needs to know how to recognize painful conditions in these individuals. The best measures are deviations from the person's typical behavior. The person who was able to walk or move about may show reduced mobility. The person who had a good appetite may suddenly refuse to eat. The person may suddenly become restless. Poor concentration and inattention may occur.

When a patient with advanced cancer and dementia exhibits behavior changes, an evaluation of his mental and physical status is required.

If the conclusion is reached that the person probably is experiencing pain, a trial with analgesics may reverse the behavior and allow him to be comfortable.

## Side Effects of Opioids

In addition to analgesia, the use of opioids may cause several side effects such as somnolence, confusion, hallucinations, nausea, constipation, agitation, delirium and respiratory depression. If possible, all should be prevented; if side effects occur, they should be treated and reversed.

Sometimes the early sedative effects are the result of sleep deprivation that may disappear when the person's fatigue and pain are relieved. Confusion and hallucinations, which are not uncommon in the elderly, can be reversed with the use of haloperidol. If they persist, a different opioid analgesic such as hydromorphone may be substituted.

Nausea, a problem that may occur at the start of opioid use, can be controlled with prochlorperazine. Haloperidol, which also acts as an antiemetic, may be preferred in treating the elderly because it has fewer anticholinergic and cardiovascular effects.

If no preventive measures are taken, constipation always accompanies the use of opioids. Stimulating cathartics, such as senna compounds combined with stool softeners, should be added to the regimen. Bowel movements should be monitored before and during the use of opioids to be certain that normal bowel function is maintained.

Agitation may be relieved by the use of anxiolytic agents such as lorazepam or alprazolam. These drugs also may relieve anxiety attacks brought on by a feeling of suffocation, which may occur with lung cancer or pulmonary metastatic disease.

If respiratory depression occurs, it can be reversed with naloxone, an opioid antagonist. It is important to administer this drug in small increments so that when respirations return to normal, analgesia is maintained (Burchman 1989).

Delirium evidenced by restlessness, confusion and discomfort is common in persons with advanced cancer during the last weeks of life. Small doses of haloperidol may help the person to become more comfortable. The delirium may worsen if it is misdiagnosed as increased pain and treated with larger doses of opioids (Coyle 1991).

Some degree of tolerance occurs in those who take opioids for long periods of time. Increasing doses may be needed to relieve the same level of pain. Except for constipation, tolerance to side effects of opioids occurs at a faster rate than that for analgesic effects.

Addiction does not result from using opioids for cancer pain relief. Addiction is a psychological dependence on opioids that may lead to illegal behavior to obtain the drugs. Persons who have both conditions—cancer pain and drug addiction—are a small minority.

## Intractable Pain

Pharmacologic approaches alone are not effective in about 15 percent of persons with advanced cancer. Neuropathic pain, in particular, may be opioid-resistant. Anesthetic and neurosurgical approaches such as cordotomy or rhizotomy may be needed. It is important that each LTC facility develop referral services so that persons with refractory pain will have access to these alternative measures (Coyle 1991).

## Nonpharmacologic Approaches

The LTC facility is ideally suited to provide some of the alternative approaches to pain control. Physical and occupational therapies such as stretching exercises, heat therapy and transcutaneous electric nerve stimulation (TENS) may reduce musculoskeletal complications such as shortening of immobilized muscles and joint ankyloses that predispose to pain. Orthotic devices may reduce incident pain brought about by movement of specific regions. Cognitive techniques such as relaxation therapy and distraction may be useful in controlling pain (Portenoy and Hagen 1989).

## CONCLUSION

The distress caused by poorly relieved cancer-related pain is one burden that LTC residents should not have to bear. They have already lost their struggle to stay at home. They are experiencing multiple losses while facing an uncertain future and death. A greater understanding of analgesic drugs by health care workers and policymakers as well as the general public would improve the quality of life of those with cancer. Table 2 lists several key facts that should be widely disseminated in order to raise the level of awareness about cancer pain and palliative care.

*Table 2.*

Facts about Cancer Pain

---

1. Palliative care will improve the quality of life of patients with cancer, even though the disease may be incurable.

2. Cancer is not always painful.

3. Treatments exist that will relieve pain and many other symptoms in advanced cancer.

4. Drug therapy is the mainstay of cancer pain management.

5. There is no need for patients to suffer prolonged and intolerable pain and other distressing symptoms.

6. Psychological dependence ("addiction") does not result from the use of opioids to relieve cancer pain.

---

Reprinted with permission from *Cancer Pain Relief and Palliative Care*. Geneva: World Health Organization, 1990.

## REFERENCES

Bonica, J.J. Cancer Pain. In J.J. Bonica, ed., *The Management of Pain*, 2nd Ed. Malvern, PA: Lea & Febiger, 1990.

Brescia, F.J., R.K. Portenoy, M. Ryan, L. Krasnoff and G. Gray. Pain, opioid use, and survival in hospitalized patients with advanced cancer. *J. Clin. Oncol.* 10:149-154, 1992.

Burchman, S.L. Hospice Care of the Cancer Pain Patient. In S.E. Abram, ed., *Cancer Pain*. Boston: Kluwer, 1989.

Coyle, N. Initial assessment and ongoing evaluation of cancer pain. *Am. J. Hospice Palliative Care* 8(6):27-35, 1991.

Daut, R.L. and C. Cleeland. The prevalence and severity of pain in cancer. *Cancer* 50:1913-1918, 1982.

Daut, R., C. Cleeland and R. Flanery. Development of the Wisconsin brief pain questionnaire. *Pain* 17:197-210, 1983.

Ferrell, B.A. Pain management in elderly people. *J. Am. Geriatric Soc.* 39:64-73, 1991.

Fishman, B., S. Pasternak, S.L. Wallenstein, R.W. Houde, J.C. Holland and K.M. Foley. The Memorial pain assessment card: a valid instrument for the evaluation of cancer pain. *Cancer* 60:1151-1158, 1987.

Foley, K.M. The relationship of pain and symptom management to patient requests for physician-assisted suicide. *J. Pain Symptom Management* 6:289-297, 1991.

Howard-Ruben, J., L. McGuire and S.L. Groenwald. Pain. In S.L.Groenwald, ed, *Cancer Nursing: Principles and Practices.* Boston: Jones & Bartlett, 1987.

Harkins, S.W., J. Kwentus and D.D. Price. Pain and the Elderly. In C. Benedetti et al., eds., *Advances in Pain Research and Therapy,* Vol. 7. New York: Raven Press, 1984.

McCracken, A.L. and L. Gerdsen. Hospice care principles for terminally ill elders. *J. Gerontol. Nursing* 17(12):4-8, 1991.

Portenoy, R.K. and N.A. Hagen. Breakthrough pain: definition and management. *Oncology* 3(8):Suppl., 25-29, 1989.

Portenoy, R.K. Drug therapy for cancer pain. *Am. J. Hospice Palliative Care* 7(6):10-19, 1990.

Wall, R.T. Use of analgesics in the elderly. *Clin. Geriatric Med.* 6:345-363, 1990.

Wilkie, D.J. Cancer pain management. *Nursing Clin. North A.* 25:331-343, 1990.

World Health Organization. *Cancer Pain Relief and Palliative Care.* Technical Report Series 804. Geneva: WHO, 1990.

Yancik, R. Frame of Reference: Old Age as the Context for the Prevention and Treatment of Cancer. In R. Yancik et al., eds., *Aging,* Vol 24. New York: Raven Press, 1983.

# 19

# Disability, Rehabilitation and Long-Term Care

*Stanley F. Wainapel, MD, MPH*

Old age and physical disability have been part of the continuum of human experience throughout our species' documented history, but they have only become major health care and public policy issues in this century. In the United States, life expectancy at birth, which was 40 years in 1900, has nearly doubled, and the proportion of Americans aged 65 or older, only 4 percent in 1900, has almost tripled (Rabin and Stockton 1987). Moreover, the oldest of the elderly—those aged 85 or over—are increasing in numbers even faster than the elderly as a whole, and it is this particular group that accounts for the largest segment of the population who require or will require long-term care. In similar fashion, people with disabilities have grown in number until they now represent some 15 percent of the American population—more than 35,000,000 people (DeJong and Lifchez 1983).

These phenomena have a similar basis—the dramatic developments in medicine, surgery, and public health which have resulted in reductions in infant mortality and acute adult deaths from disease or trauma. Thus, the premature infant, the child with meningomyelocele, the teenager with traumatic quadriplegia, the middle-aged man with an acute myocardial infarction, the elderly woman with a hip fracture, and the elderly man with bacterial pneumonia, all of whom would probably have died 50 years ago, are now likely to survive their medical crisis and live for many years. But these victories over acute disease breed new problems—chronic illness and functional disability. Long-term care (LTC) is a reflection of this shift from acute to chronic illness in modern society. We have been able to add years to life, but can we add life to the years?

Katz and colleagues (1983) have illustrated this paradox in their concept of "active life expectancy." By dividing life expectancy into "active" and "dependent" segments they have demonstrated that a significant portion of the lifespan beyond age 65 is spent in a nonindependent state that requires community-based or institutional LTC. This is particularly true of elderly women (see Table 1). In this context rehabilitation can be seen as an intervention strategy whose goal is to maximize active life expectancy while minimizing dependent life expectancy or, in Rusk's striking phrase, to live within the limits of one's disability but to the hilt of one's ability (Rusk 1977). Before discussing the rehabilitation process, however, we need to examine the nature and prevalence of the functional disabilities that are such a major component of the needs of older people receiving LTC services.

## THE SEMANTICS AND DEMOGRAPHY OF GERIATRIC DISABILITY

Pivotal to the understanding of the nature of rehabilitation is a clear distinction of the terms impairment, disability and handicap. The World Health Organization (1980) has defined these terms as follows:

| | |
|---|---|
| *Impairment:* | Abnormality or absence of an organ, body part, or physiologic system. This represents disease at the *organ* level. An example might be the lens opacification associated with cataract formation. |
| *Disability:* | The *physical* disadvantage, or problem in performing tasks, associated with an impairment. This represents disease at the *personal* level. An example might be reduced visual acuity to 20/100 with inability to read printed material resulting from cataract. |
| *Handicap:* | The *social* disadvantage resulting from an impairment, affecting an individual's ability to satisfactorily perform his or her social role. This represents disease at the *societal* level. An example might be the inability to maintain written correspondence or to read mail resulting from a cataract. |

*Table 1.*

Percentage of Independent Years
(Active Life Expectancy/Total Life
Expectancy) for Elderly Men and Women

|              | *Percentage of Independent Years* | | |
| Age (yr.)    | Total | Men | Women |
|--------------|-------|-----|-------|
| 65-69        | 61    | 71  | 54    |
| 70-74        | 57    | 69  | 50    |
| 75-79        | 59    | 68  | 54    |
| 80-84        | 53    | 65  | 49    |
| ≥ 85         | 40    | 51  | 36    |

Reprinted with permission from S. Katz et al., Active life expectancy. *N. Engl. J. Med.* 309:1218-1224, 1983.

Implicit in these definitions is the role of environment and social expectations in determining the degree of disability and particularly handicap. Identical impairments can result in very different handicaps depending on an individual's social role or physical environment. For example, an arthritic hip may not pose much of a handicap to someone living in a first floor apartment or an apartment with elevators, but it may become a nearly insurmountable handicap if the individual lives in a third floor walk-up apartment.

These semantics are not merely academic; they have implications for the distribution of rehabilitation and LTC services. As indicated in Table 2, which lists the 15 commonest chronic conditions (i.e., impairments) among older men and women, arthritis is by far the most prevalent impairment among the elderly (over 40 percent have it to some degree), while heart disease is considerably less prevalent (approximately 27 percent of the elderly). Yet the magnitude of these two common conditions is about equal in terms of prevalence of the disability they produce, and in fact, heart disease exceeds arthritis as a cause of major disability (Fulton and Katz 1986).

About 80 percent of noninstitutionalized people aged 65 and older have one or more chronic conditions, with arthritis, hypertension, hearing loss and heart disease accounting for 60 percent of the total. Nevertheless, the great majority of the community-based elderly have no problems performing basic activities of daily living (ADLs) such as dressing, grooming, feeding and toileting, or in performing instrumental activities of daily living (IADLs) such as shopping, cooking and money management. One 1979 study reported that 9 percent of the elderly needed help with one or more ADL tasks, with 11 percent needing help with one or more IADLs, but these proportions rose to 35 and 40 percent, respectively, in those aged 85 or older. A 1982 survey of Medicare enrollees found that 19 percent had functional disabilities in ADLs or IADLs of at least three months' duration.

*Table 2.*

Fifteen Common Chronic Conditions in Elderly Men and Women

| | Condition | Male Prevalence (percentage) |
|---|---|---|
| 1. | Arthritis | 35.5 |
| 2. | Hearing impairment | 32.7 |
| 3. | Hypertension | 31.5 |
| 4. | Heart conditions | 26.6 |
| 5. | Chronic sinusitis | 13.5 |
| 6. | Arteriosclerosis | 12.2 |
| 7. | Visual impairment | 12.0 |
| 8. | Orthopedic impairment | 7.7 |
| 9. | Diabetes | 7.4 |
| 10. | Hernia | 7.1 |
| 11. | Emphysema | 6.8 |
| 12. | Prostate disease | 5.8 |

| | Condition | Female Prevalence (percentage) |
|---|---|---|
| 1. | Arthritis | 50.4 |
| 2. | Hypertension | 43.4 |
| 3. | Heart conditions | 28.1 |
| 4. | Hearing impairment | 25.0 |
| 5. | Chronic sinusitis | 17.1 |
| 6. | Varicose veins | 12.6 |
| 7. | Arteriosclerosis | 12.5 |
| 8. | Visual impairment | 11.8 |
| 9. | Orthopedic impairment | 10.9 |
| 10. | Diabetes | 8.4 |
| 11. | Constipation | 8.0 |
| 12. | Hemorrhoids | 7.6 |

Reprinted with permission from D.L. Rabin and P. Stockton, *Long-Term Care for the Elderly: A Fact Book.* New York: Oxford University Press, 1987.

One should not overlook the acute-care hospital when reviewing the degree of functional disability among the elderly, for it is frequently the transitional stage between community living and permanent institutionalization for older patients. These patients are not only ill when admitted to hospital, they also have significant functional deficits. Warshaw and colleagues (1982), in a survey of 279 hospitalized patients aged 70 or older, found that 34 percent had impaired hearing, 40 percent had impaired vision, and 5 percent had speech impairments. More than one-half of the patients aged 75 or older required ADL assistance. More recently, Hirsch and colleagues (1990) did multiple assessments of function in 71 patients over age 74 admitted to Stanford University Hospital: an estimate of function two weeks prior to admission, an assessment two days after admission, another on the day prior to discharge, and a final estimate one week after discharge. Statistically significant declines from preadmission function occurred in mobility, transfers, toileting, feeding and grooming; none of these had improved significantly by the day prior to discharge, and there was even some further decline in certain functions (e.g., mobility) between day 2 and the day prior to discharge.

What do the foregoing studies tell us? They document that the great majority (80 to 90 percent) of noninstitutionalized elders are physically functioning at a relatively high level that is compatible with independent living with little or no need for LTC services, and that most of those who function suboptimally and do need LTC services are likely to be 85 or older. They also indicate that hospitalization may contribute to the downward spiral of functional dependence that leads to the need for institutional LTC in a nursing home or similar facility.

But is this downward spiral inevitable, and is a similar progressive decline in overall function (disability or handicap) to be accepted as the norm for an aging individual? Bortz (1982, 1989) has argued forcefully against such a pessimistic view. Citing evidence in the cardiovascular research literature that demonstrates the potential reversal in aerobic fitness (maximal oxygen consumption) that has been formerly judged as a normal aging change, he points out that a maximally fit 70 year old may have the same oxygen carrying capacity as an unfit 30 year old. Calling upon the laws of thermodynamics he has propounded the concept of aging as entropy and has stressed the central role of disuse in the development of aging-related changes. By doing so, Bortz has provided the ideal link between aging, its associated disabilities, and the role of rehabilitation as a therapeutic intervention. Disuse atrophy and deconditioning have long been the focus of rehabilitation research and therapies, so it should come as no surprise that the rehabilitation paradigm should fit neatly into Bortz' conceptual model of aging.

## THE REHABILITATION PROCESS

Rehabilitation can be defined in the most literal way as the process of making a person able once again. This implies that at some point a previous homeostatic level of function has deteriorated to the extent that affected individuals are no longer capable of functioning adequately based on their physical (disability) and social (handicap) needs. Any impairment can cause this change; in fact, a social change (e.g., death of a spouse or significant other) can result in a similar homeostatic imbalance. In some cases, as with a limb amputation, the impairment is permanent and total; in others, as with a stroke, some degree of recovery may take place. In any event, these patients become immediately or progressively unable to perform ADLs and IADLs, and to maintain their prior social existence.

The rehabilitation process was developed in the 1930s and 1940s by pioneering physicians such as Henry Kessler and Howard Rusk. It was utilized mainly for disabled children and young adults, particularly those injured during World Wars I and II. What made the rehabilitation model unusual and distinct from the more traditional medical model was its focus on function rather than disease (disability versus impairment), its concern for psychosocial consequences (handicap), its interdisciplinary team, and the participatory role of the patient within the team itself. Despite the younger clientele in the early days of medical rehabilitation, with their clear vocational goals, the rehabilitation model was found to be highly appropriate for the treatment of disabling diseases in the elderly.

Rusk conceptualized rehabilitation as the third stage of medical care (prevention and acute care being the first and second): "when the fever is down and the stitches are out," but in the case of the elderly patient with functional disability this separation should not be taken too literally. Based on the aforementioned study by Hirsch and colleagues (1990) on hospitalized patients, rehabilitative therapy is indicated by day 2 of an acute hospitalization, since it could prevent or even reverse the functional deterioration associated with acute illness. It may be more helpful to think of the rehabilitation process as a triage point for the LTC system. The elderly person with functional disability needs to be evaluated for the potential for those disabilities to be altered or eliminated through treatment. Remediation through rehabilitation may avoid the need for community-based LTC or for institutionalization. Conversely, the failure of a trial of rehabilitation may ultimately result in a decision to resort to institutional LTC. Thus, rehabilitation is a major component of geriatric assessment.

Where does rehabilitation take place, and who does it? Much has been written about the rehabilitation milieu, with the utopian ideal being a modern purpose-built rehabilitation department (for outpatients) or rehabilitation unit (for hospital inpatients), but the process can be independent of such facilities. The personnel and their philosophy take precedence over the environment. Successful rehabilitation can take place in a nursing home, on a general medical-surgical hospital floor, in an outpatient setting, or in a person's own home. Regardless of locale, the following professional personnel need to be part of the evaluating team: (1) a physician with interest and preferably expertise in rehabilitation of the elderly (geriatrician, physiatrist); (2) a physical therapist; (3) an occupational therapist; (4) a speech-language pathologist; (5) a social worker; (6) a psychologist or psychiatrist and (7) a nurse. Others (e.g., dietician, pastoral counselor, recreation therapist) may also be part of this team as indicated by the case under consideration. The essential requirement for the effective operation of this team of specialists is that it be not just multidisciplinary (everyone gives an opinion) but truly interdisciplinary (opinions are mutually communicated among team members).

The team process generally consists of (1) individual assessments by selected members of the team, (2) conference to discuss assessment results and establish goals, (3) ongoing treatment and (4) periodic reassessment and conference discussion. Though this procedure is a straightforward one, it is actually extremely difficult to organize and maintain a truly interdisciplinary team held together by bonds of unanimity of mission and mutual respect.

## SPECIAL ISSUES IN GERIATRIC REHABILITATION

When the rehabilitation process briefly outlined above is applied to elderly patients there are several special factors that must be borne in mind. The first is the multisystem nature of the pathologic processes associated with aging, which leads to multiple rather than single impairments. It is not unusual to encounter a 75-year-old diabetic who has visual problems from diabetic retinopathy, a below-knee amputation, a previous myocardial infarction, and some degree of hearing loss. Given this complex of problems one cannot simply pick a "generic" rehabilitation program like "amputee rehab," "cardiac rehab" or "vision rehab." Each impairment and its attendant disability needs to be given equal attention, and their potential interactions must be considered. For example, the hypothetical (but wholly plausible) patient above may or may not be capable of using a prosthesis, with the primary determinant being not the strength of his remaining leg but the adequacy of his cardiac reserve to tolerate the increased energy expenditure associated with prosthetic ambulation. Notwithstanding the multiple nature of geriatric disability, the literature attests to the considerable rehabilitation potential of these individuals. To give but one example, 75 percent of 12 blind elderly amputees became ambulatory with a prosthesis despite their double disability (Altner, Rusin and DeBoer 1980).

Another special consideration in elderly patients undergoing rehabilitation is their reduced tolerance for certain activities and environments. Many require rest periods during the day, particularly when undergoing a rigorous day-long series of treatments on an inpatient basis. Reduced tolerance of temperature extremes may require the avoidance of relatively warm environments such as a heated therapeutic pool. Circulatory insufficiency in the legs may even make it unwise to use local forms of heat that could increase oxygen demand to the area being heated.

Osteoporosis is very common among the elderly, particularly in postmenopausal women, and its presence places the patient at risk for fractures of the femur and distal radius. Because of the increased fragility of osteoporotic bone, vigorous types of physical or occupational therapy, such as the passive stretching used to reduce joint contractures, needs to be performed with caution or with reduced force.

Psychosocial considerations loom large in the assessment of elderly patients. Many are widowed and therefore lack the personal assistance that a spouse or significant other can provide as a form of informal LTC. Moreover, the children of these elderly people often live considerable distances away and cannot provide direct care either. Friends in the neighborhood may also be elderly and therefore unable to physically assist in IADL tasks like shopping or cleaning.

## CONCLUSIONS: THE ROLE OF REHABILITATION IN LONG-TERM CARE

Elderly people usually require LTC services because (1) they lack social support, (2) they are mentally incapable of managing themselves safely, or (3) they are physically unable to care for themselves. The first of these problems can only be remedied by the provision of personal services or institutionalization, that is, by having recourse to the LTC system. The second problem is more often than not irreversible except if there is an underlying medical cause (e.g., anemia, hypoglycemia) or a treatable psychiatric diagnosis (e.g., depression). The functional disabilities associated with aging are by far the most amenable to successful treatment of the major contributors to the need for LTC. The rehabilitation paradigm, forged in the crucible of World War II as a way to restore wounded young veterans (mostly male) to productive life and gainful employment, is equally pertinent to the plight of elderly disabled civilians (more often female) whose frailty places them at heightened risk for institutional placement. The face of health care has been forever altered by the conquest of most acute illnesses, leaving in their wake a new challenge in the many chronic diseases which increasingly dominate hospitals and doctors' offices. This modern epidemic of chronic illness is to some extent iatrogenic—the side-effect of our medical progress—and it has spawned the LTC revolution that is now of such concern to health care planners and providers alike.

Rehabilitation is not a panacea for the chronic problems facing the disabled elderly, but it offers an opportunity to halt the functional decline that often leads to institutional placement. When home-based LTC versus institutional LTC is being debated, the results of comprehensive rehabilitation intervention will as often as not cast the deciding vote.

## REFERENCES

Altner P.E., J.J. Rusin and A. DeBoer. Rehabilitation of blind patients with lower extremity amputations. *Arch. Phys. Med. Rehabil.* 61:82-85, 1980.

Bortz W.M. Disuse and aging. *JAMA* 248:1203-1208, 1982.

Bortz W.M. Redefining human aging. *J. Am. Geriatrics Soc.* 37:1092-1096, 1989.

DeJong G. and R. Lifchez. Physical disability and public policy. *Sci. Am.* 248:40-50, 1983.

Fulton, J.P. and S. Katz. Characteristics of the Disabled Elderly and Implications for Rehabilitation. In S.J. Brody and G.E. Ruff, eds., *Aging and Rehabilitation: Advances in the State of the Art.* New York: Springer Publishing, 1986.

Hing, E., E. Sekscenski and G. Strahan. *The National Nursing Home Survey: 1985 Summary for the United States.* Vital and Health Statistics, Series 13, No. 97. Washington, DC: National Center for Health Statistics, 1989.

Hirsch, C.H., L. Sommers, A. Olsen, L. Mullen and C. Hutner Winograd. The natural history of functional morbidity in hospitalized older patients. *J. Am. Geriatrics Soc.* 38:1296-1303, 1990.

Katz, S., L.G. Branch, M.H. Branson, J.A. Papsidero, J. Beck and D.S. Greer. Active life expectancy. *N. Engl. J. Med.* 309:1218-1224, 1983.

Kovar, M.G., G. Hendershot, E. Mathis. Older people in the United States who receive help with basic activities of daily living. *Am. J. Public Health* 792:778-779, 1989.

Rabin, D.L. and P. Stockton. *Long-Term Care for the Elderly: A Fact Book.* New York: Oxford University Press, 1987.

Rusk, H.A. *A World to Care For: The Autobiography of Howard A. Rusk.* New York: Random House, 1977.

Warshaw, G.A., J.T. Moore, S.W. Friedman, C.T. Currie, D.C. Kennie, W.J. Kane and P.A. Mears. Functional disability in the hospitalized elderly. *JAMA* 248:847-850, 1982.

World Health Organization. *International Classification of Impairments, Disabilities, and Handicaps (ICIDH).* Geneva: World Health Organization, 1980.

# 20

# The History of Respite for the Elderly in the United States

*Lois Grau, PhD, RN*

Describing the history and goals of respite care is, to a certain extent, a subjective matter. This is because the concept of respite is open to a wide range of interpretations as a result of its broad and functionally based definition. Although definitions vary somewhat, most have in common the notion that respite care is temporary (or intermittent) substitute care designed to provide relief to the primary caregiver (see Gwyther 1986; Meltzer 1982). On this basis, respite could encompass any type of temporary relief from the responsibility of caring for another person, whether a baby, a child, an adult or an older person. However, the concept of respite has been refined and formalized as a result of a number of factors, including technological, regulatory and reimbursement changes in the health care system; the rapid growth in the numbers and proportion of older persons in the population; and the subsequent emergence of Alzheimer's disease as a major health problem and a social and economic issue. Because little has been written on the history of respite, this chapter will attempt to piece together some of the forces and factors that have influenced the emergence of respite as an increasingly important component of the long-term care system in the United States.

## EARLY DEVELOPMENTS IN THE UNITED STATES

Historically, European countries have long provided respite or respite-like services to the families of the chronically ill and frail elderly persons. In the United States, respite care first appeared in the statutes of several states in the early 1970s as a component of services for developmentally disabled persons (Dickman and Warren 1981). In the latter part of that decade the term respite was applied to a small number of programs for the elderly. The Foundation for Long-Term Care conducted a comprehensive literature review in 1983 and found only two U.S. journal articles on respite for the elderly published prior to 1980. The first article, "Respite Care Program," published in the *Journal of Gerontological Nursing* (1977), reported on an in-home respite program in Wisconsin. The program provided services to families of developmentally disabled or elderly persons. The second article, "A Community-Based Continuing Care Program for the Elderly Disabled," published in the *Journal of Gerontology* (1977), described the continuing care program for severely disabled elderly in Oxford, England, which included in-home care as well as short-term hospital readmission.

These early U.S. publications represent the first steps in the societal legitimization of respite as a specific type of formal service. However, it is important to note that this definition is functional rather than structural in kind. That is, despite having a common name, these early programs differed in their settings, staffing patterns and program activities. What they have in common is the direct acknowledgment of their major purpose, i.e., the provision of temporary relief from caregiving on the part of family members.

The need to acknowledge the use of home care, day care and hospital care as a temporary substitute for family care was the result, in large measure, of specific historical transitions in the nation's health care system and attitudes toward the care of the frail elderly. In the years prior to the advent of cost-effective strategies and cost containment measures that characterize today's health care system, service use was often a function of both health and social care needs. For example, it was not uncommon for physicians to extend a hospital length of stay, or even incur a hospital admission, when such care was not warranted in exclusively medical terms (Gwyther 1986). Such hospital stays were often triggered by an acute illness of the primary family caregiver or by social factors such as a lack of access to informal family care. Institutional care was also encouraged as a result of the lack of skilled nursing and other home care programs and services. For similar reasons, "retirement," "old age" and "nursing homes" housed persons who today would be ineligible for care as a result of their relatively uncompromised functional status.

## THE RECOGNITION OF THE ROLE OF THE FAMILY

The use of institutional care, particularly the hospital, to meet social as well as health care needs was undertaken with little fanfare. Prior to passage of the Medicare and Medicaid legislation in 1965, little attention was given to the distinction between the health care needs of the patient and the caregiving ability of the family. This was for a number of reasons. First, prior to the 1960s, hospitals were not overly taxed by the care of a disproportionate number of elderly persons, as occurred in latter years, because the demographic shift to an older population was in its early phases. Also, the lack of costly and sophisticated diagnostic and treatment modalities, and the need to employ them based on medical norms and legal pressures, had yet to come into play. Nor was there the need to rationalized health care use on the basis of medical typologies such as those employed in today's case-mix reimbursements systems.

The increasing number and proportion of older persons in the population and disproportionate utilization of hospital beds became a recognized concern in the early 1960s. The need to free hospital beds for acutely ill persons contributed to the establishment of the 1965 Medicare provision for skilled nursing home care, and Medicaid's intermediate-level nursing home care program. The unexpectedly high costs of insti-tutional care to these federal programs focused attention on nursing home quality, cost and utilization issues during the late 1960s and 1970s. During this time the myth that long-term care institutions and other service agencies had replaced the family in providing care to frail elderly persons remained intact among the general public (Shanas 1979b). However, the fact that the ratio of severely impaired in the community was twice the proportion of old people in institutions was recognized by gerontologists, as was the fact that this ratio did not significantly change following the implementation of Medicare and Medicaid (Shanas 1979a).

The growing recognition of the importance of the family's role in the care of the frail elderly generated early studies of the characteristics of family caregiving situations (Cantor and Johnson 1978; Shanas, 1977; Johnson 1979; Horowitz 1978) and the burden of providing such care (Lebowitz 1978; Rathbone-McCluan 1976; Fengler and Goodrich 1979). These studies led to investigations of the role formal services played in reducing the emotional strain associated with family care. Although the term respite itself was not used, a number of studies found that formal service use provided relief from caregiving responsibilities. For example, in a study of geriatric day care patients, families reported that the program helped to reduce family tension, alleviated the burden of care and served as a "last-ditch" effort to maintain the older person in the community (Rathbone-McCuan 1976). Horowitz (1978) found that in-home services provided the caregiver with freedom to engage in other activities and freedom from the emotional pressure of having primary responsibility for caregiving. Similarly, Gross-Andrews and Zimmer (1977) reported that the provision of up to four services resulted in self-reported alleviation of stress and emotional, physical and social disruption.

These early studies of the impact of formal service use on family caregivers did not technically address the concept of respite as it is currently understood because the length of service provision was not taken into account. Respite care, by definition, is the provision of temporary care. (However, the public policy debate continues as to what is meant by "temporary" care.) Such studies did, however, point to the efficacy of formal services in providing relief to family caregivers.

## THE INFLUENCE OF EXISTING HEALTH CARE STRUCTURES

The recognition of the crucial role of families in the care of the elderly and their need for formal services to supplement family care represented the first stage in the evolution of formal respite programs. A second factor of importance was the emergence of adult day care programs in the late 1970s and 1980s. In the U.S., major initiatives for the development of adult day care came from the community rather than from federal or state agencies or funding sources. Because of this, there were only about 617 adult day care programs in 46 states in 1980 (Palmer 1982). This number has grown during the past decade, but such programs still suffer as a result of minimal federal funding.

Adult day care programs are often described in terms of their primary functions. Three models prevail. They are restorative programs, which focus on rehabilitation; maintenance programs, which address primarily custodial care issues; and social programs, which provide social activities and stimulation. Of these, the latter two—custodial and social models—most closely approximate contemporary day care respite programs. The major difference between adult day care and respite programs is their stated mission. The former focuses on the elderly person as the client and recipient of care. That respite is provided to family caregivers is simply an artifact of the service. This distinction is also true between in-home services, such as those provided by a home health aide, and in-home respite. In-home care funded by Medicare, Medicaid and many private insurers prohibits the provision of any service or assistance to family members. For example, Medicare home health aides are not allowed to wash other than the client's laundry or to clean areas of the home not used by the client.

Nursing homes have also contributed to the development of respite programs by providing a logical environment for the provision of overnight respite care. Once again, however, the issue of temporary care has limited the utilization of nursing homes as sites for respite care. Because nursing homes are long-term care institutions, regulatory requirements create barriers to the admission of short-stay patients. Staff time required to meet admission documentary requirements, coupled with the need for medical examinations and laboratory studies, makes short-term admissions a costly enterprise beyond that which most nursing homes can afford. Inpatient respite is also disadvantaged by the lack of predictability of admissions and the consequent likelihood of empty beds. Another issue is the need of such programs to provide support and assistance to family members to comply with the stated philosophy of respite. Such services typically focus on the need of family members for information about community-based services and programs and permanent institutional placement, areas that are typically not germane to social service departments within nursing homes.

## THE FORMALIZATION OF RESPITE CARE

The formalization of respite care rests on two sets of understandings. As discussed earlier, the first evolved from the recognition of the crucial role families play in the provision of care to older persons and the burden of this care on the emotional, physical, and financial well-being of families. The second foundation is the scope of formal services upon which respite care is built. They include adult day care programs, in-home services and nursing home care. The major distinction between these traditional services and respite care is the later's exclusive focus on the client, rather than on the client and the family caregiver. A second, less clear-cut distinction is duration of service. Respite care is defined as temporary supportive care. Adult day care and in-home care may or may not be temporary, while nursing home care is generally not.

Respite care developed in the United States to meet two needs: to fill gaps in the continuum of care and to support family members involved in primary care. The second purpose, the care and support of family members, has emerged as most important in distinguishing respite care from other services. The recognition that the service is geared toward both patient and family member has important public policy implications. For example, in Medicare home care services, service use is exclusively determined by the patient's medical health status vis-à-vis service entitlement. Similarly, access to Medicaid-funded nursing home care is a function of the patient's health care status (and financial resources). In contract, because respite's primary function is the relief of family caregivers, the patient's mental and physical functional status is of secondary importance. It can simply be assumed that the provision of family care reflects the fact of a need for this care and for periodic relief from the burden it engenders for family members.

The focus on family need rather than the patient's health care status may, in part, be the result of the strong association between respite care and Alzheimer's disease. The "discovery" of Alzheimer's disease by the public in the 1980s, and subsequent public knowledge of and sensitivity to its devastating consequences, provided general support for the need for various types of supportive services by both patients and families. This awareness, coupled with the strong support of respite programs by national and state Alzheimer's Associations, has resulted in most respite programs limiting their services to families caring for persons with Alzheimer's disease or a related disorder.

This focus on Alzheimer's patients and their families makes sense from a number of perspectives. First, targeting programs to this group results in a patient/family population with similar needs. As a result, program staffing and activities can be tailored to the needs of this particular group of clients. In addition, regulatory and reimbursement public policy can be shaped in accordance with the generally known symptomatology of dementing disorders and consequent resources needed by programs to provide appropriate care.

The expressed need for respite care by families who care for Alzheimer's patients has also encouraged the link between respite and dementia. For example, the 1987 Report of the U.S. Congressional Office of Technology Assessment (OTA) notes that of the top ten services rated as "essential or most important," six could be construed as related to respite care. In addition, California's five-year Family Survival Project recorded respite care as one of the most needed forms of service for caregivers of people with brain impairments (Petty and Wolf, 1982-85).

Despite the perceived need for respite care by families caring for persons with Alzheimer's disease, access to respite remains limited. A study by George (1986) found respite care was cited as the most desired but least available community service. Similarly, a study of both active and former caregivers of persons with Alzheimer's disease found that fully 46.5 percent of active caregivers cited in-home respite care as the "most useful but not available" service (Fortinsky and Hathaway 1990).

Although respite programs have evolved slowly, there is a strong trend toward an increase in their numbers. Many model programs exist that range from voluntary church-sponsored day respite centers to resource centers for brain-impaired adults. The efforts of the Older Women's League (1983) in sponsoring legislation in several states in the 1980s to encourage the development of state-wide respite services brought the need for this type of care to the attention of the public. The Robert Wood Johnson Foundation, in collaboration with the Alzheimer's Association, has funded ten respite programs, each representing somewhat different models of care. These centers also receive support from the Federal Administration on Aging. In addition, respite care is mandated in some state-sponsored programs such as the Illinois Alzheimer's Disease Program, the New York State Expanded In-Home Services for the Elderly Program and California's Alzheimer's Disease Institute (Petty 1990).

Despite these gains, the perceived need for respite care continues to outstrip available resources. This is, in large measure, the result of limited governmental funding. With the exception of New York State, government funds only limited amounts of respite care. As noted by Petty (1990), because the care provided to the patient is often defined as "personal" rather than "skilled" care, Medicare does not reimburse for respite. Medicaid waiver projects did support 24 respite programs in 1985 and, in some states, the program continues to pay for limited out-of-home day care (Rabbitt 1986; Kemper et al. 1987). These programs are, however, limited in scope and subject to wide state-to-state variation in the number and funding of respite programs.

## BARRIERS TO THE DEVELOPMENT OF RESPITE CARE PROGRAMS

In the current era of cost containment in health care, major barriers to federal support and funding of respite programs are the costs of program implementation and lack of certainty as to whether these costs will be offset by savings engendered by reduced use of institutional care. The OTA reviewed several studies of home care and concluded that such community-based services do not generally substitute for nursing home care (Office of Technology Assessment 1987). The Family Survival Project found, over its five-year history, that avoiding or deterring institutional placement fluctuated from year to year. It was thought that differences in patient and caregiver age, and cognitive and physical status may account for this variation. Other studies (e.g., George 1986; Mace and Rubins 1984) found service to increase shortly before placement in an institution or death of the client. The OTA study also found that the provision of respite may postpone nursing home placement of persons who are ultimately sicker when admitted to nursing homes or hospitals, thus contributing to higher costs at that stage (Office of Technology Assessment 1987). It also needs to be noted that factors such as the availability of nursing home beds, private pay fees and proportion of Medicaid beds in the local area are major sources of influence on the timing of institutionalization. Hence, cost-containment arguments for the implementation of respite care are at best shaky. As noted by Petty (1990), "respite care cannot possible preclude the need for more intensive care in the late stages of dementing illness, in the event of severe or acute illness of the caregiver, or in other circumstances calling for more formal intervention."

The provision of respite care does represent a cost-effective strategy vis-à-vis the provision of 24-hour in-home care. However, it is unlikely that persons who require this level of care would be able to be supported by respite care alone. The lack of adequate family care, as suggested by the need for round-the-clock in-home services, most likely would result in respite serving only as a supplement to formal in-home care.

Another barrier to the growth and utilization of respite programs by Alzheimer's clients and their families is the lack of appropriateness of this type of care for some individuals. Family caregivers may fear that even short-term respite will disrupt their caregiving routines and open the door to institutionalization. Other families fear exposing their loved one to strangers because they are afraid of inadequate care or hesitate to expose their loved one to the behavior of other demented persons. It may also be that patients or caregivers are too ill or disabled to be cared for at home or to attend a day care program. To deal with this problem, some agencies require home visits prior to admission to determine the appropriateness of the program for individual clients and their families (Ellis 1986; California Health and Welfare Agency 1987; Quinn and Crabtree 1987).

An area of potential debate that may eventually thwart the implementation of respite programs is the growing linkage between the concept of respite care and Alzheimer's disease. Although respite care is an obviously important resource for families caring for persons with

Alzheimer's disease, the establishment of a specific set of services on the basis of medical diagnostic criteria raises a number of questions and concerns. First, the use of diagnostic criteria compromises the hard-fought battle to shift entitlement and reimbursement from disease-based criteria to functional status and behavioral descriptors. To limit or even suggest a limitation of services to persons with Alzheimer's disease and related disorders ignores the functional and behavioral variation that occurs during the course of a dementing illness. It also fails to take into account the extent to which symptom expression and family need during the course of a dementing illness may be similar or identical to that experienced by persons with other disorders such as Parkinson's disease, stroke and multiple sclerosis.

A second danger is the possibility that a disease-specific focus blankets the need of families caring for elderly persons with other disorders for some form of respite care. An obvious analogue is the development of Medicare hospice programs in the United States. These programs are limited to cancer patients who are anticipated to die within 6 months. Moreover, the inpatient component of most such programs is restricted to those who are expected to expire within two months. The strategy of limiting such care to a single diagnostic group is the result of major support by the American Cancer Society for hospice care, as well as cost-containment concerns. The ability to make relatively accurate prognostic statements for patients in the terminal phase cancer makes possible a time cap on service delivery. From a programmatic perspective, it also enables a careful delineation. One of the program goals specifically concerns pain control and quality of life. However, at the same time, other terminal patients and their families, with less certain prognostic trajectories, are not afforded the holistic, family-centered care that characterizes the philosophy of hospice. These individuals die in inappropriate acute care centers, in nursing homes that may or may not be versed in the care of the dying, or in the home with limited or nonexistent Medicare in-home services.

The implementation of disease-specific programs may also increase fragmentation within the health care system. Older persons and families with similar or identical needs may be filtered through different agencies and reimbursement systems on the basis of their major presenting illness. For example, it is likely that a very frail elderly person will be channeled into a day care program, while an Alzheimer's patient will be placed in a respite program. This may not be problematic if both programs offer similar services. However, by definition, the philosophy of respite, which focuses on family relief from care, should be reflected in specific program characteristics (e.g., flexible hours or counseling). If this is not the case, there is little justification for distinguishing respite from other programs with similar structural and programmatic characteristics.

The future of respite should be determined by the need for such services based on the assessment of family caregivers rather than on cost-containment outcomes. Whether this will occur is uncertain. However, the likelihood of the inclusion of respite as a routine and accessible part of the long-term care system will be enhanced if the need for such care is determined by the intensity, duration and burden of caregiving on the part of all family members responsible for older persons who can no longer care for themselves.

## REFERENCES

California Health and Welfare Agency, Department of Mental Health. *Regional Resource Centers for Families and Caregivers of Brain-impaired Adults Operations Manual: Policies and Procedures Pursuant to the Implementation of Chapter 1658.* Sacramento: California Health and Welfare Agency, 1987.

Cantor, M. and J. Johnson. The Informal Support System of the 'Familyless' Elderly—Who Takes Over? Paper presented at Annual Gerontological Society Meeting, Dallas, November 1978.

Dickman, I.R. and R.D. Warren. *For This Respite Much Thanks: Concepts, Guidelines and Issues in the Development of Community Respite Services.* New York: United Cerebral Palsy Association, 1981.

Ellis, V. Introducing Patients and Families to Respite. In R.J.V. Montgomery and J. Prothero, eds., *Developing Respite Services for the Elderly.* Seattle: University of Washington Press, 1986.

Fengler, A. and N. Goodrich. Wives of elderly disabled men: the hidden patients. *Gerontologist* 19(2), April 1979.

Fortinsky, R. and T.J. Hathaway. Information and service needs among active and former family caregivers of persons with Alzheimer's disease. *Gerontologist* 30(5), October 1990.

Foundation of Long-Term Care. *Respite Care for the Frail Elderly: A Summary Report on Institutional Respite Research and Operations.* Albany: The Center for the Study of Aging, 1983.

George, L.K. *Respite Care: Evaluating a Strategy for Easing Caregiver Burden.* Durham, NC: Center for the Study of Aging and Human Development, 1986.

George, L.K., L.P. Gwyther, E.L. Ballard, G.G. Fillenbaum and E.B. Palmore. *Respite Care Use: Predicting Length of Use and Reasons for Dropout.* Durham, NC: Center for the Study of Aging and Human Development, 1987.

Gross-Andrews, S. and A. Zimmer. Incentive to Families Caring for Disabled Elderly: Research and Demonstration Project to Strengthen the National

Supports System. Paper presented at the Annual Gerontological Meeting, November, 1977.

Gwyther, L. Introduction: What is Respite Care? *Pride Inst. J. Long-Term Home Health Care* 5:5-6, 1986.

Horowitz, A. Families Who Care: A Study of Natural Support Systems of the Elderly. Paper presented at the Annual Meeting of the Gerontological Society, November 1978.

Johnson, C. Impediments to Family Supports to Dependent Elderly: An Analysis of the Primary Caregivers. Paper presented at the Annual Gerontological Society Meeting, Washington, DC, November 1979.

Kemper, P., R. Applebaum and M. Harrigan. Community care demonstrations: what have we learned? *Health Care Financing Rev.* 8(4), 1987.

Lebowitz, B. Old age and family functioning. *J. Gerontol. Social Work* 2:111-118, Winter, 1978.

Mace, N.L., P.V. Rabins. *A Survey of Day Care for the Demented Adult in the United States.* Washington, DC: The National Council on the Aging, 1984.

Meltzer, J. *Respite Care: An Emerging Family Support Service.* Washington, DC: Center for Study of Social Policy, 1982.

Office of Technology Assessment. *Losing a Million Minds: Confronting the Tragedy of Alzheimer's Disease and Other Dementias.* Pub. No. OIA-BA-323. Washington, DC: U.S. Government Printing Office, April 1987.

Older Women's League. *Model Legislation for Respite Care Services.* Washington, DC: Older Women's League, 1983.

Palmer, H.C. Adult Day Care. In R.J. Vogel and H.C. Palmer, eds., *Long-Term Care: Perspectives from Research and Demonstrations.* New York: Haworth, 1982.

Petty, D.M. Respite Care: A Flexible Response to Service Fragmentation. In N.L. Mace, ed., *Dementia Care: Patient, Family and Community.* New York: Brunner/Mazel, 1990.

Petty, D.M. and A. Wolf. *Annual Report of a State Pilot Project to Assist Families of Brain-damaged Family Members. Reports for Years 1982-82, 1982-83, 1983-84, and 1984-85.* San Francisco: Family Survival Project, 1982-85.

Quinn, T. and J. Crabtree, eds. *How to Start a Respite Service for People with Alzheimer's and Their Families: A Guide for Community-Based Organizations.* New York: The Brookdale Foundation and the Brookdale Center on Aging of Hunter College, 1987.

Rabbitt, W.J. The New York Respite Demonstration Program. In R.J.V. Montgomery and J. Prothero, eds., *Developing Respite Services for the Elderly.* Seattle: University of Washington Press, 1986

Rathbone-McCuan, E. Geriatric day care: a family perspective. *Gerontologist* 16(6):517-521, 1976.

Shanas, E. Social myth as hypothesis: the case of family relations of old people. *Gerontologist* 19:1, 3-9, 1979.

Shanas, E. The family as a social support system in old age. *Gerontologist* 19(1):169-174, 1979.

Shanas, E. *National Survey of the Aged, Final Report to the Administration on Aging.* AoA Grant No. 90-A-369. Washington, DC: Administration on Aging, 1977.

# 21

# Developing Long-Term Care Roles for America's Senior Centers

*Roger H. Sherman, PhD*

## ON THE SIDELINES

Despite their remarkable growth, senior centers have yet to establish for themselves clear and significant roles in America's long-term care system. From an estimated 218 centers in 1961 to the more than 10,000 estimated in 1985 (Schulder 1985), senior centers have multiplied by focusing their attention on the interests of healthy older people and by offering a great variety of activities and services. As a consequence, however, senior centers have typically failed to play critical roles in long-term care.

Such an assessment of the peripheral role of most senior centers in long-term care is certainly not original. Kane and Kane (1987), for example, remarked, "Senior centers...cannot be construed as long-term care" because they serve few individuals who are functionally impaired. They noted the "potential" of centers as focal points "for information and referral and support to family caregivers." Less explicitly but in a similar vein, Huttman (1985) identified no clear long-term care role for centers; she highlighted instead the importance of centers as a "substitute for the workplace," as a "bridge to reconnect the elderly with the community" and as an "accessible and acceptable vehicle [to] community resources." Even more telling on the incidental role of centers is that a number of important works on long-term care largely or completely overlook them (Harrington et al. 1985; Katz, Kane and Mezey 1991; Sager 1982). J.A. Krout (1990), perhaps the leading academic authority on senior centers, has discussed the importance of centers in terms of their numbers, visibility to seniors, interest to legislators, funding level and programming to the "relatively healthy and socially active." He identified some activities at some centers intended for the frail but could locate no consistent, clear, shared long-term care orientation. In the opinion of many knowledgeable observers, therefore, senior centers do not have clearly defined, significant roles in our nation's long-term care system.

## BECOMING A LONG-TERM CARE PLAYER

In view of their obvious growth in numbers, why have senior centers not established roles in long-term care? The answer seems to lie with four fundamental problems:

1. Senior centers are unclearly defined.
2. They have not focused on the needs of the frail elderly.
3. The purposes centers would serve in a long-term care system remain vague.
4. The existing analytical or conceptual models of senior centers do not focus on significant dimensions that assist in establishing clear and significant roles for centers in a long-term care system.

With such serious limitations, it is not surprising that senior centers are not included more often in long-term care discussions.

The first difficulty, the lack of a common definition, makes any attempt to pinpoint even one long-term role for centers a questionable undertaking. For if centers cannot be well defined, they almost certainly cannot be counted upon to perform in predictable ways. Krout (1990) has reviewed a number of the major definitions of senior centers and has concluded that they share the following set of criteria: (1) centers are physical entities, (2) centers are part of a community planning process, and (3) centers provide a wide variety of services and activities. Some definitions also state that centers have a regular schedule of activities and services; a few add that they have paid, professional staff. But what points out the general inadequacies of most definitions is the failure to identify any clear purposes or goals for centers. Moreover, many definitions are so vague that they cannot distinguish clearly between senior centers, senior groups and senior clubs. The definitional problems are clearly a handicap in trying to position centers in a long-term care system that has many clearly defined and highly regulated players, e.g., nursing homes, home health care agencies, hospitals, rehabilitation centers and hospices.

Numerous studies have highlighted the second problem area centers have in establishing a long-term care role. Most centers serve individuals who are healthy (Krout 1983; Leanse and Wagener 1975; Tissue 1971; Tuckman 1967). Most center participants are under age 75 and most are not suffering from impairments in activities of daily life. Although growing numbers of senior centers are reporting the "aging in" of their members, research has yet to confirm a sizable transformation of center clientele from the well to the impaired.

Also notable when examining the literature on senior centers is a third serious problem: centers have had no clear long-term care mission or goal. Some experts assert that the purpose of centers is to address the "unmet needs" of seniors (Maxwell 1962), a phrase sufficiently broad to embrace any number of different services and activities. Others identify the goals of enhancing older people's dignity, supporting their independence and encouraging their community involvement (National Institute of Senior Centers 1978). Still other observers focus on the attempts of the centers to meet older people's recreational, health, educational, informational or socialization needs (Frankel 1966; Leanse and Wagener 1975). These varied statements of purpose are sufficiently broad to permit almost any type of activity or service at centers. They do not help focus centers upon any clearly identifiable set of long-term care services.

The lack of a clearly identified mission for senior centers has contributed to the fourth and final difficulty. Relatively few analytical models of senior centers exist (Krout 1983; Ralston 1987) and of those available, most have focused on aspects of centers that are largely irrelevant to the goals of senior centers. Existing models of centers have, for example, highlighted aspects of their physical structure (Jordan 1978), the number of services offered (Maxwell 1962), their size and complexity (Leanse and Wagener 1975), or the characteristics of their users (Taietz 1976). By not focusing on the purposes of centers, such models have deflected attention from what centers *could do* for healthy or impaired older people to less critical considerations of where the centers' services are provided, how many services are offered, or who utilizes the services.

If senior centers are to assume valued long-term care roles, all four of these major deficiencies need to be addressed. Improved and more rigorous definitions of centers must be offered. Targeting of center services to the frail elderly must occur at least to some extent. Significant and realistic long-term care goals need to be identified and models of centers that focus on clear and significant long-term care purposes need to be proposed. While such fundamental issues have certainly not impeded the past growth of centers, they may do so in the future as scarce resources are increasingly targeted to the functionally impaired and the poor. Without further efforts to identify the roles of centers in long-term care, retrenchment rather than expansion may be in the offing.

## ON THE PLAYING FIELD

In order to develop models depicting long-term care roles, the four stated shortcomings of senior centers need to be addressed. The starting point for developing useful models begins with an improved definition. For the purposes of this discussion, a senior center will be defined as:

> A physical structure in which a set of activities, programs and services with a common long-term care purpose are provided to older people by a professional staff on a frequent and regular basis and as part of a community planning process.

The terms "multipurpose" and "multiservice" will not be used in this discussion because centers by definition must offer multiple services and most in fact have been found to be multiservice; it is therefore redundant to refer to them as such.

To remedy the second difficulty—the present focus of centers on the well elderly—this chapter will direct its attentions largely to the impaired. Although many services are appropriate for either the well or the impaired, the focus in any long-term care model needs to be on the latter group. However, such a focus obviously does not mean that healthy older individuals are inappropriate candidates for center services.

In this discussion, the purpose of senior centers, the third area of difficulty, will be the effort either to maintain, restore or improve the health of functionally impaired older people or to ensure their access to appropriate long-term care services. In order to address these purposes, centers must provide a number of specific health and social services, ones that primarily include (1) access, (2) health care and chronic or rehabilitative care, (3) health promotion, (4) nutrition, (5) community-based services, (6) in-home services, and (7) caregiver supportive services. Noticeable by their absence from this list are the more traditional senior center activities of socialization, recreation and education. By themselves these activities are not sufficiently health- or access-related to warrant being the sole foci of centers. But they may be included as appropriate center services in a long-term care model if they are integrally related to one of the aforementioned areas, like health promotion or nutrition.

Finally, one of the most critical needs of senior centers is for analytical or conceptual models that get them to focus on long-term care services. To do so, an analytical model must satisfy a number of conditions. These conditions arise not only out of the roles centers have traditionally performed, but also out of the need to focus on the concerns of the functionally dependent, to broaden the bases of funding and to work more closely with existing long-term care institutions. Long-term care models for senior centers will specifically need to:

1. Focus on a clear and well-defined set of services, programs or activities.
2. Locate an important role for senior centers to play in the long-term care system.
3. Provide senior centers with the opportunities to address the long-term care needs of a broad array of older people, e.g., healthy and frail, minority and non-minority, low-income and middle income.
4. Maintain the traditional roles senior centers have had for older people in providing information, referral, congregate meals and home-delivered meals.
5. Offer centers the opportunity to obtain funding for their new long-term care roles from a variety of revenue sources.

Models that fulfill these requirements, along with an improved definition of senior centers, a focus on the functionally impaired and a clearer sense of purpose, should be able to help forge clear and significant long-term care roles for senior centers.

## LONG-TERM CARE MODELS FOR SENIOR CENTERS

### The Early Senior Center Model

The first senior center in the United States, the William Hudson Community Center, was founded in 1943 in New York City. It had two primary goals: (1) to provide nutritious, midday meals to low-income elderly who lived alone and (2) to offer these individuals opportunities to socialize. This original model of senior centers still holds such influence that it forms the core of many center programs. These early goals recognized not only that many seniors have nutritional deficiencies, but also that they appreciated regular opportunities for social contact. This original center model addressed both of these needs and did so with an understanding, often overlooked, that individuals tend to eat better when eating with someone than when eating alone.

## The Current Senior Center Model

With the growth of senior centers, this original model evolved relatively quickly into an eclectic model in which the goals of centers became highly diversified. Exactly what senior centers were trying to achieve became less recognizable. The goals of centers became so numerous and diverse—from nutrition, access, recreation and health to education, socialization, community service and supportive services—that activity upon activity was added and justified as appropriate for a center. This expansion of activities, services and programs has made more evident the overall lack of clear center goals, particularly in long-term care, and the centers' lack of programmatic cohesion.

To alter this situation and establish roles for centers in long-term care, a number of different analytical models are proposed. Each model attempts to address a central purpose, such as health promotion or improved nutrition, and each and every service, activity or program offered by a center operating under one of the proposed models must conform to the intended purpose. Adherence to a particular model would not only provide centers with a clearly identifiable, cohesive group of services, but it would also eliminate the propensity of centers to offer services that were irrelevant to a central mission. One caution is in order. These models are not static but dynamic and the types of services appropriate in the model may therefore expand or contract depending upon the needs of the seniors, the characteristics of the local long-term care system and the availability of funding. Moreover, the models are offered as ideal types and are not meant to be interpreted as requiring senior centers to conform to only one model or to prohibit the development of alternative models or of multimodels.

## The Health Promotion Model of Senior Centers

The first model for senior centers is designed to address the widely recognized gap in the nation's present health care system: the need for preventive health care and health promotion services (Belloc and Breslow 1972; Burdman 1986; Kane and Kane 1987). Under this model, centers would offer only services, programs and activities that are considered important to the health maintenance or health improvement of functionally dependent older people. The purposes of the center's services would be threefold: (1) to provide access to health and long-term care services, (2) to foster health-oriented attitudes and behaviors, and (3) to offer services and programs to reduce the risk of injuries, illnesses and diseases. The types of senior center programming offered in this model would be access services, community-based health-related services or in-home health-related services. Centers, in short, would take on a clear health orientation and, as a result, hire appropriate staff, offer only health-related services and focus on health-related issues. They would provide such services as health information, health assessments, health monitoring, individual and group health counseling, special health programs and home health care. Such a model would clearly result in dramatic substantive changes at most centers.

**The Nutrition Model of Senior Centers**

Although most senior centers provide congregate meals and some offer nutrition education, centers typically have done little else to try to meet the nutritional needs of older people. The next model attempts to address this shortcoming by focusing on the following specific purposes: (1) to provide access to nutrition-related programs and services, (2) to provide congregate and home-delivered meals as well as programs on meal preparation and provision, and (3) to provide nutrition-related activities and services. The list of appropriate center activities, programs and services in this model would therefore embrace a range of older people's nutritional needs, not simply that of a midday meal. Centers would conduct nutritional assessments, provide nutrition counseling, offer weight control or weight reduction programs, sponsor cooking classes, organize cooperative food purchasing programs, support gardening in order to produce edible fruits and vegetables, offer food-related trips and encourage research on the nutritional needs of the elderly. Senior centers in this model would become "nutrition assistance centers" in the fullest sense of the term.

## The Long-Term Care Community Service Model

Senior centers have traditionally offered a range of community services to the well elderly. Under the next proposed model, centers would expand these community services and design them so that they would assist the frail to continue to live independently in their homes for as long as possible. This community service model would have three general purposes: (1) to provide access to long-term care services, whether in-home, community or institutional; (2) to offer a range of community-based long-term care services, including health, personal care, rehabilitation, economic and nutritional services and (3) to provide in-home services. Centers could and would sponsor adult day care programs, respite care, rehabilitation services and home care under this model because all are likely to promote independence and reduce the risk of institutionalization.

## The Access Model of Senior Centers

Much has been made of senior centers serving as points of entry or "focal points" to the social service system. However, what is considered by some to be access often may be nothing more than the passing on of an address or a telephone number. The next proposed model of a senior center attempts to ensure that frail older people have "full service access" to the long-term care system. "Full service access" means that centers will provide a range of services, not just access services, to ensure that older people are screened, assessed, placed appropriately, and when placed, are monitored. Under this model, if a center does not provide a needed long-term care service, it will be able to access the service directly from another agency or institution because of formal written agreements. If an older person requires services that other agencies do not provide, e.g., adult day care, home care or home monitoring, the center will make them available. A center operating under the access model will make much more than just information available.

## The Caregiver Support Model

The final model of senior centers shifts their focus from the frail older person to the caregiver. Under this model, centers would be designed to assist caregivers in keeping the impaired older person at home for as long as possible. The centers would attempt (1) to provide caregivers with access to health and long-term care services and (2) to provide in-home and community services. Centers would provide counseling to the caregiver, legal assistance, rehabilitation services, respite care, long-term care system education, home-delivered meals and in-home monitoring. Services would be offered to the caregiver or to the frail older person either in the home or at the center. Senior centers would consequently be looked upon as tangible sources of support for the millions of caregivers to the frail elderly.

## CONCLUSION

Senior centers have served the needs of thousands of older Americans for approximately half a century. They have done so in spite of a number of significant difficulties. Because the centers lack a standardized definition, they have assumed a variety of structures and functions. Because they have focused largely on the interests of well older people, they may have allowed the frail to not attend centers or to look elsewhere for appropriate programming. In addition, senior centers have taken on such a wide variety of purposes that many do not have a clear idea of their principal mission. Finally, centers have been operating with a dearth of analytical or conceptual models to orient them to the needs of the functionally impaired. These are major problems and they are so severe that they continue to limit the influence centers have in the long-term care system. In the less regulated area of social services, these shortcomings have not proved so detrimental; centers have been able to grow and expand. But in the long-term care arena they must be remedied.

Senior centers could in fact assume very important roles in the nation's long-term care system, roles that are not now being performed by other institutions or roles that are being taken care of in an uncoordinated fashion. For example, under the health promotion model, senior centers become the major players in promoting good physical health and in reducing the likelihood of accidents. Under the nutrition model, they could work to improve the eating behaviors of older people. Under the long-term care community service model, they could expand the number and types of community-based long-term care services they offer to the frail. If centers sought to be true access points to the long-term care system, as in the access model, they could assist older people not only in negotiating the health and long-term care systems, but also in obtaining vital supportive services. Finally, centers could be the principal sources of support for millions of caregivers under the caregiver support model. Any of these roles would fill significant gaps in the present long-term care system. The opportunities are certainly available to senior centers, and the time is right for them to leave the sidelines and step onto the playing field.

## REFERENCES

Belloc, N. and L. Breslow. Relationship of physical health status and health practices. *Preventive Med.* 1:409-421, 1972.
Burdman, G.M. *Healthful Aging.* Englewood Cliffs, NJ: Prentice-Hall, 1986.
Frankel, G. The multipurpose senior citizen center: a new comprehensive agency. *Gerontologist* 6:23-27, 1966.
Harrington, C., R.J. Newcomer, C.L. Estes et al., eds. *Long-Term Care of the Elderly: Public Policy Issues.* Beverly Hills, CA: Sage Publications, 1985.
Huttman, E.D. *Social Services for the Elderly.* New York: The Free Press, 1985.
Jordan, J. *Senior Center Design: An Architect's Discussion of Family Planning.* Washington, DC: National Council on the Aging, 1978.
Kane, R.A. and R.L. Kane. *Long-Term Care: Principles, Programs, and Policies.* New York: Springer Publishing, 1987.
Katz, P.R., R.L. Kane and M.D. Mezey. *Advances in Long-Term Care,* Vol. 1. New York: Springer Publishing, 1991.
Krout, J.A. Correlates of senior center utilization. *Res. on Aging* 5:339-352, 1983.
Krout, J.A. *Senior Centers in America.* Westport, CT: Greenwood Press, 1990.
Leanse, J. and L. Wagener. *Senior Centers: A Report of Senior Group Programs in America.* Washington, DC: National Council on the Aging, 1975.
Lowy, L. and J. Doolin. Multipurpose Senior Centers. In A. Monk, ed., *Handbook of Gerontological Services,* 2nd Ed. New York: Columbia University Press, 1990.
Maxwell, J. *Centers for Older People: Guide for Programs and Facilities.* Washington, DC: National Council on the Aging, 1962.
National Institute of Senior Centers. *Senior Center Standards: Guidelines for Practice.* Washington, DC: National Council on the Aging, 1978.
Ralston, P. Senior Center Research: Policy from Knowledge? In E. Borgatta and R. Montgomery, eds., *Critical Issues in Aging Policy: Linking Research and Values.* Newbury Park, CA: Sage Publications, 1987.
Sager, A. Improving the provision of long-term care. *Perspect. Aging* 11:16-27, 1982.
Schulder, D. Older Americans Act: a vast network of public, private agencies. *Perspect. Aging* 14:5-7, 1985.
Taietz, P. Two conceptual models of the senior center. *J. Gerontol.* 31:219-222, 1976.
Tissue, T. Social class and the senior citizen center. *Gerontologist* 11:196-200, 1971.
Tuckman, J. Factors related to attendance in a center for older people. *J. Am. Geriatrics Soc.* 15:474-479, 1967.